The Kings and Queens

of England

THE KINGS

AND QUEENS

OF ENGLAND

A TOURIST GUIDE

BY

Jane Murray

Charles Scribner's Sons   New York

Grateful acknowledgment is made to the following copyright owners to quote as indicated:

William Heinemann Ltd., *Ballade Tragique, A Double Refrain,* reprinted from *Max in Verse: Parodies and Rhymes* collected and annotated by J. G. Riewald, published by Stephen Greene; John Murray, a verse from *Long Shadows* by Shane Leslie; W. W. Norton, Inc., New York, N.Y., quotations from *Richard the Third* by Paul Murray Kendall, copyright © 1955, 1956 by Paul Murray Kendall; Harper & Row, Publishers, Inc., a quotation from *Civilisation* by Kenneth Clark; Constable Publishers, quotations from *Horace Walpole's England*, edited by Alfred Bishop Mason, 1930.

Library of Congress Cataloging in Publication Data
Murray, Jane.
    The kings and queens of England.
    Includes bibliographical references.
    1. Great Britain—Kings and rulers—Biography.
I. Title.
DA28.1.M8   942'.00992 [B]   74–8019
ISBN 0–684–13889–1

1 3 5 7 9 11 13 15 17 19 C/C 20 18 16 14 12 10 8 6 4 2

Printed in the United States of America

Contents

Contents

Contents

Preface

Good tourists going to England undertake to read a book about the kings and queens. These books are of two kinds. One kind begins with William the Conqueror, and tourists wander pitifully around Westminster Abbey thumbing it for Edward the Confessor. The other kind begins back with the earliest *Rex totius Anglorum patriae*, King Offa (d. 796), and about the time tourists get to King Harold Harefoot (d. 1040) they lose their courage and read no more.

So this book begins at neither of those points back in time, but now.

Please try the English kings and queens this different way, reading backwards from now. If you find yourself disliking the device you need not use it. Start again, with the last chapter instead of the first, and read chronologically.

But to go backwards in time is, really, the normal way. We all look at continuing history from where we stand ourselves. We say: "My grandfather's name was John. He was the son of Robert, who settled in this town. Robert's father was named Thomas; he came from England. . . ."

So in this book we begin with Queen Elizabeth II, who "succeeded to the throne upon the death of her father, George VI. . . . He succeeded . . . upon the abdication of his brother, Edward VIII. . . ."

And we go back not even a thousand years—beyond the Conqueror, necessarily, but only as far as the Confessor, the first king to be buried in Westminster Abbey, the last of the old English line.

It is too bad not to go a century or so beyond him, back to Alfred the Great (d. 900). Alfred bears a familiar, expected name. But to reach this landmark king who codified the laws, beat back the Danes, and burned the cakes, we plod through barren country —not only Harold Harefoot and Canute but Edmund Ironside, Ethelred the Unready, Edward the Martyr, Edgar the Peaceable, Edwy, Edred, Edmund the Magnificent, Ethelstan, and Edward the Elder. Some superstitious magic seems to have resided in the letter "E." Perhaps rising above it helped to make Alfred great— he himself was the son of Ethelwulf and youngest brother to three successive kings named Ethelbald, Ethelbert, and Ethelred I.

All of these "E" kings are far too dim to be fascinating. They have scarcely any identifying marks. Was Harefoot deformed, or merely a fast runner? We do not know. And some of the few things we did think we knew about them are not so. Ethelred, for instance, was not really Unready but "Redeless—without counsel." Furthermore, they have no imprint on England in the physical, guidebook sense. Their graves are unmarked. There is not a single castle or monument or church standing that we know they lived in or built. It was thought once that the big white horse cut into the Downs at Uffington marked a victory of Alfred the Great—but now the experts say it is a thousand years too old for that, first century B.C.

This means that even Alfred, for all his greatness, has left us no trace.

Edward the Confessor, on the contrary, is the most prominent person in Westminster Abbey; his great upstanding tomb is its central shrine. And as English history goes, his day was almost yesterday—only a thousand years.

It was presumptuous of me to undertake even that thousand years of English sovereigns. I am a narrow-minded specialist and this is "not my field." Only one of all these centuries is "my century." Even since I have been going to England in earnest I have confused Edward I with Edward III, and Henry of Bolingbroke with Henry of Monmouth, and Mary II with her aunt, another Mary Stuart who also married a Prince William of Orange. No literate English person would do that—and yet up to 1776 and all that I too am English. All these English kings and queens up to and including George III are my kings and queens. Obviously I could not settle down, at this late date, to the original, *immer Quellen lesen* research which is the only right kind; and the secondary sources, particularly the thesis-dissertation ones, are as divergent as Yorkists and Lancastrians and often as acrimonious. But what I have been reading has helped to clear my own mind. Perhaps it will help other people, too, to distinguish among the Richards and Henrys and Margarets and Catherines, and between the Duke of York who fought against his king and the one who is merely on top of a London column to escape his creditors.

Attempting to pass my findings painlessly on, I took counsel from Sir Kenneth Clark, now Lord Clark of Saltwood. He wrote *Civilisation* for a television audience, and television audiences and tourists, it seemed to me, have much in common. They are all rather simple people. Even those who are ordinarily intellectuals or sophisticates are simplified by being in these groups at all. They sit before the screens, they stand before the castles, to be entertained rather than improved; they are not prepared to make much effort to retain, evaluate, or become authorities on what they see and hear. So, as Lord Clark says, "every subject must be simplified . . . and what is said . . . must usually be said without qualification. Generalisations are inevitable and, in order not to be boring, must be slightly risky. There is nothing new in this. It is how we talk about things sitting round the room after dinner; and [the idea is to] . . . retain the character of the spoken word, with the rhythms of ordinary speech, and even some of the off-hand imprecise language which prevents conversation from becoming pompous."

Risky generalizations—off-hand imprecise language—if this book helps tourists to relax and enjoy England, it has succeeded.

JANE MURRAY

April 11, 1974

The Kings and Queens of England

Elizabeth II

1926–

SHE succeeded to the throne in 1952, upon the death of her father George VI.

Queen Elizabeth II is the first English ruler in centuries to have more than a teaspoonful of English blood.

In the six hundred years following William the Conqueror, royalty made many foreign marriages but, also, many marriages with their own subjects at home. Queen Mary II and Queen Anne were both the daughters of an English lady, Anne Hyde. Queen Elizabeth I's mother had been English Anne Boleyn. (Four out of her father's six wives, in fact, were English.) Henry VII, Richard III, Edward IV, and Henry IV all had English mothers and all married English wives.

But when in 1714 Queen Anne died—the last of the Stuarts—the Royal Family turned German overnight. The Act of Settlement (1701) had provided that a German branch of the family would get the crown. George of Hanover, who became George I of England because his grandmother had been a Stuart, James I's daughter, showed no trace of that strain of blood. He had no knowledge of English or of Englishmen and no desire to learn. Obviously he could not have declined the throne and the revenues of England, but he surrounded himself with Germans, spent as much time as he could in his German principality of Hanover, and died unreconciled and unreconstructed.

His son, George II, did learn to speak some gutteral English, but he had even less non-German blood—an eighth, now, instead of George I's quarter-portion. And since his wife, like his mother, was another German princess, his son Frederick inherited only a sixteenth.

Frederick married still another German princess and died before his father did, never becoming king. His son (31/32 German) succeeded George II as George III. He too married a German, so George IV and William IV, his sons, had only 1/64 non-German blood, their niece Victoria only 1/128—because everybody right down the line married still another German princess. Queen Victoria was 127/128 German.

Victoria married Albert of Saxe-Coburg-Gotha, than whom nobody in history has been more German, so their son Edward VII was 255/256 German.

But it was like the frog that jumps a certain distance across a table, and then half that distance, then half the second distance, and so on. Does this well-trained frog ever fall off the edge? Theoretically he does not. Even though Edward VII was 255/256 German, the 1/256 of blood from his Stuart line justified him on the English throne.

And with Edward came a leavening of the German lump. He married the beautiful Princess Alexandra of Denmark who was only half German. This was fine, but the next royal generation—George V—was still almost three-quarters German, and when in World War I Mr. H. G. Wells wrote the *Times* protesting England's "alien and uninspiring Court," and King George said he might be uninspiring but he was damned if he was alien, this "was not a statement of fact; it was a profession of faith." *

George V, too, contributed toward making the Royal Family less German, if not more English. His wife, Queen Mary, had, improbably, a Hungarian grandmother. (This was through a morganatic marriage, but somehow Queen Mary was the most royal of the lot. We easily say Alexandra and Elizabeth and even Victoria; we always say Queen Mary.) But it was George VI who really broke the family pattern. Reverting nearly three hundred years to a precedent, he married as

* Lord Altrincham and others, *Is the Monarchy Perfect?* (London: John Calder, 1958), p. 4.

Duke of York one of his father's subjects, the Earl of Strathmore's daughter, all Scottish and English. Their daughter Elizabeth II, thanks to the maternal half of her blood and the few (but valuable) Stuart drops from her father's side, is an English queen.

There were many other auspicious things about Her Majesty when, in 1952, she suddenly and dramatically succeeded her father. She was young and pretty and charming, a model of royal deportment and devotion to duty; inevitably Englishmen, recalling as earnest and transparently good a little Queen, wondered if they were not standing on the verge of a new Elizabethan Age as great as the Victorian.

Like Victoria, Elizabeth had her Melbourne, a remarkable old man, the authentic hero of World War II. Winston Churchill, back in power after the electorate had dismissed him but failed to teach him humility, was the most suitable of prime ministers for these times and this Queen.

He did not, Mr. Churchill had said, propose to preside over the dissolution of the British Empire. Yet that is exactly what he had to do. The optimism that the hard postwar years were over lasted for a little while. The coronation focused the most favorable of lights upon the British Empire and its institutions; the world, enraptured before its television sets, sighed with pleasure as the Queen's handsome husband— so much more attractive and palatable than Prince Albert—knelt to pledge his fealty. The nine-hundred-year-old Abbey, the glittering crowd, the ritual that had come in with Richard Coeur-de-Lion were reality, with no dreamlike quality; it was austerity which they made seem like a dream.

But austerity closed in again. Having been a victor in World War II, Britain was not eligible for the helping hands so generously extended to the defeated foes. While Germany's and Japan's economies grew steadily and finally boomed, Britain struggled painfully to provide the comforts and security of the socialist dream. The pound was devalued. There were hideous Mau Mau troubles in Kenya. The Suez crisis loomed and then dimmed, but it did not disappear; nor did the Cyprus problem. France, the former ally, made it plain that Great Britain was not wanted in the Common Market. And the colonies had begun to slip away.

India, the diamond in the crown, had gone in the Queen's father's time. Earl and Countess Mountbatten of Burma, representing King George VI, had carried the ceremony off magnificently, smiling as if losing India were the most desirable dynastic thing in the world. But the death-blow to Empire was plain. The African colonies were lost with, perhaps, no great loss of face. The rest of the world had often wondered what England saw in those still-savage outposts of Empire—beyond their adding to the gratifying splashes of red all over the map. But it was painful for England to lose the Empire on which the sun had never set, and though some of the colonies were very small the cumulative effect was that of drops of water, one after another, wearing away a stone. In the early years of the Queen's reign we looked constantly, it seemed, at pictures of her former colonies' independence celebrations.

Mr. Churchill, Sir Winston since the coronation, had retired full of years and honors, getting out of the game while he was winning again. Mr. Macmillan in his place spoke euphemistically about "the winds of change." But in terms of Empire all the winds were blowing in the wrong direction. "Commonwealth" in place of "Empire" is a euphemism in itself; it is only their acknowledgment of a common Queen that holds many disparate countries loosely together.

As this book will do, people have always said "English" even after, to be perfectly correct, they should have said "British." But in these early years of her reign calling Elizabeth Queen of England sounded more and more accurate, as if before long England might be an island again.

Through all the changes (which still go on, though the pace has slackened) the Queen has been the calm center, the eye of the hurricane. Her poise has never failed. No outsider knows how she feels about it, no outsider knows what she is really like. The official biography, perhaps with revealing letters, will be posthumous; meantime, neither the barley-sugars of court reporters nor the acid-drops of Lord Altrincham and others have been very helpful. There is more criticism than at the beginning of the reign—this is routinely so, for monarchs as well as presidents—but most people in and out of the Commonwealth admire Elizabeth. Within the narrow limits she is constitutionally allowed, she moves and speaks with great suitability. She handles horses better than Boadicea and dresses like a lady. Her private life is exemplary, her way of life not ostentatiously but sufficiently regal. (Her subjects would hate it if, like the Dutch and Scandinavian royalties, she bicycled down the street.) She has, through devotion to duty and application to the red boxes of official papers which—under her father's guidance—she learned to read and digest every day, largely made up for unfortunate gaps in her education.

Whereas the Dutch heiress, now Queen Juliana, always competed in school with other children and studied law at the University of Leyden, Queen Elizabeth's parents wanted her to have "a happy childhood." Walks and games and pets and treats and casual instruction—she shared with her little sister, four years younger, a devoted governess more like a nursery-governess or a baby-sitter—are naively described by the governess, Marion Crawford, in *The Little Princesses*. (Even Queen Mary, not a bluestocking herself and most anxious not to interfere or pull rank, wondered if only half-an-hour a week for literature—?) Later sessions with the distinguished vice-provost of Eton supplemented this ingenuous regime; there were constant opportunities in horsemanship and conversational French; and, of course, living in a museum is a chance to learn about paintings and china and furniture, as Queen Mary did. Beautifully trained rather than broadly educated, Elizabeth II decided upon a different kind of preparation for her son.

When or—as many observers insist upon adding—if her son succeeds her as Charles III he will be following an expert in the field. It is puzzling that increasing numbers of people (not socialists) feel and say that this field is a foolish, anachronistic, and unnecessary one; for how can they say it is less than the field of public relations, even if they feel it is not much more? The field of public relations is considered neither foolish nor unnecessary, and very modern indeed. Yet the articles about how much the Queen is costing the Commonwealth proliferate.

It is true that some of the kings and queens who ruled England only a little while ago would be anachronistic now. It would be ironic if, now that monarchy has learned not to abuse its privileges and to give a full measure in return for its subjects' loyalty, the English Royal Family were to go the way of its royal cousins—wanderers, even though very rich ones, on the face of the earth.

George VI

1895–1952

H E succeeded to the throne in 1936, upon the abdication of his elder brother Edward VIII.

Becoming king rather suddenly, the Duke of York was advised it would be expedient for him to take a familiar name. Christened Albert Frederick Arthur George, he had always used the first one, Albert. His family called him "Bertie." But this was no time to recall the Prince Consort. Englishmen had always resented Queen Victoria's husband, always an outsider and a German though no one in English history ever worked more devotedly for the English nation. It would be far better for Albert Duke of York, succeeding to the throne of his defecting brother Edward, to recall their stable and popular father and call himself George VI.

There was already a George, so called, in the immediate family—the youngest brother, the Duke of Kent. It must have been the last straw for the new king, a shy, retiring young man with a stutter, to have to give up his very name and step out into the limelight calling himself something else.

He did it, as he did everything else it seemed his duty to do. And he did extremely well. There was nothing spectacular about him; he had not even one of the showy virtues. But England in 1936 found itself tired of café-society kings. They much preferred, they found, the solid, reliable, yes, dull young man (sixty-eighth in his Osborne class of sixty-eight) who, with his wife and two little girls, had moved into Buckingham Palace and was going about his business of laying wreaths and receiving delegations and working through the red boxes as if there had never been a transition named Edward VIII between George V and George VI.

His wife, Lady Elizabeth Bowes-Lyon when he married her in 1923, was a tremendous help to him. This Queen Consort had come to the throne perhaps as reluctantly as he; but she accepted its responsibilities with as radiant an appearance of pleasure as she accepted, after her daughter became Queen Regnant, stepping back and aside. The present Queen Mother has been given hundreds of bouquets since 1936; she has opened hundreds of dreary bazaars and listened to hundreds of tiresome speeches and inspected hundreds of factories and battleships which could not possibly interest her; and in every picture her smile is still one of delight. Some few people may find this priggish; most people feel it is a pleasure to see anyone doing a job so really well.

Encouraged all the way by his Queen, George VI managed with increasing triumph things he had never thought he could do—like speeches in which he did not stutter at all.

It must have been a relief to him and everyone that Stanley Baldwin did not stay on as prime minister. He had been too instrumental in removing Edward VIII. He retired with a peerage in favor of Neville Chamberlain, and Mr. Chamberlain, complete with umbrella, coped as best he could with Hitler at Munich.

Too much fun has been made of that umbrella—after all, it does rain constantly in England—and too much contempt accorded his saying that, at Munich, he had achieved "peace in our time." Mr. Chamberlain was merely quoting the *Book of Common Prayer*—the order for evening services, to be exact. He was not using "peace in our time" in the "after me the deluge" sense, but in the prayer book's sense of "peace now, not at some vague time in the distant future." His fellow Anglicans, if not the American reporters, understood him perfectly, and they were very pleased with Mr. Chamberlain until Hitler moved into Czechoslovakia in 1939 and it appeared that Munich had not, after all, worked. Events then were swift—the Fall of Poland, the Fall of Norway, of Belgium and the Netherlands, the Fall of France, and, suddenly, strong prospects of the Fall of Britain.

Winston Churchill in 1940 replaced Mr. Chamberlain.

Unless Americans want to count John Paul Jones's little foray in 1778, the British Isles had not been invaded since 1066. Nor were they in 1940. Incredibly, Dowding's air arm turned back Goering's. The great courage the British showed in the Battle of Britain was not merely in the air, or in the armed services. Churchill's speeches in the House of Commons gave it a voice. London took the Blitz and began to think in terms of giving it back.

Through the war, the new sovereigns stood firm as St. Paul's. Other people's children were evacuated to Canada and "the States," but not theirs. "They could not go without me, and I cannot leave the King," the Queen said simply. The little princesses did live in the comparative safety of Windsor Castle, but their parents stayed in Buckingham Palace, even after the direct hits. After each of the London air-raids, Their Majesties could be seen picking their way through the rubble, the King in his admiral's uniform, the Queen in her pretty, dowdy pastels and pearls, inspecting the damage, commiserating with the survivors. They were not unaware that they made an incongruous picture. "I'm glad we've been bombed," the Queen said, when Buckingham Palace got it finally. "It makes me feel I can look the East End in the face." But she and her husband had not shirked facing them in any case, and the Londoners loved it. Someone wrote a poem to the Queen:

> Be it said to your renown
> That you wore your gayest gown,
> Your bravest smile, and stayed in Town
> When London Bridge was burning down,
>   My fair lady.*

And someone called across a shell-crater, "You're a good king!" "You're a good people," the King called back.

It was a good victory, after six and a half years. Its sour aftermath was the voters' dismissal of Mr. Churchill in his hour of triumph. World

---

* Quoted in John W. Wheeler-Bennett, *King George VI* (New York: St. Martin's Press, 1958), p. 470.

opinion found this inexcusable. Mr. Churchill found it a challenge. George VI found himself under the necessity of changing from a royalist prime minister, one who truly believed in the monarchy and had given his sovereign every aid and comfort throughout the war, to a socialist, Clement Attlee.

He accomplished the change without a flicker. Constitutional monarchs take prime ministers as they come, just as they take the speeches that are handed them to read. George VI's preparation for the kingship had been nil—unless you count his background in the Navy—but his on-the-job training saw him through everything.* Mr. Attlee's government meant National Health, which would have been great if Britain could have afforded it, NATO membership, UN membership, the loss of India and Pakistan. The King sent his most distinguished cousin, Earl Mountbatten of Burma, out as viceroy to wind things up in style.

The war years, much less the peace, had been hard on the King. Emotionally involved, physically under a strain, morally obligated to appear tireless and serene, he began having circulatory troubles which were hard to ignore and rise above. Being a king is a stand-up job. He had to cancel his Australian tour. Princess Elizabeth and her husband made a tour of Canada in his place. But only when it was really necessary—he could not, for instance, sit motionless on horseback taking the salute at the Trooping the Colour—did he allow her to substitute for him. With care, he escaped the amputation of his right leg, but an operation for cancer of the lung did not eliminate that disease. When he saw the Princess and her husband off for the next tour they both knew what might happen before her return.

* "I've never even seen a State Paper," he told Lord Louis Mountbatten, distressed. "I'm only a Naval Officer, it's the only thing I know about." But Lord Louis told him what *his* father had told George V when that unexpected king had expressed the same fears of being unprepared: "George, you're wrong. There is no more fitting preparation for a King than to have been trained in the Navy." Wheeler-Bennett, *George VI*, pp. 293–94.

Edward VIII

1894–1972

HE succeeded to the throne in 1936, upon the death of his father
George V.

Everyone had thought that, with responsibility, the Prince of Wales
would settle down.

In a sense he did. Becoming king not too old, like his grandfather, and
not too young, like his great-grandmother, he neglected none of the
work that came in the red boxes, nor in the shape of delegations or
occasions or conferring politicians. If the prime minister he had
inherited, Stanley Baldwin, was not the prime minister he would have
chosen, he showed it no more than a constitutional monarch is supposed
to. (Victoria had been the last one to kick against those traces.) There
were signs, however, that Mr. Baldwin did not like. The news from
abroad was troubling enough—Hitler in the Rhineland, Mussolini in
Ethiopia, civil war in Spain—but it was Edward's expressed interest in
the troubles of his own country that made headlines. Visiting the
depressed areas, he emerged from the houses of the Welsh unemployed
to say, "Something must be done."

He also took a more proper interest in his approaching coronation,
approving the glass and china and souvenir items with the Royal cipher
that were being turned out for the tourist trade, conferring with the Earl

Marshal on the arrangements at Westminster Abbey. If there was a lack of enthusiasm anywhere it was laid to there being no queen to be crowned with him; the coronation of a bachelor king could hardly be as exciting socially.

England had never had a middle-aged unmarried king before. Historically there was always great pressure on the heir to the throne to marry and beget, but oddly enough, in Edward's case, he had been allowed to reach forty-one without being unduly urged. One reason, of course, was the paucity of eligible princesses. There were still plenty of German ones, but since World War I, when the British Royal Family had publicly divested itself of all its German titles, changed its German name, and washed its hands of everything German, they were no longer the solution they had been in past generations. Also, as far back as Queen Victoria they had begun to wonder if cousins had not married cousins too many times. Edward VIII's youngest brother, Prince John, had been "quite abnormal" and kept in strict seclusion. (He "had fits and died young," Loelia Duchess of Westminster says succinctly.) His father's elder brother, who also had fortunately died early, was as unmistakably subnormal, quite unable to learn.

But if one could not consider the German princesses, one could not consider the French or Spanish or Italian either. It did not matter whether or not royalty was still on these thrones, but these princesses were all Roman Catholics, and the King, as defender of the strictly Anglican faith, was forbidden to marry one. Of course this was a bit overcautious; it had been a long time since the trouble over Queen Henrietta Maria's Catholic chapel, and that tail was not likely to try to wag that dog again; but the law was still on the books.

So what with one thing and another the English people had grown into the habit of thinking that Edward VIII might not have children of his own, and that little Princess Elizabeth of York might one day be queen. There was increasing interest in her. She lived with her parents in a comfortable but unostentatious house on Piccadilly, only a little way from Bruton Street where she had been born, and she was often seen, with her governess and her little sister, in the park or at the zoo or even sightseeing on a big red bus.

Then Britain heard what America had been talking about for quite some time, but which the British press had loyally suppressed. They heard about Mrs. Simpson.

Mrs. Simpson had been born Bessie Wallis Warfield, an American from Maryland. Her family was a good one and she herself was charming. But she was a divorced woman; she had divorced her first husband, a Lieutenant Spencer, and at the time all the publicity broke was about to divorce Mr. Ernest Simpson.

This was par for the course in the circles that the Prince of Wales had not stopped frequenting when he became king. It was full of persons of good family who were not particularly staid, and numbers of them had been divorced. Divorce had been more or less acceptable in England, socially, since the days of Edward VII's raffish friends; even some members of the Royal Family had been divorced; and it was not true that divorced women could not come to court. Mrs. Simpson herself, complete with long white train and feathers, had been presented to Their Majesties King George and Queen Mary.

One is at liberty to wonder if Edward VIII would ever have thought of marrying Mrs. Simpson if nobody had put it into his head. But first there was the press, and then there was Mr. Baldwin.

Stanley Baldwin was not a brilliant but a reasonably able and conscientious prime minister. Like the King, who had many good points Mr. Baldwin did not appreciate, Mr. Baldwin had many good points invisible to the King. It was Queen Victoria and Mr. Gladstone all over again. There is no reason to doubt the bona fides of either, but also none to doubt that, if so devoted and convinced a royalist as Winston Churchill had been prime minister—or almost anyone else had been prime minister—the results might have been different. In any case, Mr. Baldwin issued his ultimatum, and Edward VIII left the throne. His speech of abdication, with its mention of "the help and support of the woman I love," became a classic.

The most amazing thing about the whole affair was how little it seemed to matter. Far from falling, the throne did not even quiver. The transfer of title and constitutional authority to the King's next brother, as George VI, was smoothness itself. Edward VIII had not been crowned and consecrated, and it was like annulling an unconsummated marriage. The man in the street, who had cheered him so heartily and liked him so much as Prince of Wales, let him go with only momentary regrets. He had behaved badly, Englishmen thought. He had let them down. Imagine putting aside duty and the crown of England for a woman—any woman. Englishmen might not have minded—though Mr. Baldwin had told the King they would—the kind of morganatic marriage King Leopold contracted later in Belgium, giving a non-royal lady an impressive title and all respect and courtesy. Mrs. Simpson herself, brought up in the Episcopal Church which like the Anglican frowned on remarriage after divorce, had never expected to be crowned queen in Westminster Abbey. Further, entering her fifth decade without having borne either of two previous husbands a child, she could not have minded too much the King's renouncing the throne on behalf of any morganatic children.

But the whole point was that nobody really cared. After the nine days' wonder was over and the King—now the Duke of Windsor—had married his charming American abroad, the basics were unchanged. It was one in the eye for those socialists who might have thought the English were longing to abolish royalty. After an interval, the Duke of Windsor started coming back to England occasionally, first to see his mother, then to go to accustomed doctors. He passed almost unnoticed in the streets. Growing older, he was looking more and more like his second cousin the last Crown Prince of Germany, and some people recalled that almost all his blood was German, not English, and quoted the Duke of Wellington to the effect that being born in a stable does not make a man a horse.

Even when his wife came with him they were received (so Mollie Panter-Downes recorded in 1939) "in a blaze of public apathy."

But his marriage was a success. The people who had cried "Infatuation!" and "It won't last!" were perfectly still. Thirty-five years later, when His Royal Highness the Duke of Windsor died—in France where he had lived—the Duchess of Windsor was at his side. She had never been granted her husband's style of Royal Highness.

George V

1865–1936

H E succeeded to the throne in 1910, upon the death of his father Edward VII.

Death had previously removed his elder brother "Prince Eddy," the Duke of Clarence; there was relief over this and a special welcome therefore for Prince George. Prince Eddy had been strikingly inadequate. But that was all—he was not clever enough to have been Jack the Ripper, as recent sensational articles in the London *Sunday Times* and other papers wanted us to believe. He did not have criminal tendencies. There had to be general concern, however, about the "abnormally dormant condition" of his mind. Various English kings, back in the mists of history, had not been able to read, but this was from lack of opportunity and not "weakness of brain." One of his tutors reported that Prince Eddy "hardly knows the meaning of the words *to read*"; another related that, unable to "fix his attention to any given subject for more than a few minutes consecutively," he failed in school "not in one or two subjects, but in all." As a constitutional monarch, Prince Eddy could never have harmed England the way such a defective could have done in the days of real power; but since his mental weakness was "manifested . . . also in his hours of recreation and social intercourse," he would certainly have been an embarrassment.*

* Philip Magnus, *King Edward VII* (New York: Dutton, 1964), pp. 158, 169, 178.

As he grew up he gave, of course, increasing cause for apprehension, because he was physically normal and healthy. Fortunately he was gentle and tractable, too, and the best thing seemed to marry him off promptly to a kind-hearted, common-sense princess who would manage him for his own good, keep him in line, and tell him which foot came first.

The royal choice fell upon Princess Mary (or May) of Teck, also a grandchild of Queen Victoria, who was pretty as well as practical and good. The Queen could not resist keeping the consort's crown in the family—and as head of the family, of course, she, rather than the two sets of parents, was the matchmaker. But one of the things she liked best about Princess May was the fact that a quarter of her blood was Hungarian, a fresh strain. Her father's father, Duke Alexander of Württemberg, had married, morganatically, a Countess Rhédey.

It was not quite as bad as sacrificing a maiden to the Minotaur, but it was not good, and some of the courtiers, at least, felt very sorry for Princess May. They did not "anticipate any real opposition on Prince Eddy's part if he is properly managed and told he *must* do it," one of them wrote to another, ". . . but do you suppose Princess May will make any resistance?" *

She did not, nor did she when Prince Eddy rather suddenly died, in 1892, and Queen Victoria at once began promoting her marriage to the next brother, now in direct line for the throne. They were married a year and a half later.

Only a princess who truly believed in the mystique of royalty, in her dynasty and its destiny, could have smoothly accepted this otherwise rather crude substitution. Princess May did so believe. Being human, she must have been grateful for the turn of fate which had given her a nice normal young husband instead of a subnormal one, and George Duke of York had many attractive qualities. Theirs was a thoroughly happy marriage and they became one of the most successful couples ever to occupy the throne.

With no expectation that he would ever be king, the Duke of York had been trained in the Navy. Though he had to give that up—and

* Magnus, *Edward VII*, p. 239.

always missed it—order and discipline remained his way of life, his quarterdeck voice became the terror of his well-drilled, sailor-suited children, and his devotion to duty set a high standard for everyone around him. He was forty-four when he came to the throne. Not a brilliant man—there was really no branch the Royal Family could derive brilliance from—he had nevertheless plain, cool common sense, a blunt way of dealing with problems and questions, and a grasp of detail that was a pleasure to his successive prime ministers. Overnight, the atmosphere of the court changed. There were no more enormous Sodom-and-Gomorrah dinners, no more discreet and beautiful ladies, no more house-parties, race-horses, Jewish bankers, attractive hangers-on, backstairs gossip, trips to Paris and Marienbad. Instead there was just a retired naval officer going doggedly through his red boxes, not merely glancing at the documents but reading every word; and, on the other side of the fireplace, a lady with a curled fringe doing needlework.

Queen Mary was to become quite famous as a needlewoman; a carpet she worked brought a staggering £35,000 when it was auctioned after World War II, the Queen's contribution to the National Debt; and she also made herself a professional-level authority on antiques, cataloguing the great royal collection, filling in its gaps, bringing the good things down from the attics and banishing the bad, and rearranging all the palaces. When you go to Windsor Castle and see, for instance, the Van Dycks all beautifully displayed together in one room, with the triple portrait of Charles I over the mantel, you can thank Queen Mary and her sense of history. On a much larger scale, for she did all the royal residences, literally hundreds of rooms, it was the same kind of thing Mrs. Kennedy did later for our White House.

Eventually everybody got to be terribly proud of Queen Mary, and of King George and his ability to pot his partridge with every shot; but at first, right after "good old Teddy," they did seem rather dull. Max Beerbohm circulated to this effect a *Ballade Tragique à Double Refrain*, in which a lady-in-waiting and her opposite number compare their horrid lives:

SHE: . . . The Queen is duller than the King. . . .

HE: Lady, you lie. Last evening
I found him with a rural dean

Talking of District visiting. . . .
The King is duller than the Queen.

SHE: At any rate he doesn't sew;
You don't see him embellishing
Yard after yard of calico. . . .
The Queen is duller than the King.
Oh, to have been an underling
To (say) the Empress Josephine.

HE: Enough of your self-pitying;
The King is duller than the Queen.

SHE: The Queen is duller than the King.

HE: Death, then, for you shall have no sting.
 (*Stabs her, and as she falls dead produces phial from breast-pocket of coat*)
Nevertheless, sweet friend strychnine,
The King—is—duller than—the Queen.
 (*Expires in horrible agony*)*

It was said that Sir Max postponed his knighthood twenty years by writing this; but actually he seems lucky to have got it at all, even in a subsequent reign.

George V had been on the throne only four years when the Archduke Franz Ferdinand was assassinated and war burst out all over Europe. Tireless and tremendously involved, he spent 1914–1918 between England and France, checking progress there and inspecting the troops. Kings were no longer leading armies into battle—and anyway King George was a Navy man—but it was certainly a service-connected disability when Field Marshal Sir Douglas Haig's horse reared, lost its balance, and fell backward onto the King's horse, knocking him off and breaking his pelvis. From his hospital cot, King George continued pinning medals on soldiers as usual.

His wife and daughter worked as tirelessly, making surgical dressings, visiting the wounded. The younger sons were too little, still in school, but Prince Albert was on the *Collingwood* in the great Battle of Jutland, and the Prince of Wales, kept seething at first in safe spots, finally made

* The English also say appendiceetis. This poem is quoted in S. N. Behrman, *Portrait of Max* (New York: Random House, 1960), pp. 100–101.

it overseas with his regiment, the Grenadier Guards. "What does it matter if I am killed? I have four brothers," he would say, and Lord Kitchener would spell it out to him that it was not his death but his capture they could not risk. The enemy was said to be hoping for a royal hostage.

It was awkward that the enemy, Kaiser Wilhelm II, the Emperor of Germany, was the King of England's first cousin. Their branches of the family had not been congenial; King George's father loathed the Kaiser because he had condescended to him when he, King Edward, was only Prince of Wales, while his mother, a Danish princess, had loathed the whole country and connection ever since Prussia took Schleswig-Holstein from Denmark in 1866. But the Kaiser had, conversely, been a devoted grandson to Queen Victoria and often visited; the surface was kept smooth and King George's subjects did not know about any family unpleasantness. All they knew was that the Kaiser was his first cousin; and with the whole country emotionally involved, spies everywhere, Englishmen were more and more unhappy about the King's German kin—saying, for instance, that it was unsafe for another cousin, Prince Louis of Battenberg, to be First Sea Lord.

King George acted firmly. Within the constitutional limits there were not many big, sweeping gestures he could make, but he could make this one. He issued a proclamation (July 17, 1917) "Declaring that the Name of Windsor is to be borne by His Royal House and Family and Relinquishing the Use of All German Titles and Dignities." And it was not only "for Ourselves and for and on behalf of Our descendants" that he did this, but also on behalf of "all other the descendants of Our Grandmother QUEEN VICTORIA. . . ." * There went Saxony, Saxe-Coburg and Gotha, Battenberg, Hesse, everything German, at one stroke of the pen.

Even with Prince Louis of Battenberg translated into an English Mountbatten and created Marquess of Milford Haven, he had to give up First Sea Lord, and his whole career, and (he thought) his good name. This was terribly unfair to Prince Louis, who was only a cousin-in-law anyway, who had been a naturalized Englishman since he was fourteen,

* *Burke's Peerage* (London: 1956), p. xxxiii.

and who had served in the Royal Navy almost the whole fifty years since. It was some vindiction for this branch of the family when a generation later, in an even greater war with Germany, Prince Louis's remarkable son Lord Louis Mountbatten (later Earl Mountbatten of Burma) made First Sea Lord too.

The postwar years were not much easier than the fighting years had been. Home front problems, pushed aside for the duration, had lost nothing by waiting. Class feeling, something relatively new, unless you wanted to call it a throwback to the Middle Ages, was becoming bitter. "The rich man in his castle, The poor man at his gate, God made them high and lowly, And ordered their estate," the hymn verse which high and lowly had warbled happily together in churches all over England, no longer expressed a universal view.* The Irish Revolution, only postponed by Home Rule back in 1911, achieved the Free State in 1921. After the bloodiest fighting, Eire came into being, only six counties remaining with the Empire as Northern Ireland. Women had chained themselves to the railings and gone on hunger strikes in jails to get the vote. A Labour government, if a brief one, was voted in as early as 1924. There was a General Strike in 1926, very severe; and in 1931, Britain, bearing its share in a world-wide Depression, went off the Gold Standard.

With deep divisions among his people—economic, social, the House of Commons trying now to crush the House of Lords—King George found himself a new role, the common father of them all. It was discovered that he had a real talent for radio broadcasting. He was the kind of person—and so was his wife—of whom his subjects highly approved, and as he spoke to them more and more often, in Christmas messages and the like, the approval turned into real affection. Twenty-five years on the throne, riding back through the cheering crowds from his Silver Jubilee Service at St. Paul's, King George said to Queen Mary, surprised, "I believe they really like me."

Actually he had been mellowing for quite some time. His family first

---

* This verse of "All Things Bright and Beautiful" is democratically omitted from *The Hymnal of the Protestant Episcopal Church in the United States of America*, 1940. It is still familiar in Anglican circles. Jessica Mitford quotes it on page 59 of her autobiography *Daughters and Rebels*.

noticed it the night his daughter-in-law, the sweet young Duchess of York, was late for dinner. "I'm sorry I was two minutes late, Papa," she apologized, while the others waited for the heavens to fall. "Not at all, my dear," replied the King; "I think we must have sat down two minutes early."

Edward VII

1841–1910

Hᴇ succeeded to the throne in 1901, upon the death of his mother Queen Victoria.

This king waited in the wings through most of the longest reign in English history. When he did succeed, at age fifty-nine, he was unprepared because his mother had not seen fit to show him anything in the red boxes or delegate any real authority to him or let him help her in any constructive way. Journalists and journalistic historians have thought this showed the Queen hated him because he was her heir apparent; the thesis has been expanded to assert that all Hanoverian rulers hate their heirs apparent.

Some of the earlier ones did. But Victoria did not hate her son; she loved him. It is true that she blamed him for a while, at least, for the Prince Consort's death. She held it dreadfully against him that it was getting this son out of an affair with an actress—an actress! the Queen's son!—that had weakened poor Papa so that he caught a bad cold, which aggravated his typhoid fever, which caused his death. And she did indeed have a reputation for creating and bearing grudges; when her great-grandson was born, the one who later became George VI, they were actually afraid to break the news to her because he had chosen a sacred date, the thirty-fourth anniversary of (again) the death of the Prince Consort.

Victoria was not a logical or a very intellectual woman. But she was a good woman, doing always what she really believed was right. It seems likely that she thought it would be bad enough to be succeeded by her scandalous eldest son; she could not prevent that; but she certainly could prevent his taking any part in her government meantime. So that is what she did.

Apologists for the Prince of Wales believe that his lack of occupation in these matters accounts for his colorful social and personal career. But of course he could have amused himself along more constructive and respectable lines if he had been so inclined. His mother would have given him every encouragement and aid if he had wanted to pursue art or economics like his father the Prince Consort. Dear Albert had kept very busy indeed with his studies; the present Emperor of Japan has made himself a highly respected marine biologist; the present Duke of Edinburgh is an expert wildlife photographer. The Prince of Wales who finally became Edward VII simply preferred to spend his time on food, drink, horses, gambling, and mistresses.

He had more mistresses than any English king since Charles II—Mrs. Langtry the most enduring of the actresses, the Honourable Mrs. George Keppel and the Countess of Warwick the most famous of the society beauties. This in spite of the fact that his wife was quite the loveliest queen England had had for centuries. To find one comparable it was necessary to go back as far as the 1460's, bypassing Catherine Howard because *non casta,* all the way back to Elizabeth Woodville, that "incorruptible beauty with the gilt hair" who married Edward IV. Alexandra of Denmark was beautiful, elegant, gracious, dignified, good, gay, affectionate, and generous. She had, indeed, a few faults, such as unpunctuality—she disrupted train schedules all over Europe—and a weakness for infantile, embarrassing practical jokes. But her children absolutely adored Darling Motherdear, the court circle was not far behind, and even her gross old roué of a husband "always loved me the best, I think," she said, wistfully. Before she was even middle-aged she began to grow deaf, and this rather built a wall around her; she could no longer enjoy being in groups she could not hear or talk to; and she withdrew more and more into the company of her two younger daughters. (One of them did not seem to mind staying an old maid to comfort Darling Motherdear; the other did escape, with some assistance, becoming Queen Maud of Norway.) Queen Alexandra lived on until 1925, secluded in Marlborough House; when she died numbers of people were surprised, because they thought she had died long before.

Edward VII had died in 1910, less than ten years after he came to the throne. His admirers give him great credit for the Entente Cordiale in 1904, which Viscount Esher says he had suggested to the French Ambassador a quarter-century before he became king. "Before he was thirty," Lord Esher says, "he was in the habit of requesting interviews from Ministers and begging for explanations of their policy." This thirst for information did not extend to other founts of knowledge. There are many funny stories—dialect stories, in the thick, German accent surely discreditable in a king of the seventh English generation—that show Edward's abysmal ignorance and his apparent pride in it. It seems doubtful that in his reign, which included part of the Boer War and the beginnings of a political revolution at home, he could have commanded much respect or reflected much credit upon the Crown.

But the legend of his charm persists. He could, indeed, be very nice when he wanted to be. He really loved his children, especially his heir, George Duke of York before he was Prince of Wales, and went out of his way to show him the consideration he had never had himself from Queen Victoria. This is no negative virtue; a boy who has been hazed at school often enjoys hazing younger boys, just as viciously, in his turn. But King Edward, who had never been shown (much less consulted about) the documents in the red boxes, gave his heir every chance to learn and prepare himself to be king.

He was also kind, in his own way, to his wife. It was not, of course, kind to be as openly unfaithful as he was. Everybody would have known about his affairs, perhaps, but he did not even try to be careful or considerate. His flaunting of his "friends" at his coronation, for instance, where they had a special box the court wits called the "King's Loose Box," really came under the head of bragging. (King Edward's honest opinion that these beautiful ladies loved him personally takes us back to King Henry VIII, who was even fatter.) And he did not spare Queen Alexandra the embarrassment and distress she felt, predictably, when he involved himself in the Tranby Croft, the Beresford, and the Aylesford scandals. Edward could have kept out of all of these. (He was furious when the Kaiser pompously wrote that it was unbecoming of an honorary colonel of Prussian Guards to be "embroiled with men young enough to be his children in a gambling scandal"—but the Kaiser was quite right; and it was unbecoming for the first gentleman of England, too.) Alexandra was so upset about his involvement in the Beresford matter that she prolonged some visits she had been making to her family on the Continent, not coming home until their son became seriously ill and she was sent for. But then she forgave her husband and put herself on his side again. She was too good and affectionate to be angry with him long; and he was grateful to her.

He showed this and his own real, if fragmented, affection by always making other people defer to her and show her every respect and consideration. If Alexandra were wearing a tiara, for instance, and another lady had come to dinner without hers, he would issue a stern rebuke; the Princess of Wales took the trouble to put on a tiara, why had not she? He was always particularly interested in matters like this, the details of dress and decorations.

They were, face it, just about his speed. The people around him faced this obvious if regrettable fact. William III's shrewd intelligence (from the Dutch side of his family) had gone out of the royal line when William died childless. Charles II's insight and flashing wit (from the Medici branch of his family) were lost similarly when Charles died childless. And the Prince Consort, considered by many to be the leavener of the royal lump, was industrious and painstaking rather than brilliant. A little verse about Edward VII's enduring mistress Mrs. Keppel gives a thumbnail sketch of him:

> There is peace within the palace
> At a little word from Alice.
> Send for Mrs. Keppel!
> She alone can keep the King from dumps,
> Once she's shown him how to play his trumps.
> Send for Mrs. Keppel!*

* Quoted in Ralph G. Martin, *Jennie: The Life of Lady Randolph Churchill* (New York: New American Library, 1972), vol. 2, p. 448.

Queen Alexandra herself sent for Mrs. Keppel during the King's last illness. It showed, everyone said, how truly good she was. She waited at the palace door for her husband's mistress, took her upstairs, left them alone. But she may have felt gratitude to Mrs. Keppel for sharing the burden of a difficult husband—as Queen Caroline may have felt gratitude to the women who shared George II's affections.

She could not show him how to play his trumps, but Queen Alexandra's loyal affection for her husband has helped his reputation. Edward VII is still as controversial as George IV. A choice is still to be made between blaming Queen Victoria for bringing him up badly and giving him no responsibility and sympathizing with Queen Victoria because her heir was a throwback to his two grandfathers and to his limited and idle great-uncles. In either case he ascended her throne still a juvenile delinquent in his sixtieth year. Possibly if he had had more time as king— But more probably not.

Victoria

1819–1901

SHE succeeded to the throne in 1837, upon the death of her uncle
William IV.

It was only toward the end of her uncle's reign that Princess
Alexandrina Victoria was taken very seriously. The children Queen
Adelaide had borne had died, but she was still young; she might have
borne more. Or she could have died and the King had children by a
second wife. Instead King William himself died, and Victoria at
eighteen ascended the throne.

The Sully portrait of her actually doing so is a familiar one, and the
first years of her reign well remembered. The childlike, tiny Queen,
receiving their momentous news and presiding at her first council,
impresses her ministers with her royal dignity and heartfelt wish "to do
what is fit and right." She has her bed moved out of her mother's room
and accepts no further guidance from the Duchess of Kent. Instead she
listens with adoration to her prime minister, Lord Melbourne, who only
occasionally—as in the Lady Flora Hastings case—fails to steer her well.
She marries a handsome young German and has an enormous family;
then her husband dies and she all but commits suttee. Suddenly not only
her youth but her life is over; the Widow of Windsor, crepe-hung,
half-cracked (that adjective is the Victorians') becomes a recluse who
thinks it no part of her duty to make public appearances. A whole new

generation grows up that has never seen the face of the Queen. Meantime her popularity, high in the first few years, has swooped to a dangerous low. It is not until she is very old, having her Golden and then actually her Diamond Jubilee, that her people love her again.

No matter how many biographies you read, you will never understand Queen Victoria until you have saturated yourself in her own journals, especially the *Leaves from the Journal of Our Life in the Highlands* which (to the embarrassment of her family) she published late in life. They are unbelievable. The simplicity of her mind is unbelievable. Queen Victoria lived to be old, very old, but she never matured. Her journals are always those of ingenuous adolescence. Like other members of her line before and since, her chief acquaintance with books was from the outside, but dear Albert had tried so hard to improve her mind, and she had tried so hard to learn from him, and nothing happened.

But if her mind never changed neither did her character. That was strength itself. Black was black and white was white; right was right and wrong was wrong. She does not deserve having the achievements of the Victorian Age called after her—it was dear Albert who encouraged the scientists and literary men and promoted the Great Exhibition—but for the Victorian virtues she does. Not only did Queen Victoria have convictions, she had the courage of them, and down the long years of her reign she stood up firmly for every one.

In her simplicity, she cut straight to the heart of many matters. And by repetition—she had a splendid memory—she learned much. Among England's foolish laws (like the one quaranining dogs with rabies shots, while smallpox and diptheria epidemics still flourish in London) is one making a prime minister's papers unavailable to his successor. No wonder English politicians are always reinventing the wheel. But the sovereign, who sees all the papers of succeeding governments, can furnish continuity. Thus when Mr. Wilson succeeds Mr. Heath he cannot go back and read Mr. Heath's papers, but Queen Elizabeth II has already read them—they were in her daily red boxes—and she can, if she likes, fill Mr. Wilson in. So Queen Victoria was a useful liaison between her successive prime ministers.

And the longer she reigned, the more useful she became.

This upright lady had an upright husband whose virtue, like hers, had triumphed over a rather sordid and shady heritage. Albert of Saxe-Coburg-Gotha had a father who was, one biographer says candidly, "an unmitigated disaster." * As for his mother, she had been banished and then divorced for adultery. Albert was four when he saw her last.

By rights, he should have emerged from this violently broken home an emotional and a behavioral problem; instead he was a faultlessly regular young man. His only weakness was that he could not convince his adopted country, as he convinced its queen, of his perfections. England disagreed with her opinion that dear Albert was always right. Particularly England disagreed with her opinion (Albert's) that the Queen should be a force in constitutional matters and the relations with foreign countries; it did not wish the Queen (Albert) to have any more power at all. Perhaps because he pushed too hard, Albert may have reduced Victoria's already insignificant powers. She was really, as everyone knew, nothing but a figurehead. The American ambassador's wife, for one, was always commenting in her letters home on the immense amount of deference paid to this little woman who had so little real power.

With no authority to wield as far as the country was concerned, Victoria became a petty domestic tyrant, ruling her family and her court with a heavy hand. Never tired of standing herself, she kept everybody else standing until feet nearly broke off at the ankles. Never cool enough—this and her protruding eyes and her volatile temper suggest, perhaps, an overactive thyroid—she forbade fires to those who found their rooms in damp, stone Windsor Castle nothing above zero. Above temptation herself, she was so strict and judgmental with her children that it was hard for them to develop. A justly famous cartoon of Queen Victoria in old age—Beerbohm again—shows her sitting in conscious rectitude while her son the Prince of Wales, almost as fat and old, stands in the corner with his face to the wall.

The people who got along with Queen Victoria were the ones who learned to manage her—Melbourne, of course, at first; Albert above all; Disraeli; John Brown. It was in Disraeli's prime-ministership that she

---

* Elizabeth Longford, *Queen Victoria* (New York: Pyramid Books, 1966), p. 172.

became Empress of India. Queen Empress—and the British Empire covered the globe, the sun never set on the British flag. The Suez Canal (in 1875, Disraeli had bought up large quantities of shares) made management and coordination easier, and if the natives were restless the British Army, dressing for dinner in the outposts of the Empire, could put them down. The Boers were troublesome too, but only they and the brief Crimean War marred the peacefulness of the longest reign.

Victoria was so emotional a sovereign, so decided in her likes and dislikes, that her being only a constitutional monarch saved many a head from rolling on Tower Hill. She despised Mr. Gladstone as heartily as she loved dear Mr. Disraeli, later dear Lord Beaconsfield. When Mr. Gladstone was prime minister, the Queen could not work with him at all. Mr. Gladstone for his part found her equally difficult; he went around predicting the end of the monarchy because the Queen meddled in politics, and after his resignation (he refused the usual earldom) he actually suggested that the best way the Queen could celebrate her Diamond Jubilee would be by abdicating.

It had been bad enough, the Opposition thought, when Queen Victoria had let herself be unduly influenced by that fawning, flattering mountebank Disraeli—"we authors, ma'am," he would say to her, after her publication of her Highland journals—but he at least had the duty of conferring with her, he at least, as prime minister, was in a position to shower her with Indian titles and Indian diamonds. It was the Queen's insignificant favorites who really upset first the court and then the country. One of these was the Munshi; another was John Brown.

John Brown became a real scandal. A thoroughly ordinary (the Queen's family and courtiers thought) Scottish servant, he soon came to exercise an almost uncanny influence over her. His pay and his privileges increased rapidly; his rude manners, even toward Her Majesty, were considered by the Queen only forthrightness and honesty; and she was willing to call indisposition what everybody else called plain, sodden drunkenness. The wildest stories, inevitably, spread: the Queen was a madwoman, a spiritualist, and (remembering her father and the wicked uncles) a lewd Hanoverian. John Brown was, respectively, her keeper, her medium, and her lover—even her morganatic husband. Nobody who knew the Queen's character believed any of this, of course, especially that she should so far forget her royalty as to marry a servant. But her continued seclusion made her a mystery to her kingdom at large.

John Brown himself did much to end this seclusion, for with dear faithful Brown on the box Queen Victoria was increasingly willing to drive out. With him to pin her shawl (and sometimes her chin: "Hoots, then, wumman, can you no hold yerr head up?" he was heard shouting at her) she could dispense with her lady-in-waiting. Brown was all the companion she needed on these excursions. At home, it was said, Brown even went into her room without knocking. And when finally Brown did die, Queen Victoria not only erected overlapping statues and memorials to him (asking the poet laureate Tennyson for verses to carve) but was with difficulty restrained from publishing a memoir of him. She had written it herself. Whether this sort of thing was worse than her meddling in politics, or not, it was hard to say.

When in turn Queen Victoria herself died, Edward VII made the removal of the statues of good faithful Brown one of his first kingly acts. He also burned the papers of the Munshi, her favorite clerk Abdul Karim, who began by blotting her letters for her and ended helping to compose them. (He was also supposed to be her teacher of Hindustani but even dear humorless Albert, leaning out from the gold bar of heaven, must have snickered at that; he had tried to teach her too.) King Edward could not, of course, get rid of all the evidences that his mother the great queen was in her old age—indeed, all through her life—a contradictory woman capable of embarrassing her family and country as well as making them very proud. But as time has passed she has been laughed at always more gently.

Perhaps Queen Victoria's most quoted saying is the one from her childhood, when she first understood that she was in the line of succession and would one day be England's Queen. "I will be good," she said then, and all her life, according to her lights, she did her very best to be a good queen. "How I wish I could have done more," she said on one anniversary of her coming to the throne. The frequently quoted "We are not amused" recalls a stiffness which indeed there was in Queen Victoria; but it is less often remembered that most of the stiffness was in her spine. Something better to remember her by is what she said to Mr. Balfour when he came to see her at Windsor during "Black Week" of the Boer War: "Please understand that there is no one depressed in this house; we are not interested in the possibilities of defeat; they do not," said Queen Victoria, "exist."

William IV

1765–1837

HE succeeded to the throne in 1830, upon the death of his older brother George IV.

Sometimes a second son shares the educational and social opportunities of the heir to the throne, an understudy in case one is needed to take over. But it is not anticipated that a third son will ever become king. This one, therefore, was given no preparation and, really, scarcely any education. He was only thirteen when he was sent into the Navy as a midshipman. Everything he learned there was bad, and the fact that he had the command of a frigate, when he came of age, meant only that he was the king's son.

Fortunately for the Navy, the Duke of Clarence (as Prince William soon became) disliked it and gave it up. He established residence at Richmond with the actress Dorothea Jordan, who gave him ten children—FitzClarences who married later into the legitimate English aristocracy. Since Mrs. Jordan had four illegitimate children already, it was quite a household.

Clarence was right to stay so long with Mrs. Jordan, for she was the only person in his long life who seemed even to like him. His father, of course, despised him, his shipmates had found him obnoxious, and the high command agreed he was not cut out for a naval officer. Subsequently, when the French Revolution broke out, his father refused to allow him to serve afloat, and the ministers chimed in by refusing to allow him in the Admiralty. Again because he was the king's son he was given high commissions, but no authority went with his rank of vice-admiral in 1794 and admiral in 1799.

He had a third chance, too; by that time George III was sunk in hopeless insanity and could not forbid him anything. Under Canning the office of Lord High Admiral was revived for him, but under the succeeding prime minister, the old Duke of Wellington, he was out the following year. His quarrels at the Admiralty had been unceasing.

His success as a suitor had been no greater than his success in the Navy. Nobody wanted him there, either. There was never any question of his marrying Mrs. Jordan, but half a dozen more eligible ladies, English heiresses as well as foreign royalty, were given the chance to reject him. Finally, when he was almost fifty-three, he was accepted by Princess Adelaide of Saxe-Meiningen, less than half his age.

He was no more attractive than he had ever been but he had better prospects. Suddenly he was third in line for the English throne, directly after the Prince Regent and the Duke of York, who were now both childless.

The Prince Regent had had one child, Princess Charlotte, by his hated and soon abandoned wife Caroline of Brunswick. Charlotte had married Leopold of Saxe-Coburg, later King of the Belgians, under the best of auspices; they were a hearty, happy, popular young couple; but in 1817 Charlotte had died in childbed, and her baby with her.

There was a great rustling around then among the Prince Regent's six younger brothers. It seemed ridiculous that they had not an heir among them, but this was exactly the case. The Duke of Cumberland, like the Duke of York, was married to an apparently barren wife. The Duke of Sussex was unwilling to abandon his illegal arrangement for a dynastic marriage. The others—the dukes of Clarence, Cambridge, and Kent—were more than willing. The Duke of Kent, who would become Queen Victoria's father, had lived with his Madame St. Laurent for nearly twenty-eight years, but he gave her up for the good of the cause.

It was well that he did, for Adelaide of Saxe-Meiningen bore his brother William no long-lived child. She had two little girls who lived less than three months between them. But Adelaide was so much younger than her husband, and he was so very proven a sire—those ten FitzClarences—that England was never sure she would not provide an heir. She was made regent, when William became king, just in case she did.

When William came to the throne, at sixty-four, "a bursting, bubbling old gentleman, with quarterdeck gestures, round rolling eyes, and a head like a pineapple, his sudden elevation . . . after . . . years of utter insignificance . . . almost set him crazy." * And, of course, his father George III had actually been crazy; everyone had a watchful eye on poor old "Silly Billy" as he made his long, embarrassing speeches or went into his periodic rages, wondering just when he too would cross the line.

However, he never did. Nothing very good could be said for him as a king, but he was much less trouble to his ministers than they anticipated. He had never seemed to realize, when he was Lord High Admiral, that he was supposed to be a figurehead only and not give orders and make changes. But as king he was ductile. He felt reluctant, for instance, to create enough Whig peers for the Reform Bill of 1832 to be pushed through the House of Lords, but he did as he was told; and also during his reign, with no credit to him but with no temper tantrums from him either, the Poor Law was amended, the law governing the choice of municipal officers was modernized, and slavery was abolished throughout the British Empire. There was even a gesture toward the reformation of virtual slavery in factories—the Factory Act of 1833 prevented children under nine from working at all, and limited those thirteen and under to forty-eight hours a week. Adolescents eighteen and under, however, could still work sixty-eight hours.

Also under eighteen, the Princess Alexandrina Victoria (called Drina when she was younger, but by now Victoria) was heiress presumptive to the throne. Her father the Duke of Kent, King George's fourth son, Edward, had been winner in the race to produce George III's legitimate grandchild. He had died when Victoria (then Drina) was a baby and her upbringing had since been in the hands of her formidable mother. From this extremely trying lady stemmed all the troubles and trials of

---

* Lytton Strachey, *Queen Victoria* (New York: Harcourt, Brace, 1921), pp. 53–54.

Queen Victoria's adolescence—not, as one would expect, from the rather awkward situation in which she and the King and Queen found themselves, the Queen still hoping to produce a living child, the court swarming with FitzClarences who had only one thing the matter with them, and the young princess waiting modestly at one side. It is much to the credit of King William and his quiet, unobtrusive Queen that they were all so kind and polite to one another.

But the Duchess of Kent, Victoria's mother, was neither kind nor polite, and she brought out the very worst in the King. Encouraged by the comptroller of her household, the upstart Sir John Conroy whom many people believed to be her lover, she thrust herself and her shrinking little daughter crudely forward, making practically regal progresses without the King's knowledge and consent, and appropriating a suite of seventeen rooms in Kensington Palace which he had expressly forbidden her to use. It was this last that proved the final straw for the King. He went into one of his tremendous rages—in public, at his birthday dinner in front of a hundred guests—declaring it was his greatest wish to live until the Princess Victoria reached eighteen, so that she could succeed him directly, without her mother's regency. It was one of the worst scenes an English king ever made, worse than George II's when he used to kick his hat, or his wig, all around the room. Really it was more comparable to the temper tantrum King John had had, actually frothing at the mouth, when he came back from Runnymede.

King William did live till Victoria was eighteen, but barely so. The lasting impression of this "foolish, disreputable old man," as Strachey calls him, is the figure he cut at that public birthday dinner. He was a horrid sight at best; he had taken to covering his pineapple-shaped head with a black wig, and to painting his face. The black wig was askew, the painted jowls shook with fury as he lost all control and shouted at the Duchess of Kent, neither noticing nor caring that he had reduced the Princess Victoria to tears.

George IV

1762–1830

H<small>E</small> succeeded to the throne in 1820, upon the death of his father George III. But as Prince Regent he had been virtually king since 1811.

His mad old father had been outworn. But the new King was worn, too, and his reign lacked some of the brilliance of his Regency.

Regency and Regent should not be confused. Subjects—not only English subjects—are commendably anxious to admire royalty, and on sometimes slight pretext deck it out in largely imaginary virtues and talents. Mildly pretty princesses are routinely called beautiful, and mildly attractive princes, especially heirs to the throne, emerge charming, talented, and cultivated. In the case of George IV, it is hard by now to distinguish the legend from the man. He gets full credit for all the graces and beauties of Regency architecture and decoration and society; there is a biography of him called *The Great Corinthian* because, like the Renaissance Man, the Corinthian was supposed to combine every talent and accomplishment.

George IV's young portraits show him attractive in the way a plump, pouting, wide-eyed baby can be attractive. Without his aureole of royal light (the point is that he never was without it) his attractions were unimpressive. In any case they were soon buried in physical, emotional, and intellectual fatty tissue.

He was one of fifteen children of George III, and by no means the one his father would have chosen to succeed him on the throne. Frederick, the second son, was the one he outspokenly preferred, and this view, expounded in lucid periods as well as insane ones, no doubt depressed the heir and hurt his feelings. But he remained the heir—there was nothing George III could do about that—and while he was waiting there was plenty he could do to divert his mind.

He did almost everything—except, of course, work or study. Some of his companions were brilliant—like Sheridan and Charles James Fox—but he derived no liberal education from association with them. His interests were, chiefly, gambling, dress, extravagant and ostentatious building, and women.

One of his early indiscretions was the beautiful actress Mary Robinson, more often called Perdita from the role she was playing in *The Winter's Tale* when, as she wrote in her autobiography, "my eyes met those of the Prince of Wales." The Prince not only showered money and jewelry on Perdita, he wrote her letters actually promising to marry her, and George III paid a very large sum indeed to get those foolish letters back.

Young George had marriage on the brain. If he had not mentioned it Perdita would never have thought of it. Mrs. Fitzherbert was a different matter; she did think along the lines of holy and respectable matrimony; but even she would not have expected marriage with the Prince of Wales unless he brought it up.

Mrs. Fitzherbert was a lady. Though still quite young, she had been widowed twice. She was a Roman Catholic. The Hanover line, which owed its position on the English throne to the very fact that it was not Roman Catholic, was obligated to make Protestant marriages only. It was also expected to make royal marriages only, and Mrs. Fitzherbert, of course, though of a very good and old family, was a commoner. Even before the Royal Marriages Act, George III had forsworn the beautiful Lady Sarah Lennox because she was a commoner. So surely George III felt some sympathy for his son when he in turn fell unsuitably in love; but he felt only rage when that foolish young man actually married Mrs. Fitzherbert.

Mrs. Fitzherbert, of course, acted far more foolishly than the Prince did. She was—usually—a sensible and intelligent young woman. She may have been in love; more probably, she was the kind of royalist who cannot say no to a Royal Highness. Like the kind of Catholics who melt into nods and becks and wreathèd smiles whenever a priest speaks to them, she went all to pieces when the Prince of Wales went into a decline, declaring that he would die unless his Maria, his only love, married him. Whether he faked or actually made a suicide attempt—in any case there was blood on the bandages—Mrs. Fitzherbert was, in spite of herself, persuaded.

Of course it was not really a marriage. It was strictly against the law. The Royal Marriages Act, in 1772, made the king's permission necessary to any member of the Royal Family. The King himself had got this Act through Parliament, after two of his brothers had married non-royally without his permission, and he would have had to ask for an Act repealing it even if he had wanted to make an exception for the heir to the throne. This, of course, he did not want to do. He disapproved of Mrs. Fitzherbert for the same reason he had disapproved of his own beautiful Sarah: she was non-royal.

Mrs. Fitzherbert's male relatives did what they could to make the ceremony respectable and binding—witnesses, a regular clergyman, documentary evidence—but legally it was a farce, legally it was inexcusable.

On Mrs. Fitzherbert the marriage was binding. She may (or may not) have borne the Prince a discreet child or children. She had his respect and admiration all his life and, as far as he was capable of it, his love. They had estrangements and finally a permanent one, but (having asked the Pope for a ruling) she always considered the Prince, the Regent, and King George IV her husband in the sight of God, and he (in his fashion) considered her his wife.

He was not faithful to her, of course. He took mistresses, and their final estrangement came through the influence of one of them, the vulgar, cowlike Lady Jersey. But the worst thing was his taking another wife.

He did so under pressure, on the promise of having all his monumental debts paid.* The princess chosen for him was his first

---

* All of George III's sons were wastrels. When a tall column was topped with a statue

cousin, Caroline of Brunswick, the niece of King George III.

This marriage was a disaster. Princess Caroline had many of the family faults and perhaps it was by projection that the Prince hated her on sight. Also, she was frankly dirty—whereas Mrs. Fitzherbert, though not strictly a beauty, was "always like a fresh rose." Eventually, the Princess would also show herself less like Caesar's wife than the wife of the heir to the throne was expected to be.

But there was no question about the paternity of the child of this disreputable marriage. Coming to his wedding almost falling-down drunk, dripping with tears throughout the ceremony, and spending, so said the bride, most of his wedding-night out cold in the luckily cold bedroom grate, the Prince of Wales managed to beget the Princess Charlotte. The probability is that he never approached his wife again.

Caroline consoled herself; she was flagrantly indiscreet if not actually adulterous; and when finally old King George died and the Prince succeeded as George IV, he tried to divorce her by a Bill of Pains and Penalties. It was so much a case of the pot calling the kettle black that he could not put it through. He did succeed in barring her from Westminster Abbey the day of his coronation. Poor Caroline—discreditable as she was, she deserves some sympathy—had come there in queenly attire hoping she would be crowned too.

Much of the London we see today—the sightseer's London—dates from the time of George IV, the regency 1811–1820, the reign then till 1830. He was a compulsive builder, decorator, spender. He was fortunate in its being a great time for architects; John Nash is only the most famous of the fine ones we call "Regency"; but unfortunately it was often the Regent's personal taste which prevailed. The monstrosities of the Brighton Pavilion ("Looks as if St. Paul's had gone down to Brighton and pupped," the Reverend Sydney Smith said of this famous eyesore) are sure to be all his. Perhaps it was just as well George never built his projected palace in Regent's Park, to which Nash planned the beautiful curve of Regent Street and which he rimmed with the great terraces, Cambridge and the rest. But then—be fair—George's taste did

---

of one of them, the Duke of York, it was said that he had gone up there to escape his creditors.

swing from the sublime to the ridiculous, from the beautifully chaste to the vulgarly new-rich, from Mrs. Fitzherbert to Lady Jersey—and, no doubt, back again.

Politically, George IV proved an impotent king. As Prince of Wales, much under the influence of his friend Fox, he had been an outspoken Whig; as prince regent and king, he found this indiscretion had not been forgiven by the Tories. During most of his regency and reign it was the Tories who were in power. Lord Liverpool was prime minister but it was Castlereagh, and later Canning, who set the seal on this era. Canning succeeded Liverpool when he finally resigned, but died soon after, and the old Duke of Wellington became prime minister.

What a study in contrasts they made, the hero of Waterloo and the non-hero on the throne!

George IV will always have his apologists. As with Edward VII, his much-alike great-nephew, the legend of his charm persists. Much allowance can be made for him; his father's method of child-rearing was questionable, perhaps even touched with madness; perhaps much of his own erratic behavior was symptomatic of the same disease, porphyria, his father had; his conduct toward Mrs. Fitzherbert reflects discredit, but Mrs. Fitzherbert acted like a fool in "marrying" him and deserved everything she got; he was very ugly indeed to the princess he legally married, but surely she should have taken a bath, or even baths; he was always blubbering like a baby, great disgusting tears rolling down his fat cheeks, but then he was always, or at least often, drunk. And he was vain and extravagant, but all royalty is surrounded by sycophants who can turn stronger heads than royalty's have often been.

What Leigh Hunt wrote about him—being sent to prison for "libel" when he did—was perfectly true; George IV was indeed "a violator of his word, a libertine . . . a despiser of domestic ties, the companion of demireps . . . without one single claim to the gratitude of his country, or the respect of posterity." But then Leigh Hunt was not making allowances.

George III

1738–1820

He succeeded to the throne in 1760, upon the death of his grandfather, George II.

He was only twenty-two when he became king; dying at eighty-one, he had the second longest reign in English history. But during much of it he was either insane or borderline, and at his very best he was not too bright. This was unfortunate, because he was a politically active king.

"Be a king, George!" his mother exhorted him. She had never had a chance to be a queen herself, for his father, Frederick, had died while still Prince of Wales. She tried to compensate by ruling through her son.

She had watched the royal power, during the reign of George II, slipping more and more into the hands of his ministers. Older people at court had watched it even longer; it went back through the reign of George I. It was the kind of thing that usually happens when a head of state, or a head of a business, is not very interested in the state or the business and he is surrounded by people who are. The trouble was not, as has often been said, a lack of communication because the Hanoverian kings did not speak English. They spoke French, and so did the ministers; besides, George II did learn some English, though George I never bothered. The trouble was rather one of laissez-faire. The first two Georges had been, a contemporary wrote, each "a royal ward to his state guardians." They had been content to let their ministers do the work.

But now came this young George III, setting out "to eradicate the deep system of ministerial power . . . and to fulfill the executive trust vested in him by the laws. . . ." He wanted the royal power himself. He did not go so far as to want figureheads for ministers, but he did not believe in "referring his government wholly" to them.*

All this was very healthy and commendable—though of course the ministers did not like it—and George III did seem to be a very nice young man. Not only because he was young was he considered promising. He had virtues that his Hanoverian predecessors had never even dreamed of; he enjoyed an active, outdoor life with particular emphasis on farming; he had no bad habits; and he was utterly faithful to his young wife. This last was particularly a triumph of mind over matter because the Queen, Charlotte of Mecklenburg-Strelitz, was a decided contrast to the girl George had wanted to marry. He had fallen in love at first sight with beautiful Lady Sarah Lennox, and would have married her at second if she had only been royal. Charlotte was a thoroughly nice girl with a mouth like a circus clown's. Even in her portraits, and royal portraits tend to be flattering, it is a slash straight across her face. But it was part of the young King's exemplary character that he married her with good grace and immediately became devoted to her. He gave her nine sons and six daughters, which was perhaps overdoing it.

George was only twenty-six, only a few years on the throne, when he had his first significant illness. It is significant because it is famous. Many historians have called it his first attack of insanity. Two authorities now refute this. These English psychiatrists, Ida Macalpine and Richard Hunter, in 1969 published a long book called *George III and the Mad-Business* which introduces to most of us a disease called hepatic porphyria. It is too bad that Queen Victoria had no chance to read this book, for she was very sensitive indeed about her grandfather's being called "the Mad King" and she would have been gratified to know that his madness was only a symptom of a highly respectable physical

* Quoted in Herbert Butterfield, *George III and the Historians* (New York: Macmillan, 1959), pp. 45, 46.

disease. Of course mental diseases are respectable now, but they were not respectable then, and even in our enlightened century nobody wants an ancestor with manic-depressive psychosis, which is what George III has always been thought to have had.

Instead he had, it seems, a genetic metabolic anomaly "due to overproduction of the porphyrin precursors. . . . An increased quantity of porphobilinogen (and porphyrins) accumulates in the liver." Acute intermittent porphyria, as hepatic porphyria is usually called, is chronic; it runs, as we laymen say with refreshing simplicity, in families; and "Paroxysms of abdominal pain, . . . vomiting, distention, and diarrhea or constipation, are the most common manifestations. . . . Neurologic disturbances may be sudden in onset. . . . Convulsive seizures may occur. . . . Most patients develop psychiatric manifestations which vary from mild (e.g., irritability, anxiety, confusion, restlessness) to severe (e.g., delirium, hallucinations, psychoses)." *

Laymen may think this brings us back to where we started. If George III had psychoses as a consequence of porphyria, that still makes him (to us) psychotic. And we are always being told not to make our historical judgments out of context. We are not supposed to apply twentieth-century standards to the Duke of Marlborough's taking money from his mistress to get started in life (this was perfectly all right in the seventeenth century) or to Richard Coeur-de-Lion's killing women, children, and "babies at the breast" (this was perfectly all right in the twelfth). We would certainly be judging George III and his circle in terms of our century, not his, if we thought of him as the victim of a physical disease.

In context, George III was a madman. This is what he thought he was, this is what his doctors and family and court and country thought. History developed on the basis of this premise.

But no matter now; the important thing is to remember that Macalpine and Hunter have established through impressive research that this is not what George III had in 1765. Porphyria is what he would have later, in 1788, in 1810, etc. The point is that George III was not psychotic for any reason in 1765, the year of the Stamp Act.

* David N. Holvey, M.D., ed., *The Merck Manual of Diagnosis and Therapy*, Twelfth Edition (copyright 1972 by Merck & Co., Inc., Rahway, N.J.), pp. 1108–09.

He did find this and the subsequent American War upsetting. His accession (1760) had found the nation apparently on the brink of a successful phase, with the Peace of Paris, in 1763, ending the Seven Years' War. Then the Stamp Act caused excitement in America which was all out of proportion, King George and his ministers thought, to its actual effect on the colonists' purses and "rights."

American refusal to accept the Stamp Act quietly was offensive to the young King. Then as always he was well-meaning and well-motivated, but stubborn and, if crossed, sullen. He took it as a personal insult. He was indignant that his colonists should question his knowing, and doing, what was best and just for them. His indignation mounted, naturally, with the Boston Tea Party (1773), the battles of Lexington and Bunker Hill (1775), the Declaration of Independence (1776), and the entrance into the war, on the colonists' side, of France, Spain, and Holland (1778, 1779, 1780). He was personally bitter against the rebels, and the rebels, enthusiastically pulling down his statues in public squares, felt personally bitter about him.

Naturally George III took the news of Yorktown surrender very hard, and at first refused to receive the new American ambassador, John Adams. But it was not the loss of the war, as is so often said, that drove him mad. He did not show the first signs of derangement until 1788, and it was not until 1810, after the death of his favorite daughter Princess Amelia, that he permanently lost his mind.

Even then, in the light of the researches of Macalpine and Hunter, the events were not connected. It was only by coincidence that the King's illness, porphyria, reached a climax at that time. But his contemporaries knew nothing of this and their natural inference was that "his troubles had gone to his head."

He suffered, and everybody around him suffered, from the psychotic symptoms of his disease both when it was active and when it was merely anticipated. In the years between 1788 and 1810 nobody ever knew when the King was likely to "go off." The King knew least of all, and took full advantage of this to get his own way. When anyone tried to cross him or disagree with him he would point significantly to his head, and that settled that. Nobody, politician or progeny, wanted the responsibility of sending the King into one of his spells of insanity.

It was hardest of all for the Prince of Wales, who, persona non grata with the King at best, was damned if he did and damned if he didn't; but much sympathy was also felt for the Queen. She had borne him all those children and in every way made him the best of wives, but after his madness began she was physically terrified of him and it was no kindness when, by the Regency Act of 1811, she was awarded the custody of the King.

Perhaps it would have been easier for everybody if the doctors then had known what the doctors know now, that the King's ailment was not one classified as a mental disease but was a physical disease which merely had psychotic manifestations. But nothing would have altered the fact that the King did things like leaping out of his carriage, seizing and shaking the branch of a tree, and carrying on a conversation with it thinking it was the King of Prussia. Such conduct was not suitable in a reigning king, obviously he was not able to attend to the duties of his position, and it was accordingly quite rightly decided that he would have to be shut up. But his doctors had neither chlorpromazine, rauwolfia alkaloids, chloral hydrate, or meperidine with which to treat him successfully, so they had to treat him as best they knew how. The list of their remedies and procedures is distressing. The unfortunate King was purged, blistered, and exercised; he was placed in warm water with cold water dripping from a height down on his head; he was successively punished, coerced, intimidated, and rewarded; and he was confined often and long in a "strait-waistcoat." This last restraint is bad enough when it is used on a commoner; used on a king the effect was doubly traumatic; and as his doctor said, "The strait waistcoat was the offence to her pride which the Queen never could, and never did, overcome."

Sunk in madness, the King missed most of the excitement of his long reign. The revolt of the distant American colonies was nothing to the rise of Napoleon Bonaparte just across the channel. Englishmen had never feared that George Washington would come over and take England, but they had every reason to fear that Napoleon would. A whole generation of children grew up under the threat that "old Boney" would get them if they were bad. Defeating the French and Spanish at Trafalgar (1805), Nelson put down what seemed like imminent invasion, and the Duke of Wellington was victorious in the Peninsular

Campaign (1808–1813), but it was Napoleon himself who most contributed to his own downfall. His ill-advised attempt in Russia led to his abdication and exile. George III, rusticating at Kew, now blind as well as insane, never knew about his coming back from Elba and being defeated again, by the Duke of Wellington, at Waterloo.

George II

1683–1760

HE succeeded to the throne in 1727, upon the death of his father, George I.

There were a few good things to be said about George II. He was brave; at the Battle of Oudenarde, when he was twenty-five, he led a cavalry charge, was unhorsed, and put himself unnecessarily in real danger; at the Battle of Dettingen, when he was sixty, he fought at the head of his troops all day. It could also be said of him that, in his fashion, he loved his wife. And, finally, he tried—at least at first—to take a more positive attitude toward being king of England than his father had ever done, saying good things about the country and the people and not making constant and unfavorable comparisons with Hanover.

But on the whole he was not an attractive king. Inclined to lose his temper often, he would kick his hat, or his wig, all around the room. Physically unappetizing, a small, strutting man with a deep purplish-red face and a forehead that slanted back at an alarming angle, he had not been the kind of child, either, who inspired affection. His father the king frankly hated him and the court, taking its cue therefrom, had never shown him much kindness. His mother, who never was the queen, was conspicuous by her absence; long before the family came from Hanover she had been divorced and permanently locked up in prison. Her children never saw her again. Her presumed partner in adultery, a

Swedish Count von Königsmark, was as summarily dealt with; he disappeared on the first of July 1694 and nobody has ever found out what happened to him. King George I, then Elector of Hanover, was always a thorough man.

If it is true, as many novels quote Scotland Yard as saying, that criminals tend to repeat a pattern, it is legitimate to guess that Count von Königsmark may have been kidnapped and transported to America. For there is evidence that this is what King George I planned to do with his hated heir the Prince of Wales, the unattractive but surely pitiable young man who—the kidnap plot having failed—succeeded him as King George II.

At the meeting of his first Council, the Archbishop of Canterbury handed King George II King George I's will. He put it "in his pocket, and it was seen no more." Nobody ever found out what happened to the will, either, or what was in it. It was as gone as Count von Königsmark.

This was in 1727, when George II was forty-four. He had married, many years before in Hanover, a princess far above him in intellect and maturity. Caroline of Anspach had also, a heart—"a rare thing as times go," a contemporary said. She was not brilliant, but she was a student and a thinker; as a young girl she had carefully weighed (and found wanting) the merits of an early suitor's Roman Catholicism; and she took an interest in politics. She also enjoyed managing the King. Managing his personal life was beyond her, or perhaps she did not even try; at any rate he had a succession of mistresses, mostly right in the palace. ("You must love the Walmoden, for she loves me," he told the Queen naively, when the Countess of Walmoden replaced Henrietta Howard.) But politically the King presented no problems. All Caroline had to do was to feed ideas into his ear, and presently they emerged from his mouth as his own.

She herself worked in close collaboration with Sir Robert Walpole, the brilliantly able minister who, first dismissed by George II because he wanted nothing of his father's, had contrived his own reappointment. She was soon a power to be reckoned with. It was known throughout England that the Queen was really the king.

She was not altogether an admirable woman, Caroline of Anspach. One can make allowances for King George, who had been hated by his own father; but why did Queen Caroline hate Frederick the Prince of Wales? When he and his wife and newborn child were turned physically out of St. James's Palace, just as she herself, and her husband the then Prince of Wales, and *their* newborn child had been turned out by George I, surely sympathy might have been expected from Queen Caroline. Instead "the Queen thanked God that the business was over and uttered a devout hope that she might never see the monster's face again," and this comes strangely from any mother, much less one pointedly described as having a heart.

The truth seems to have been that Caroline echoed her husband in all things—this was how she managed him, by building up his self-esteem and never, of course, contradicting him. The reader of history is torn, as the onlooker at court must have been, between siding with the surely unnatural parents and siding with the son who, at thirty, was still breaking people's windows for the fun of it. That was a bit unnatural too. Still, when Frederick unexpectedly died, it would have been nice if the King had expressed some conventional sentiment. But he merely expressed surprise. "Countess," he said mildly, leaning over his mistress's shoulder as she sat at the card-table, "Fred's gone."

But the Queen's death was a very different matter. It is a familiar story: how she advised him to marry again, and how, "between hoarse sobs, he had some difficulty producing an answer. 'Non—j'aurai—des—maîtresses,' he assured her brokenly. 'Ah, mon Dieu! cela n'empêche pas,' replied the Queen." * But his grief was really very serious and sincere and certainly permanent. The Princess Amelia went through packs of cards removing the queens, so that the King would not suddenly be confronted by a reminder which had made him break down completely. Hearing of a portrait of the Queen she had given to someone, he sent to borrow it, had it put in his bedroom and, in tears, gave orders not to be disturbed. Hours passed. Sending the picture back finally, "I never yet saw a woman worthy to buckle her shoe," the King said.

Caroline had died in 1737; in 1742 Sir Robert Walpole lost power and resigned. It was wartime, and he was not the kind of prime minister

---

* Peter Quennell, *Caroline of England* (New York: Viking, 1940), pp. 226, 237, 249, 250–51.

who feeds and grows on war. He had shone in the matter of the South
Sea Bubble, in the first George's time, when cleaning up the mess
required a master hand; he was particularly interested in tax reform and
promoting trade; and his study was to avoid war. Unfortunately, an
obscure shipmaster named Robert Jenkins, who went around London
showing everybody where he said the Spanish had cut off his ear,
provoked a public clamor for war with Spain. Actually Spain was the
injured party, not England; if Englishmen like Captain Jenkins had not
been consistently violating that part of the Treaty of Utrecht which let
England ship slaves to Spanish South America but restricted other trade,
nobody would have lost an ear.

The worst thing about the two-year War of Jenkins' Ear (its official
historical name) was its leading to greater wars because Spain and
France were allies. Thus England became embroiled in the War of the
Austrian Succession, fighting against both France and Prussia on the
side of Maria Theresa's Austria. Frederick the Great, who was George
II's nephew, had seized Silesia from her in defiance of the Pragmatic
Sanction. George II was not very interested in the merits of any of this,
but unlike Walpole he rather liked wars. He led his own troops to
victory in the Battle of Dettingen, 1743.

As it turned out, this was the last time in English history that an
English king did so, and the people of London celebrated as if they
realized it. Months later, when the King finally got home, their
enthusiasm was still at peak; "you would have thought," the diarist
Horace Walpole said, "that it had not been a week after the victory at
Dettingen. They almost carried him into the palace on their shoulders;
and at night the whole town was illuminated and bonfired. He looks
much better than he has for these five years, and is in great spirits. The
Duke limps a little." (The Duke of Cumberland, the King's younger
son William Augustus, had been wounded slightly in the leg.) "The
King's reception of the Prince, who was come to St. James's to wait for
him, and who met him on the stairs with his two sisters and the privy
councillors, was not so gracious—*pas un mot*. . . ." * This was poor

* Alfred Bishop Mason, ed., *Horace Walpole's England* (Boston: Houghton Mifflin,
1930), pp. 33, 31.

Frederick, of course, who could never do anything right even when his father was victorious, happy, and glorious.

Much closer home, in every way, than the War of the Austrian Succession was the bid of the deposed Stuarts to get back their throne. This uprising—the year was 1745—was a far more serious matter than the attempt of 1715. Then James Stuart whose friends called him James III of England, and whose enemies called him the Old Pretender, had succeeded in having himself proclaimed in Scotland, but the uprising had failed. Now, thirty years later, James Stuart was still James III and the Old Pretender respectively, but there was also a Young Pretender, his son Prince Charles Edward, and much reason for fresh hope.

Bonnie Prince Charlie was twenty-five, and easily the most attractive Stuart since Charles II. Exuding charm, he landed with no trouble, moved on to Edinburgh, and from Holyrood Palace issued manifestos and received, as Prince of Wales, the homage of the clans.

In London they circulated a ballad: "Pray consider my Lords, how disastrous a thing, To have two Prince of Wales's and never a King!" For King George, advised now by Lord Granville instead of Sir Robert Walpole, could not seem to take the rebellion very seriously. " 'Pho: don't talk to me of that stuff!' " was his reaction. Even after the English under Sir John Cope lost the Battle of Prestonpans the hero of Dettingen did not take the field. The Duke of Cumberland—the Scots called him "the Butcher"—went instead and won a great and decisive victory at Culloden Moor. "The Young Pretender escaped. . . . The defeat is reckoned total, and the dispersal general; and all their artillery is taken. It is a brave young Duke! The town," said Horace Walpole, "is all blazing round me as I write, with fireworks and illuminations." *

If Sir Robert Walpole was indispensable to the first two Georges, his son Horace is no less so to the historians of their reigns. Horace's own "illuminations" are accepted as gospel now, though they were only gossip then; they are in any case highly readable and quotable, but actually he seems to have been remarkably exact in his reports and judgments.

The Seven Years' War, breaking out in 1756, did not particularly

* Mason, *Walpole*, p. 57.

excite George II either, though of course he kept up with the news, and his comment on one bulletin, from America, has been particularly remembered. A young major named George Washington, who had had his first fighting experience at little Fort Necessity and loved it, was quoted as saying, "I heard the bullets whistle, and, believe me, there is something charming in the sound." Said George II, remembering the larger operations of Oudenarde and Dettingen, "He would not say that, if he had been used to hear many."

King George had shut up many of the rooms in Kensington Palace, after the Queen died, and one of his mistresses set the place on fire trying to keep warm there. He was not as generous with his mistresses as he had been as a younger man. For one of them, then, he had built Marble Hill House at Twickenham, one of the most beautiful things in London; the assumption is that he merely paid for it and neither designed nor chose anything about it, but the Prince Regent is on no more evidence given much credit for "his" buildings and at Marble Hill you should perhaps spare a kind thought for poor old George II who never got much credit for anything. After the death of the Prince of Wales much of the hostility seems to have gone out of him; he did not transfer it elsewhere. He got along decently enough then with the rest of his family, providing suitably for the next generation and creating Frederick's eldest son, who would become George III, Prince of Wales in his turn. He went in costume to a masquerade at Ranelagh and was "much pleased with somebody who desired him to hold their cup as they were drinking tea." (People then drank out of the saucer, not the cup.) He had such a good time with nobody knowing him in his disguise that he decided to give another "jubilee-masquerade" for Miss Chudleigh, the maid-of-honor who had caught his, and everyone's, eye by coming as "Iphigenia, but so naked that you would have taken her for Andromeda"; and there "at one of the booths he gave her a fairing for her watch, which cost him five-and-thirty guineas,—actually disbursed out of his privy purse, and not charged on the civil list." But in spite of Elizabeth Chudleigh and all the other diversions which Horace Walpole set down for ours, he never forgot his Caroline till the day he died.*

* Mason, *Walpole*, pp. 69, 70.

Caroline's biographer, coping as needs he must with the question of why, if George was so much in love with his devoted wife, he kept all those mistresses, just as his father had done with better reason, says, "Both father and son were extremely conventional in matters of love. A prince owed it to himself to appear as a man of gallantry, and a mistress was as important a part of his household as a valet, coachman or page of the back-stairs." * But George II seems to me more like a kindly and considerate husband who hires a maid to help his wife with the work.

He had arranged when Caroline died to be buried with her. Her coffin was made so the side panel would slide out, when the time came for his to be set beside it; and when his subjects heard this he recaptured, briefly, some of the popularity he had had after Dettingen. Except for this he was as unloved and unattractive as ever and even more German, for he had forgotten long since his early resolutions of amiability and freely expressed his disgust with England and Englishmen. He died an old man, seventy-seven, the year after Wolfe captured Quebec, and his coffin was made like Caroline's, with a removable side panel, so that their remains could be mingled in the passage of time. He had left explicit directions for this. Fortunately *his* heir did not put this paper in *his* pocket, so George II got his desire.

* Quennell, *Caroline*, pp. 13–14.

George I

1660–1727

H E succeeded to the throne in 1714, upon the death of his second
cousin Queen Anne.

This was in accordance with the Act of Settlement of 1701, passed in
the reign of William III to exclude the male Stuart line, which was
Catholic, and give the throne instead, after the deaths of William and his
sister-in-law Anne, to the Protestant descendants of a female line. The
Electress Sophia of Hanover, the granddaughter of James I of England,
was to get the throne—Sophia and "the heirs of her body being
Protestants."

Unfortunately, Sophia died two months before Queen Anne did. The
transition from Stuart dynasty to Hanover dynasty would have seemed
less abrupt if she, not her son George, had succeeded. She was a woman
of many attractive qualities and she showed her English blood; she was
not quite a foreigner. George had no attractive qualities and did not
show his English blood. He was, and remained, a foreigner.

"An honest blockhead," Lady Mary Wortley Montagu called him. It
was one of the kinder comments.

A presentable queen might have improved the impression he was
making, but George (now George I) brought with him no queen to be
crowned. He had divorced Sophia Dorothea of Zell in 1694 and he kept
her locked up in a castle prison until she died. Instead he brought two

mistresses who became famous for their ugliness, rapacity, and broken English. "Good peoples, we have only come for all your goods!" the Duchess of Kendal, ingratiatingly, told a mob that surrounded her carriage. "Yes, damn you, and for all our chattels, too!" came the reply. It was true; the Duchess profited vastly from her stay in England, and the other chief mistress, the Countess of Darlington (called "the Elephant"—Kendal was "the Maypole") was not far behind.

George I also had unashamedly come to England for what he could get out of it. He did not like the place, he did not like the people, and naturally nobody liked him. He never seemed to worry about that or whether he had the right to sit on the English throne, possibly because he did not really care whether he sat there or not. He went back and forth to Hanover as often as he could.

He was able to do this because he had had a clause in the Act of Settlement repealed—the one that prevented the king from leaving England. The King had every intention of leaving England whenever he chose.

He did wait until after the Jacobite insurrection of 1715. It was soon over. In September the Stuart royal standard was raised in the Highlands and clansmen rallied to it. (This was what they literally did; following a custom perhaps as old as monarchy, the flagstaff was planted in the ground or fastened on top of a castle and the men who intended to follow it gathered round.) In October James was proclaimed king in the town of Warkworth in England—James III, by the grace of God. . . . In November there was a clash of arms at Sheriffmuir. In December he himself arrived in Scotland.

In one way his appearance did his cause immeasurable good. Only the most bigoted and the most credulous could say now, after seeing him, that he was a warming-pan baby smuggled into the royal bed to provide a Catholic heir. Experts had known for a long time that James III was the true son of James II; the court painter Sir Godfrey Kneller, who had done portraits of all the Royal Family and was an authority on the shape of their noses and the set of their eyes, could see the resemblance even when he painted James III as a baby.

"Wet de devil de Prince of Wales te son of a brickbat woman," he said at the time, and his heavy accent was faithfully set down with his words, "begot it is a ly. I am not of his party, . . . I am satisfet wit wat ye parliament has done, but I must tell you wat I am sure of. . . . His fader and moder have sate to me about 36 times a piece, and I know every line and bit in their faces. . . . I sayh this child is so like both, yt there is not a feature in his face, but wat belongs either to his fader or his moder; this I'm sure of, and be got, I cannot be mistaken. Nay ye nails of his fingers are his moders ye Queen yt was. . . ." *

Now everyone could see for himself the familiar Stuart features, and personality as well as physical proof. James III, so proclaimed at Warkworth, was just as foolish, just as feckless, just as proud and obstinate and unreasonable as his father James II.

He did not even come promptly to put in his bid for his father's throne. Dithering in France, he waited over a year after the death of Queen Anne. But perhaps the outcome would have been no different. James was an ineffectual leader—in addition to his other faults. Born to misfortune and exile, he accepted them as the natural order of things; his was "the melancholy pride of never choosing the winning side." There have been few men in history who would really rather be right than president, but James III—the Old Pretender—was one of them. His father was another. Their adherence to the Roman Catholic faith was creditable indeed, for it cost them the crown.

It was plain, when James finally arrived in Scotland, that he had come in vain. Scotland was divided for and against him; many who were not already disgusted with him became so. The English adherents to the Stuart cause had failed to materialize. There had been some troops raised for him, true, but even before Sheriffmuir those had laid down their arms at Preston. So no later than February 1716 King James III took ship back to France, and King George I made his plans for a nice trip to Hanover.

There was a little delay in his getting off, because of a quarrel about the regency. His son the Prince of Wales, thirty-two years old, was the logical person to act in his absence, but unfortunately King George loathed the Prince of Wales. Finally it was settled that the Prince would be "Guardian of the Realm and Lieutenant," though denied the title of regent.

* Lord Killanin, *Sir Godfrey Kneller* (London: Batsford, 1948), p. 18.

Thus began the rival court, that of the Prince of Wales, that would make the rest of King George I's reign an exciting contest between father and son, and between the Princess of Wales and her father-in-law's imported mistresses.

His spies did their best to spoil King George's stay in Hanover. They faithfully reported to him how popular the Prince and Princess were making themselves; how regally they dined in public at Hampton Court; and how they had put up a red damask canopy in the Queen's Audience Chamber where, there being of course no queen, they held their state receptions. They were behaving, George I heard, exactly as if they were reigning monarchs already. When they moved back to St. James's, from Hampton Court, it was in the gilded state barge with musicians playing at a respectful distance in another boat—quite like Henry VIII or one of those autocrats. The Princess was being graciously charitable (always where it would do the most good) out of her own money, while the Prince was making an almost-regal "progress" through the southern counties.

But the King was enjoying himself so much in Hanover, and so disliked England and everything about it, that in spite of such troublesome reports he was many months in returning.

The explosion was surprising only in that it was delayed. But there were other matters for the King to attend to. First there was a fresh Jacobite conspiracy, and then the prime minister, Sir Robert Walpole, resigned. King George could not believe that he was really losing this excellent man. "As often as Walpole laid his seal upon the table" he "took it up again and dropped it into the Minister's hat. It was not until the tenth repetition of this comedy"—Sir Robert may somehow have hidden the hat—that the King gave in and accepted the resignation.* But it put him in a very bad mood. He was put in a bad mood, again, at the christening of his newest grandson, and there is no doubt that the Prince of Wales did behave badly himself on this occasion. The King had him arrested, which was, however, rather extreme, and the next day sent the vice-chamberlain with an order of eviction. The Prince and Princess of Wales were to get out of St. James's Palace by seven that evening.

* Quennell, *Caroline,* pp. 46–47.

They were forced to leave their children, including the newborn baby; and this little boy soon died.

It was a harrowing time for the whole court, who now had to choose between allegiance to the King, who would not live forever, and to the Prince, who would succeed eventually but could do nothing for anybody now. Many chose the Prince, and his rival court, set up finally at Leicester House, was a credit to his wife.

The Princess, Caroline of Anspach, was a bluestocking as well as a carefully trained royal lady. She had a decided talent for politics, and an even greater talent for managing her husband while pretending to defer to his greater wisdom in all things. Finally she was a friend of Sir Robert Walpole, who with her great assistance succeeded in patching up the breach between father and son.

Walpole returned to power in consequence of the South Sea Bubble's bursting. Almost alone among the so-called wiser heads of England, he had inveighed against this get-rich-quick scheme by which the National Debt (a mere matter of fifty million pounds) would be transferred to the South Sea Company, a trading company to be given monopoly of South American trade. The company would then sell stock—and this they did, to practically everybody. Court cleavages were forgotten as both the Prince and Princess of Wales and the King's mistresses bought stock. People in all walks of life bought stock. It was like the American boom in 1929. Walpole himself bought it, though he was satisfied to sell out at "1000 per cent" profit. The shrewd old Duchess of Marlborough also got out in time and made a fortune. Others bought as compulsively as the stock climbed—it rose from 128 in January to 1,050 in June—but could never bear to sell; and then the "South Sea Bubble" burst.

The King was one of the few people who had had more important things to do than play the market. He was taking one of his nice vacations in Hanover. Summoned back by the emergency, he could not, of course, reassure anybody. He had been away six months this time. Sir Robert Walpole, however, was a tower of strength; his was the calm and moderate voice in the House; he was the remarkable man who had predicted trouble and had been smart enough to sell at the right moment. His bill for the restoration of public credit was passed by a large majority, and not long after this he returned to power as prime minister. He remained in power for the rest of the reign.

It was during this reign, and with this minister, that the office of prime minister as we now understand it emerged. Importing a foreign dynasty into England, a king who was as isolated and insulated from his people as George I was, made it necessary for someone else to take up the power that kings of England had formerly held. There had already been a certain amount of natural attrition with time and with what passed for increasing civilization—thus the Stuarts were less effective than the Tudors, the Tudors less effective than the Plantagenets—but this change was more sudden and more complete. Unlike the barons, unlike the Commons, when the ministers got the upper hand they kept it. And they have it now.

Nobody could have cared less than King George I did. He not only liked and admired Sir Robert Walpole, he found him amusing. What Walpole thought of King George I is not recorded.

In spite of the surface reconciliation Walpole had brought about, the King did not like his son George, the Prince of Wales, any better than he ever had. It made him lose his temper every time he remembered that there was nothing he could do to keep him from succeeding as king. (Or was there? There was at one time a plot to kidnap the heir to the throne and ship him to America.) The thing was that the King and his son were almost exactly alike, and since they were, indeed, unattractive, it is possible to see why they loathed each other.

History would repeat itself in the next generation and for the same reason. George I had evicted his son and his wife, forcing them to leave a newborn child; George II in his turn would evict *his* son and wife and newborn child. It is unbelievable but it happened. Perhaps the most unbelievable thing about it is the way the younger George, though hating his father as heartily as he did, imitated him in so many ways.

Though George I disliked his legitimate son and heir, his daughter by the Duchess of Kendal, now Lady Walsingham, was a familiar figure at court. So, of course, was the Duchess herself. King George I occasionally added a new mistress, but his mainstays were still the old faithfuls he had brought from Hanover in 1714. It was even said that after his wife died, when he was sixty-six and she, poor woman, had been thirty years in prison, he secretly married the Duchess of Kendal. "The Maypole"—she still merited the nickname—had in any case his loyal affection until he died.

He would never have admitted to affection for his daughter-in-law Caroline, but there was no doubt that she had earned the King's grudging respect. He received such protégés of hers as Voltaire, and once, coming back from Hanover, he had brought her a present— "Peter the Wild Boy," a child twelve or thirteen years old who had been found running around the German forests on all fours. It was a bizarre present, certainly, from a man who had separated her own children from her to give his daughter-in-law.

We understand this king so little, in spite of all the facts and gossip we have about him, that it is anybody's guess what went on in his mind when he did this kind of thing.

The trips to Hanover were what had made George I's life in England bearable. He never did like London, but moving from it to Herrenhausen every year, with the regularity that the Queen now travels to Windsor or Balmoral or Sandringham, was something to look forward to. He moved comfortably if cumbrously, taking his whole court, plenty of baggage, and of course his mistresses, and once started he did not wish to stop this side of the Promised Land. Thus in 1727, having eaten "several watermelons" for his supper in Delden, Holland, and not feeling quite as well thereafter, he insisted on pushing on anyway. He was determined to get to Hanover, and he did. But there, presumably happily, he died.

Anne

1665–1714

SHE succeeded to the throne in 1702, upon the death of her brother-in-law William III, who, having ruled jointly with his wife Mary II from 1689, ruled alone after her death in 1694.

The little gentleman in the velvet coat—the mole the Jacobites toasted because his excavations caused William III's horse to stumble and so caused his death—benefited Queen Anne rather than their wishfully called James III. The backers of this fourteen-year-old boy were not ready; Anne's backers were.

They and she thought she was getting the throne none too soon, at that. She should have succeeded her sister Mary. William III had no immediate right to the throne except through Mary; he had no right to sit on it alone after she died; but it had been understood when they accepted it jointly that he would do this in case she predeceased him. There was no love lost between him and Anne, however, and the last eight years had passed in a sort of armed truce.

Anne had spent them, like the ten before, in childbearing. In 1683 she had married (in lieu of Prince George of Hanover who came to visit but did not stay to propose) Prince George of Denmark. He was an insignificant, agreeable young man—"little *Est-il possible*," Anne's father called him, from the polite and noncommittal response he made to everything—who kept her constantly pregnant. The record is unbelievable. She bore him seventeen children—except for one, they all soon died—and her miscarriages are unnumbered.

Anne was a husky, hearty young woman, over six feet tall, like her famous ancestress Mary Queen of Scots. There the resemblance was thought to stop, for there was nothing glamorous about Queen Anne and nobody ever thought of dying for her. But now the researches of Macalpine and Hunter, the psychiatrists who studied George III's recurring malady and reported it not manic-depressive psychosis but porphyria, indicate that Anne, too, may have suffered from this "family disease." It may have accounted for her otherwise puzzling inability to bear a healthy child. Except for the Duke of Gloucester, who lived precariously to be eleven, none of them survived long. To lose sixteen children almost at birth is something besides bad luck. Anne was never as healthy as she looked when she was young. "Gout in the stomach," as she called it, gave her indigestion and "hysterical affections" and an occasional convulsive "Fitt." She also complained of "gout in the bowels." It may have been real gout, of course, in her knee and her foot which, later, made her need a stick or even two sticks for walking—but this is a symptom of porphyria too. In her last illness she had occasional fits of delirium—George III's most prominent symptom.

"Her life was repeatedly stabbed by pain, disappointment, and mourning," Winston Churchill says.*

Obviously this pathetic woman needed a friend, and there was not much sympathy between her and her sister Mary. Anne's constant pregnancies were a direct affront to Mary's inability to conceive; and anyway, long before Mary returned to England as queen, Anne had sought and found an intimate friend. She had a strong emotional need to look up to and adore someone.

Her choice was Sarah Jennings, later Mrs. John Churchill and finally, as her husband rose in rank as well as fame, the Duchess of Marlborough. They had played together as children. Sarah had come to court at twelve, under the wing of her sister Frances, who was in the household of Anne's young stepmother. Charles II was king then—the

---

* Winston S. Churchill, *Marlborough*, abridged by Henry Steele Commager (New York: Scribners, 1968), p. 87.

year was 1673—and Mary of Modena still only Duchess of York, a kind, beautiful, and virtuous young woman. Princess Anne was eight. The friendship was obviously, then as always, more exciting for Anne than it was for Sarah; Sarah always had a cool eye for royalty, as she did for anything and everybody except John Churchill, and Anne had nothing but her royalty to make her attractive, certainly not to a girl four years older.

Sarah, beautiful, intelligent, almost uneducated, and frighteningly ambitious, was born to rule and command. She began by ruling the Princess Anne and, when Princess Anne became queen, ruled, with the help of her husband, Queen Anne and all of England. The great period in English history called the reign of Queen Anne was not hers at all, but theirs.

They made a remarkable quartet, Sarah and John, who would have been vividly outstanding characters in any company, against any background; dull, fat, ailing Anne; poor little *Est-il possible*. To rid both couples of any stiffness which the acknowledgment of royalty might impose, Anne suggested that they call each other by play-names, Mr. and Mrs. Freeman and Mr. and Mrs. Morley. She thought of these names all by herself. One may imagine what Sarah (Mrs. Freeman) thought, and in privacy said to John.

Mr. Freeman had to be often away from the fun and games. He was a soldier and there was a war on. Not because of his royal friends but because of real brilliance in the field—and putting down the Monmouth Rebellion for King James—he had made lieutenant-general. His deserting James and going over to William of Orange was not the sort of thing a gentleman now would do, but it was like Churchill's taking, when he was a young man and before he met Sarah—he never looked at another woman after that—money for a start in life from his rich mistress. It was the kind of thing that was perfectly all right to do then. Of course one had to have a thick skin. "You're the first deserter of the rank of lieutenant-general I've ever met," General Schomberg told him, offensively, when Churchill joined William of Orange. Sarah would have clawed his eyes out; John Churchill only smiled.

In the wars to put down William's great enemy Louis XIV, William and Churchill had worked well together, though they disliked and mistrusted each other. (And with reason—Churchill made advances to exiled King James while in the pay of the usurper William, whom he had helped bring to England.) But when William died, his work unfinished, there was only one soldier he could recommend to his successor Anne. Under Anne, Churchill—Marlborough—achieved the victories William had dreamed of.

Marlborough fought ten campaigns, "during which he had won four great battles and many secondary actions and combats, and had taken by siege thirty fortresses. In this process he had broken the military power of France. . . . During the whole of these ceaseless operations of war on the largest scale the world had seen or was to see for several generations, confronted by the main armies of France and their best generals, he had never sustained a defeat or even a serious check. . . . The annals of war contain no similar record." *

No wonder the Age of Anne was a famous one. For most of it she was besottedly proud of Mr. Freeman and his wonderful accomplishments. After his capture of Venloo, Maestricht, Liège, and the rest of the chain of enemy strongholds, she wrote Mrs. Freeman—Sarah— what seems to Marlborough's biographer a "gracious, charming letter." To me it seems a pathetic and ridiculous one:

"It is very uneasy to your poor, unfortunate, faithful Morley to think that she has so very little in her power to show how truly sensible I am of all my lord Marlborough's kindness, especially at a time when he deserves all that a rich crown could give. But since there is nothing else at this time, I hope you will give me leave as soon as he comes to make him a duke." †

It would have tempted anyone, much less the strong-minded and arrogant Sarah, to push this "poor, unfortunate, faithful Morley"—the Queen of England—around.

But finally Sarah pushed her too far.

Anne would never have noticed it herself. It had to be pointed out to her. Sarah had made the mistake of finding a place at court for a poor cousin of hers, Abigail Masham, and Abigail had gradually, subtly

* Churchill, *Marlborough*, p. 828.
† Churchill, *Marlborough*, p. 303.

supplanted her in the Queen's affections. The only wonder is that something of the kind had not happened sooner. Sarah's "friendship" had always been abrasive. She had always quite openly shown her contempt of the Queen, and the Queen had always accepted it with smiling meekness as just Mrs. Freeman's way. But finally Abigail and Sarah's enemies—she had many, and had earned them all—convinced the Queen that the contempt was sincere and that all the biting words were intentional.

She stripped Sarah of all her offices and emoluments, and removed her husband Marlborough from the command of the army. What this would do to the army did not worry her—at least not enough. Louis XIV knew at once what the effect would be. "The affair of displacing the Duke of Marlborough," he said, "will do all for us we desire."

Sarah was beside herself, of course, as furious as Marlborough was calm. But it was harder on Queen Anne than on the Marlboroughs when they left her court. They were retiring to much more than comfort. They had grown rich in the service of the Queen, her father, and her brother-in-law. They had in the process of building—Queen Anne could not halt this—the palace of Blenheim, named in honor of Marlborough's greatest victory and voted him at public expense. And they had each other. John and Sarah Marlborough, each so full of flaws in character and in other relationships, had one of the great unflawed love stories in history, and they were allowed to live into old age together. Anne had lost her husband, whom she at least always took very seriously, and every one of her incredible brood of children. But in losing Sarah she had lost most of all. Her adoration of her beautiful, brilliant, dynamic friend had been the big thing in her life. Being a queen, seeing her armies conquer the Sun King's, giving birth to her children and watching them die—none of it had been as important to her as Sarah was. This is hard to believe, but if you hope to understand Queen Anne at all you must believe it.

After the Marlboroughs left her court she gave herself up to unhappiness. Physically she had long been the most miserable of mortals. She is described in 1709: "The poor lady . . . was again under a severe fit of gout, ill-dressed, blotted in her countenance, and surrounded with plaisters, cataplaisma, and dirty-like rags." * The Queen of England!—but all the descriptions agree: "Her Majesty was labouring under a fit of the Gout, and in extream pain and agony, and . . . everything about her was in much the same disorder as about the meanest of her subjects. Her face, which was red and spotted, was rendered something frightful by her negligent dress, and the foot affected was fixed up with a poultis and some nasty bandages." †

She was so wretched that she did not care how she looked, what she was doing to her subjects' ideas of majesty; and emotionally she was as distressed. As the end of her life neared, she was truly unhappy about the succession.

She had always had a conflict about it. She had always known, really, that the child she had been told to think of as the warming-pan baby was her father's true son and the heir to his throne; she knew herself and her sister and brother-in-law to be usurpers. On the other hand, she knew as firmly as her fanatical Protestant upbringing could teach her that it was her duty to uphold the Church of England. "Was she to deliver her realm to civil war? Above all, was she . . . to give up her Crown? No—a thousand times no!" ‡

James III made her decision easier for her. In her last days he was written to, asking if he would change his religion as a condition to getting, finally, his father's throne. Of course there was the Act of Settlement which gave it to the Hanover line, but that was a scrap of paper to these experienced double, triple, and quadruple dealers. James showed them how a gentleman, even in the wrong century to expect it, keeps his word. He indignantly refused.

So Queen Anne's leaving the crown to her half-brother would have been tantamount to dividing England again, and of course she did not do it. But she still remembered how George of Hanover had come to court, all those years ago, and had not stayed to propose to her. After his mother Sophia—Anne did not like her either—he would sit on her throne. And now it was being suggested that George even come to

---

* Churchill, *Marlborough*, p. 755.

† Sir John Clerk's memoirs, quoted in John Fleming, *Robert Adam and His Circle* (Cambridge, Mass.: Harvard University Press, 1962), p. 19.

‡ Churchill, *Marlborough*, p. 250.

England early—before she died!—and take his seat in the House of Lords as Duke of Cambridge. Her ministers had had the effrontery to send this proposition to Hanover, without consulting her. This roused Anne from her miserable lethargy. She announced with vigor that none of that Hanoverian tribe would set foot in England while she lived.

Her cousin the Electress Sophia was roused in her turn. On receipt of this message she stamped angrily back and forth the length of her garden, back and forth, her face getting redder all the time. Then she had a stroke and died, two months before Queen Anne.

William III

1650–1702

AND

Mary II

1662–1694

THEY succeeded to the throne in 1689, upon the abdication of Mary's father, James II.

Or was it abdication? Was it merely departure? Had King James merely left, without forfeiting his rights? This is what Alfonso XIII did when he left Spain in 1931; he did not sign away anything. Neither did James II. He considered himself King of England until he died, and his son considered himself and was called, by the Jacobites at least, James III.

There was no question, of course, who was in control of England. William of Orange was. He had come over from Holland in 1688 and taken over. But it was a military dictatorship only. There was no lawful government, and many questions arose.

Was the throne vacant? Could the throne ever be vacant? Was there a contract between the King and the people which James had broken? Had he abdicated by flight, or merely deserted? Could he be deposed by Parliament? Arising from all this, should William become Regent, governing in the name of the absent James? Should Mary become Queen in her own right? Had she not, in view of the virtual demise of the Crown, in fact already become Queen? Or should

William be made sole King; or should William and Mary reign jointly; and if Mary died, should Anne forthwith succeed, or should William continue to reign alone as long as he lived? Both Houses, both parties, and the Church applied themselves to these lively topics with zest and without haste.*

But it boiled down, of course, to what William decided. He was not willing to be any ruling wife's consort; he was not willing to step aside for her sister, if his wife predeceased him; and in fact he would really have preferred to be king to Mary's queen consort. It was much more tactful, however, to set up a joint reign, and there was nothing whatever for him to lose by it, for Mary was governed by him in all things.

It was not ever thus. Eleven years before, Mary had married him under protest. She wept throughout the ceremony. Nobody could quite see why she minded so much. William was not handsome and he was said to be cold, hard, and stingy, but he was her own cousin, the son of her aunt, another Mary Stuart who had married another William of Orange, and anyway royal princesses might not expect to marry for love.

Her uncle the king, Charles II, tried to cheer her up with a little joke. At one point in the service, where the groom said, "With all my worldly goods I thee endow," several coins were spread out on the open Bible or prayer book, and the King whispered in the bride's ear, "Gather it up and put it in your pocket while you've got the chance." But Mary did not think that was at all funny, and cried harder.

So it was surprising when, after the wedding, Mary fell deeply and lastingly in love with her husband. He was no more attractive than he had ever been, but now everything he said she agreed with, everything he did was exactly right because he did it. When he decided to take over the throne of England, which by that time belonged to her father as King James II, she was with him heart and soul.

Mary was evidently not a very sensitive young woman. Even her entourage—usurpers too—were shocked at her frank pleasure as she ran from room to room in Whitehall Palace, exclaiming over well-remembered things and over pretty newer ones her young stepmother, who had been so kind to both the little Stuart girls, had left behind in her hasty flight.

---

* Churchill, *Marlborough*, p. 142.

Mary was not a very bright young woman, either. She would have
ruled England through her husband even if he had not shared the throne
with her. It was fortunate that William was very intelligent. It was
perhaps not so fortunate for England that he was one of the best haters
in history and that, like Richard Lion-Heart who considered England
"the milch-cow of the Third Crusade," he thought of England as a
source of money and men and supplies with which to carry on his war
with his enemy.

William's enemy—now England's—was France. His particular,
personal enemy was Louis XIV—his first cousin once removed, and his
wife's too. (This relationship did not bother Mary either; if William
hated Louis that was enough for her. She would hate him too.) He
immediately moved to muster the resources of England against France.

The fighting was between 1689 and 1697, until the Treaty of
Ryswick, and between 1702 and 1713, when the Treaty of Utrecht was
signed. In between there was an interval of uneasy peace. Several
historians have compared these wars with the two World Wars in our
century. They too were separated by an interval; they too aimed at
stopping the domination of Europe by one upsurging power. William
III would have stopped Louis XIV more quickly and more successfully
if he had not preferred to have the great Marlborough serve under lesser
generals, instead of at the head of his armies; but his reasons are
understandable, and in any case the results were very good. By the
Treaty of Ryswick, Louis recognized William as King of England.

But then when James II died, an exile in France, Louis went to his
cousin's deathbed and recognized him again as King of England and his
son as James III. This was in 1701, and in 1702 war broke out again.

Mary had died meantime. She was not much missed. She had never
been a force in government or policy, only her husband's adoring echo.
The most strong-minded thing she ever did was collect the blue and
white china which makes her remembered at Kensington Palace and
Hampton Court.

William was by no means an interim king while he ruled alone. He
was a very forceful one. He had his limitations, his foibles, and his
jealousies (as of Marlborough), but he was an able man. And he really
believed in his own cause. William was one of the extremely rare kings

in whom personal ambition was not the motivating force; he cared nothing for England, would have much preferred to go back to live in Holland, and stayed where he was only because he needed English resources to support the Protestant Cause.

One of the attractive things about him was his affection for his wife's nephew, the little Duke of Gloucester, Anne's son. (This is the child for whom the main streets in Annapolis and Williamsburg are named.) In his portrait he looks hydrocephalic. But there was much hope that he would live to succeed, and his death in 1700 (Burke says fever, others smallpox) was a crushing blow.

Two years later William died with his work unfinished. He had promoted in 1701, after little Gloucester's death, the Act of Settlement that would give the crown, after the death of Anne, to the Protestant branch of the family descended from her great-aunt, the daughter of James I. But it was all very unsatisfactory. To him, and to England.

Winston Churchill puts it, as always, very well. "A queer, unnatural interlude in English history had reached its end." *

* Churchill, *Marlborough*, p. 246.

James II

1633–1701

He succeeded to the throne in 1685, upon the death of his elder brother, Charles II.

"Don't worry, Jamie," Charles had said to him once, when James had remonstrated about his lack of security precautions. "They'll never kill me to make you king."

Nor did they; and even after Charles had died in his bed there was considerable reluctance to accept James as king. Nobody really believed that Charles's son the dashing young Duke of Monmouth was legitimate; Charles denied repeatedly the stories of a secret marriage. And Monmouth would not have made a very good king, but there were people who supported him because anyone, they felt, was better than James. James put down the Monmouth rebellion handily because he had, at the moment, the great soldier John Churchill fighting for him. Monmouth was captured and executed. But there was no great upsurging of loyalty when the crown came to rest where it belonged, on the head of King Charles I's second surviving son.

He had had, of course, a difficult childhood—in civil war, in exile, in poverty and tragedy and uncertainty, and it affected him far more than the same things affected his very different brother Charles. Perhaps it was because he was younger; the younger of the little French princes,

Francis I's sons, had been the one who showed the scars of their Spanish imprisonment. James, like Charles, was a Frenchman in looks—black-visaged Bourbons, both of them, and with the Bourbon sexual proclivities. And they both believed firmly in the divine right of kings. But where Charles was light-hearted and lax James was rigid and dour. Everybody liked the one; many people respected, but hardly anybody liked, the other. Yet the war memoirs he left, written when he was a young soldier of fortune in other kings' armies and before he felt himself burdened by the whole responsibility for the Holy Catholic Faith, show him as rather attractive—and a good soldier, too.

His mother had been strictly forbidden to bring him up a Catholic. But Queen Henrietta Maria, exiled, widowed, resigned to being a poor relation at the court of her nephew Louis XIV and never having regal power again, could not resist the chance to proselytize. She had succeeded openly with her young daughter Henrietta Anne; rather well with her son Henry, who died, however, in the year of the Restoration; and all too well with her son James, who because he was heir to the throne was duty bound to stay in the Anglican Church. Outwardly he did stay, and he had his daughters Mary and Anne brought up in it. But he himself was received into the Roman Catholic Church as early as 1668 or 1669—quietly, but it became more and more an open secret. He refused outright to take the Test Act oath, in 1673, and his promoting King Charles's deathbed conversion to Catholicism was boldness itself.

Charles had been stricken suddenly, but he was, as he said himself, apologetically, "an unconscionable time a-dying." James had time to make his arrangements, not only for preserving the kingdom as his brother wished, but for saving his soul.

First he cleared the sickroom of all but two witnesses, and barred the door. Up the little private staircase which "Old Rowley" (as a bawdy song called him, after a famous stud-horse) had often found so convenient for his ladies, now came a disguised priest. Father Hudleston, James reminded his brother, was the same priest who had saved his life after the Battle of Worcester. "Now he comes to save your soul."

"He is very welcome," Charles said weakly. And received by his own wish the rites of the Church which was his mother's, his wife's, his mistress Louise's, and (now that politics was behind him) his own preference.

But you would never get Englishmen to believe that. They preferred to call what James had done proselytizing, the taking advantage of the weakness of a dying man to force on him a conversion he did not want or intend. And, indeed, the way that James, now king, went about forcing the conversion of England lent support to this view.

King James, greatly increasing the army, appointed Roman Catholic officers to the new regiments. Parliament, hitherto amiable, cooperative, and generous, quarreled with him over this and James prorogued it in November 1685. It never convened again in his reign. This was like the reign of his father Charles I all over again; James II was making precisely the same mistakes. In 1686 the judges of the King's Bench (James having made several replacements on it first) ruled that the king had the power to dispense individuals from the Test Act oath. Roman Catholics were then admitted to high office again, and the King—still, though a professed and practicing Roman Catholic, supreme governor of the Anglican Church—suspended the less than pliable Bishop of London.

All that was needed was a male heir to the throne, so that a Catholic succession could be assured. James's two daughters by his first wife, the Earl of Clarendon's daughter, had been brought up strictly as Protestants, and the heiress presumptive, Princess Mary, now married to Prince William of Orange who was himself fourth in line for the English throne, snubbed her father soundly when he tried to convert *her*. So did his younger daughter Princess Anne. But they were the last Protestant children King James intended to have.

After the death of his first wife Anne Hyde he had remarried, an Italian princess, Mary-Beatrice of Modena. She had been unlucky, so far, but she was not barren like the poor little Queen Dowager. She was pregnant again and, surely, the luck was due to change. It was confidently expected by James and those around him that the new baby would be a boy.

It was indeed a boy, and it was indeed the son of King James and his young Queen. Later everyone realized and believed this. But at the time James himself did everything he could to put the issue in doubt. His procedure was unbelievably stupid, even for him. Required by law and custom to fill the delivery room with witnesses to the birth of his son, he chose Catholic witnesses. When they said they had seen a boy baby born to the Queen, Anglicans said they lied. They said a baby boy had been smuggled into the Queen's bed in a warming-pan.

James and the Roman Catholics had so much to gain by the birth of a male heir to the throne, and the Anglicans and the friends of his daughters Mary and Anne had so much to lose, that the issue split cleanly along party lines.

William of Orange, Mary's husband, had long since been sounded out, and had indicated that he would, indeed, be available if a Protestant Champion was needed. Obviously a Protestant Champion was—unless the Protestant heirs to the throne were to be tamely passed over in favor of this doubtfully warming-pan, but certainly Roman Catholic, baby boy.

So a messenger was dispatched to William in Holland. Whigs as well as Tories, bishops as well as worldly peers, signed an invitation asking him to invade England, overthrow the government of James II, and ascend the throne.

William accepted the invitation with the alacrity of one who has already worked out the details. In November 1688 he landed at Torbay. King James had planned to meet him on the field of battle; he assembled a strong force at Salisbury; but one by one, and then in a steady stream, the key people he had thought were on his side began to desert him. His daughter Anne disappeared during the night. Her husband, little *Est-il possible,* left. The Duke of Grafton left. The Earl of Bath left. The Earl of Devonshire left. Sir Edward Seymour left. But the worst blow came with a letter from John Churchill, the Earl of Marlborough, not yet proven the greatest soldier of his time, because the big wars were still in the future, but certainly the general James had most depended upon. Marlborough, too, was casting his lot with the Protestant Champion.

Marlborough, of course, was no more interested in Protestantism than were the rest of the turncoats. But he knew a rising from a setting sun.

So James decided to flee instead of fight. He had been a good fighter once, when he was younger, but he too knew a rising sun when he saw one.

Fleeing, he was captured by "a band of self-appointed frontier guards," which did not suit William's purposes at all. It was no part of his plan to have his wife's father harmed physically. Permitted to escape, James could be counted on to solve the problem himself. So it was arranged for him to escape again, and this is what he did. France was the logical place for him to take refuge; his first cousin Louis XIV, a good Catholic among other things, ruled there, and Louis was the bitter enemy of William of Orange. James's wife and son had already made their way to France. Queen Mary of Modena had hidden behind a buttress of a parish church, waiting for dark and a small boat to take her and her baby to safety. Now James joined them there. En route in his own small boat, he dumped the Great Seal into the Thames.

Charles II

1630–1685

H E succeeded to the throne in 1660, upon the death of Oliver Cromwell and the failure of the latter's son, Richard, to hold England together under a Commonwealth. Public opinion had steadily been growing toward the restoration of Charles to the throne of his father Charles I, whom Cromwell had put to death in 1649.

Of course from a loyalist and royalist point of view Charles II had been king ever since then, ever since the day when his courtiers broke the news by addressing him as "Your Majesty," and he burst into tears. Pathetically poor, burdened with responsibilities he could not fulfill, unable to trust either Anglicans or Catholics or Presbyterians, buffeted from one foreign country to another, defeated, betrayed, baffled, and unlucky, he was thirty years old before his luck changed. The comment he made when, finally, he came back to cheering, roistering, ecstatically happy London was Charles to the life. It must have been his own fault, the new King said, that he had stayed away so long—because he met nobody now who had not always wished for his return.

He was a very imperfect man and far from being the excellent king he had the potential to be. But he was certainly the most attractive, sophisticated, and intelligent king England has ever had. In any century he would have to be considered a very civilized human being; in his century, the seventeenth, he was remarkable. He was truly kind and considerate; he truly had concern for his fellow human beings, not just their welfare but their feelings. If the vicissitudes of his first thirty years had made him cynical, he was cynical in a very nice way. He could not, having watched their maneuverings and cruelties and treacheries and greed, consider any religious sect too sure of heaven, and he could fault them on other grounds. "Not a religion for gentlemen," he said of Presbyterianism. If he rather preferred Roman Catholicism, on the whole, it was for a very unreligious reason—because "no creed matches so well with the absolute authority of kings." Officially he showed a preference for the Anglican faith because that was the Established Church. But he would not allow any religionist to be even pushed around, much less persecuted, and there were several instances of his actually rewarding people who had served their own consciences instead of him. One of these was Dr. Thomas Ken, who was dean of Winchester when Charles's party, complete with his current mistress Nell Gwynn, arrived in town expecting to be put up at the Deanery. Doctor Ken objected to having pretty, witty, but quite unrespectable Nell in his house. Another king would have got up on his high horse. Henry VIII, for instance, would have sent Doctor Ken to the Tower. Richard III would have had him beheaded on the nearest log. Charles II merely had other quarters found for Nell, and when the bishopric of Bath and Wells fell vacant, later, he remembered a good, conscientious Anglican who could fill it well. "Who else but the little fellow who would not give poor Nell a night's lodging?"

Nell was Charles II's weak point, Nell and all the other mistresses who are so well remembered when so much else about Charles II has been forgotten. Nell and her rival actress Moll Davis, Lucy Walters who bore him his favorite son Monmouth and who always insisted there were documents proving their marriage (in a little black box, unfortunately missing), Barbara Villiers whose amours were as famous as his, Louise de Kéroualle who really concerned herself about his soul—this is to call the roll of only the most famous. Nor is the gallery of "Restoration Beauties" at Hampton Court complete. Charles had had a hard life before he came to the throne, and after he did, and Parliament granted him £1,200,000 a year, he indulged himself in, among other things, all the expensive women he wanted.

But though his mistresses were very expensive indeed—Barbara, first Countess of Castlemaine and then Duchess of Cleveland, often wore jewels worth £40,000, sometimes gambled away £25,000 of England's money in one evening, and collected thousands every year from the post office, excise, and other revenues—they emphatically did not influence him in matters of state. There was never any question about who was king. And though the legend persists that it was Nell Gwynn who influenced him to build the Royal Hospital—for old soldiers—in Chelsea, and no less an authority than Miss C. V. Wedgwood thinks she was valuable in keeping him in touch with what common people felt and thought, it seems clear that Charles needed neither his kind impulses prodded nor his insight clarified. (And anyway, Les Invalides antedates the Royal Hospital; if he had needed anybody to tell him it would be nice to do something for old soldiers, Charles learned it from Louis XIV and not Nell Gwynn.) Those early years, before he came to the throne or, indeed, had much prospect of doing so—years when he had sometimes been a fugitive disguised as a farmboy or a servant, and always an indigent living from hand to mouth—had made him like and understand his fellow-man. His kindness and his courtesy never failed him, though he was not credulous and never naive. Once, receiving the Quaker William Penn, who kept his hat on on principle, Charles removed his own. Penn stepped into the trap: "Friend Charles, why dost thou not keep on thy hat?" " 'Tis the custom of this place," blandly replied the King, "that only one person should be covered at a time."

Best of all, perhaps, if you like England, you will like Charles II's observation that it had worse weather, but a better climate, than any country.

But best known is his rejoinder to the epitaph he asked Lord Rochester to write him. The epitaph was an epigram:

> *Here lies our sovereign Lord the King,*
> *Whose word no man relies on;*
> *Who never said a foolish thing,*
> *And never did a wise one.**

* Quoted in Hesketh Pearson, *Merry Monarch* (New York: Harper, 1960), pp. 139–40.

That was easily explained, the King said: "my discourse is my own; my actions are my ministry's."

The anecdotes multiply. How he stands out, between the dull-witted time-servers who came after him and the violent opportunists who came before—and yet he was not really a very good king. It was not altogether because his actions were his ministry's. Partly it was because he was lazy, and easily diverted from the path of duty, but mostly because he had learned from others' mistakes. And especially from his father's. If he was too cynical, too cautious, too afraid of rocking the boat and upsetting Parliament, it was because he had seen too vividly what could happen to kings who took chances. He had seen how quickly cheering crowds could turn into murderous mobs. The happy Englishmen at his coronation would have, King Charles knew, come out as cheerfully to see him hanged.

It ought to be remembered how little he was an Englishman, though England is so proud and quick to claim him, and the present Queen went back three hundred years to name her son after him. Scottish, Danish, French, and Italian blood—his Bourbon mother's mother was a Medici—made a happier mixture in him than in, say, his brother James. He was highly intelligent. He could reason. He was the most objective of English kings—on second thought, maybe the only objective one. He was a very decent poet, quite as good as his ancestor, James I of Scotland, who is in the Oxford anthology. He enjoyed chemical experiments—unmistakably he profited by having as a tutor Dr. William Harvey, who discovered that blood circulates—but he dabbled at that and everything. He was a king; his main business was kingship. His being an amateur otherwise is one of the things the English like about him, that and his casual, understated approach and his offhand brilliance which is the only kind of brilliance a gentleman should really have.

His fifteen-year reign was prosperous and enjoyable—the theater, the arts, the racetrack flourished—but none too peaceful. The great dowry brought by his wife, the Portuguese Infanta Catherine of Braganza, opened up the horizons to English trade. She brought England Bombay, Tangier, the trading rights to China and the Indies; and it is from this that dates and derives the great change in English decoration, design, and tastes. A Charles II porringer, for instance, was apt to be "covered over with quaint little incised figures of a . . . Chinese intention." Silks and ivories, Chinese Chippendale and export porcelain, spices and the suddenly fashionable new drink tea—when you think of them, think of homely, unhappy little Catherine of Braganza. Always a stranger in a strange land, outnumbered and outclassed by the "Restoration Beauties," she brought her husband the king all this, but she brought him no child.

And this he badly needed, for to think of his brother James as king after King Charles was to foresee trouble. But, true to his character and conscience, King Charles never considered repudiating his plain little Queen, and soundly snubbed the few people brave enough to suggest it. (One courtier thought of having her kidnapped and transported to America, then divorced for desertion.) Nor was it in character for him to support the pretensions of his ambitious bastard Monmouth, who liked to say, and perhaps believe, that his mother Lucy Walters had been secretly married to King Charles. Charles loved Monmouth, loved all his illegitimate children by various mothers, but he was for the strictly regular and legal succession. This meant, unfortunately, his Catholic, tactless, and unattractive brother James, the Duke of York. He tried in every way he could to keep James's abrasive personality from irritating the Parliament and the people, sending him out of the country at the time of the Titus Oates excitement, issuing a Declaration of Indulgence repealing all acts against Nonconformists and Catholics including James. But Parliament rejected that and passed the Test Act instead, so that James had to resign his naval command.

It was all very annoying to James, who kept on nagging his brother to be an absolute king.

But King Charles was not that much of a gambler. He was not planning to risk the throne. It had been too hard to come by. "I will not venture a war nor travel again for any party," said King Charles.

Charles I

1600–1649

HE succeeded to the throne in 1625, upon the death of his father, James I.

He was a good, mild but stubborn, undistinguished young man, surprisingly short in stature. You would never have thought him the grandson of the six-foot Mary Queen of Scots and of the "long lad" Darnley she had (perhaps therefore) married. In every way, until it came to the very closing scenes when it was said of him that "Nothing in his life became him so well as losing it," he seemed born to be overshadowed by somebody.

First it was his elder brother Henry, who died in 1612, clever, handsome, greatly lamented, even after death a source of unfavorable comparison with Charles. Later it would be his strong-willed French wife. Meantime it was the Duke of Buckingham.

Charles had inherited the Duke of Buckingham from his father King James. James's weakness for young men was well known, but this was nothing like that. It was just that Charles needed the company and inspiration of someone more confident and dynamic than he was.

Some of the things he and Buckingham did together were entirely out of character for Charles. For instance, in his father's lifetime and with his father's permission (for James could refuse Buckingham nothing, and Buckingham wanted to go), the two young men made a trip to Spain, in disguise, so that Charles could meet the infanta there were plans for him to marry. They accomplished this ruritanian journey in safety and the infanta was, indeed, charming; but when Charles was romantically revealed as a prince she settled the whole affair by refusing to marry a heretic and move to a heathen land. She preferred to go into a convent, she said. So Charles returned without a bride and England declared war on Spain. It had wanted to anyway, because of Spain's invading the Protestant Palatinate.

Pausing in France, though, Charles had met the young—very young—sister of the King of France, Louis XIII. Henrietta Maria was the daughter of the great Henry of Navarre, who had ruled as Henri IV, and of Marie de' Medici, who now ruled France through her teen-aged son. This princess too, of course, was a Roman Catholic—her Huguenot father had deemed "Paris worth a mass" and changed his religion to get his throne—but the French were more reasonable than the Spanish. Henrietta Maria would have to have her own Catholic chapel and her own priests, unpopular as this would be in England, but there was no objection to her husband as a heretic or to England as a heathen land.

Charles married Henrietta Maria soon after coming to the throne and they became a devoted couple, in spite of many bad auspices. The little Bourbon was always difficult; she was subject to temper tantrums, and at times would even throw breakable things; and she was accustomed to having her own way. She intended from the first to rule Charles.

But though he was in love with her he did not heed or need Henrietta Maria at first, because he had Buckingham for guidance; so their married life was stormy indeed. Once after a violent quarrel he sent all her French attendants back where they came from. But then Buckingham was removed—stabbed by an unhappy assassin named John Felton who thought he was striking a great blow for his country and would go down in history a famous man. He did indeed free his king from the domination of an arrogant, thievish, and highly incompetent favorite; but he himself was hanged before he could also assassinate the Queen *pro bono publico*. For the King merely exchanged one autocratic mentor for another.

Henrietta Maria openly rejoiced at Buckingham's death. She had not been merely jealous of him; he had had the arrogance to remind her that some queens of England, her predecessors, had got themselves beheaded. Now Buckingham himself had died violently, and she had no competition for the control of her husband the king.

This was the king who thought it his duty to be "an indulgent nursing father" to his subjects. He was a babe in arms himself, always.

Though she became an accomplished intrigante later, Henrietta Maria, young and frivolous, was not at first interested in politics—except, of course, as it touched her own wishes or interests. She was violently upset, for instance, when Charles broke his word—he so often broke his word—about dispensing the Catholic penal laws. He had signed a document with his marriage treaty to this effect. The whole thing about Charles was that he would make a promise that seemed a good idea at the time and then, when circumstances changed, he thought that was reason enough to break the promise. He was utterly unreliable. He never kept his word in politics at all. This is hard to reconcile with his basic character, which was good and upright, except by considering how firmly he believed in the divine right of kings. God's lieutenant, set by Him upon the throne, was obviously not bound by promises to anyone but God.

It seems inevitable to us, considering the King and his problems by our own standards and out of the context of his times and standards, that his reign should unroll like a classic tragedy. But we should consider it, of course, in seventeenth-century terms. Many people—most people, at the outset of his reign—also believed in the divine right of kings. It did not strain credulity any more than some of the still generally unquestioned Acts of God, like natural disasters, and it was not a disaster itself. Indeed it must have been rather comforting, to an intelligent man whose fate it was to serve a fool, to feel that this was God's Will. Intelligent men are still serving, and serving under, or working for fools, and they have no such face-saving and ulcer-preventing conviction as this.

But some of the things King Charles did, out of his well-meaning stubbornness and arrogance, were hard to take. Early in his reign he had a confrontation with Parliament, when the House of Commons preferred charges against the Duke of Buckingham. Charles actually dismissed Parliament by way of stopping this. He was less successful in having Buckingham's assassin tortured before his execution. Torture, the King had to be reminded, was now against the law. Sometimes Parliament made its point rather forcibly, the Speaker having actually been held in his chair while the Commons passed a resolution calling England's enemies all innovators in religion and all those who levied or paid taxes not authorized by Parliament. They meant, of course, the King, who imposed taxes as he pleased, just the way his father had done. The Petition of Right (1628) condemned martial law, billeting of soldiers, forced loans, and imprisonment without cause.

Having dissolved his impudent Parliament, Charles ruled without it for eleven years, and the courts of Star Chamber and High Commission flourished, as they had in his father's time. England was at peace with her outside enemies but not within herself. Trying to force an Anglican prayer book on the Scots—almost anybody would have known better—Charles and William Laud, his belligerent Archbishop of Canterbury, precipitated the Bishops' Wars of 1639-40. Money was needed and Parliament had to be convened in the latter year. It was a disaster for Charles. He had to agree that he would not dissolve this Parliament against its will, and he could not keep it from passing the Grand Remonstrance—a mere 201 objections to the way he, the Lord's anointed, had been running the country.

Charles could not take this, of course. Boldly going himself into the House of Commons, he tried to arrest several members of Parliament. They escaped, and he followed them into the City. He was certainly not a coward. But here he failed. He left London and gathered an army around him. England was in a state of civil war.

It endured for four years. With Oxford as his capital, Charles's Cavaliers met the Parliamentary Roundheads at Edgehill (1642), at Marston Moor (1644), at Naseby (1645). At Edgehill his two older sons, Charles and James, came out in the charge of their tutor Dr. William Harvey to watch the battle from a safe height. It was like the First Battle of Bull Run when the congressmen and their wives and friends came out with picnic baskets to enjoy a victory and instead saw their army soundly beaten. It was fairly obvious, this soon in the King's War, as it was called, how it was going and who would ultimately win, because the Parliamentarians had everything—the money, the troops, the ships, and Oliver Cromwell. The King's nephew, Prince Rupert of the Rhine, his sister Elizabeth's son, arrived early to help and proved the most dashing of cavalry commanders, but it was not enough. Nothing was. The King's wife, barely delivered of her last baby, escaped to France, taking a great part of the crown jewels with her; there she put them to good use, and the generous allowance her French family made her too; but these were not enough. In May 1646 King Charles had to surrender himself to the Scottish army—his own people, and the army had been in his pay. They sold him to the English.

He was a prisoner for two full years. There was only one final solution to this kind of thing. The Lancastrians had found it in the case of Richard II, the Yorkists had found it in the case of Henry VI, the Wicked Uncle in the case of the Little Princes in the Tower. Queen Elizabeth had found it in the case of Mary Queen of Scots. Oliver Cromwell found it in the case of Charles I. It is not practical to leave a non-ruling ruler alive.

Many of his subjects doubted, by this time, that Charles I had been King of England by divine right. But the manner of his death must have shaken even these. Every inch a king, perfectly sure that he had done his duty and what was right, Charles established himself in his farce of a trial as a martyr and Cromwell as a murderer. Still unworried and unshaken, he stepped onto the scaffold on January 30, 1649, to show his people how a king ought to die.

James I

1566–1625

He succeeded to the throne in 1603, upon the death of his first cousin twice removed, Queen Elizabeth. When she was dying—not before—she had named him her successor.

She hated to think of any successor at all, or of England without her. But James at least was a Protestant, and now that she had cut off the stubborn Catholic head of his mother Mary Queen of Scots he was next in line for the English throne. It was not a matter of either restitution or repentance.

James I, as he became in England, was already James VI in Scotland. He was the great-grandson of that Margaret Tudor, Elizabeth's aunt and the elder of Henry VIII's sisters, who had married James IV of Scotland. King of Scotland he remained; the two traditionally warring nations now had one ruler; but he did not, as he promised, give Scotland much of his personal attention thereafter. He went "home" only once in twenty-two years.

He was a middle-aged man when he came over to England to live, and his feelings must have been very mixed indeed. He built an impressive tomb for his predecessor in Westminster Abbey, making her share it, however, with her elder half-sister, and a separate but equal tomb for his mother Mary Queen of Scots. Her body, and presumably her head also, he had brought from Peterborough, and the effigies of the two royal ladies, the beheader Elizabeth and the beheaded Mary, lie in peaceful juxtaposition.

Englishmen never knew quite what to make of James. Many of them had not expected much, but both Dissenters and Catholics had hoped that the new king, son of a Catholic mother, brought up in a Presbyterian country, might be tolerant of both their minority groups. Both were disappointed—one to the extent of trying to blow him up. (The Gunpowder Plot was foiled November 5, 1605, which the English still call Guy Fawkes Day.) His much-vaunted literary talents were a disappointment too, not up to the standards set in Elizabeth's reign. In the year of his succession to the English throne a new edition of his 1597 Edinburgh publication, *Daemonologie*, was brought out for the edification of his new subjects; they learned from this that their King believed in witches and in demoniacal possession and was interested in "unnatural diseases."

But he was indeed, in his peculiar way, clever. Bookish, certainly. "By nature he is a poor sleeper," his physician's notes say, "and often at night calls for the servant to read to him aloud."

These physician's notes are fascinating. King James was not only interested in unnatural diseases, he had one.

Without going into too many of the gruesome details (as they do) we should at least say that James I had, the researchers of George III's famous madness believe, a flaming case of the "family disease," porphyria—was, in fact, the importer of this disease into the royal English line. It is conjectured that he had it from his mother Mary Queen of Scots, who was also a great invalid.

He was a chronic invalid himself, certainly, all his life. He was subject to attacks of severe pain, but these did not manifest themselves except perhaps in irrationality. What did manifest themselves were some showy physical defects, decidedly unattractive ones. His tongue was too big for his mouth, so that he drooled, like a Great Dane. His legs were too weak to support his barrel-shaped body, so that even during "good" periods he had to lean on two courtiers, and in 1619 he lost the use of his legs entirely for four months, and had to be carried about "in a Neapolitan portative chair." Later, to strengthen his legs, he bathed them "in every stag and buck's belly on the place where he killed them." This was no more ridiculous than many of the remedies currently prescribed, but King James had the unfortunate gift of seeming ridiculous even when he was really a sick man.

Not since King John, in fact, had there been an English king who had something so ludicrous about him. There was also the matter of his undignified manners. If he had not been able to write poetry, like his ancestor the other James I, King of Scotland, if he had not been master of Latin and French (he could give the same kind of virtuoso public performances Queen Elizabeth could), if he had not sponsored (and been sponsored by) the splendid King James version of the Bible and the innovative palaces and masques of Inigo Jones, Englishmen could not have stood this newcomer.

As it was they had the greatest difficulty in standing his favorites, who were all of his own sex. Robert Carr (who succeeded Philip Herbert) was the ruling one for eight years. Even Edward VII, whose friends went in for adultery and cheating at cards and who prostrated Queen Victoria by being called to testify in a divorce case, never had a friend like Robert Carr, who was convicted of murdering Sir Thomas Overbury. Carr (whom King James had created Earl of Somerset) definitely involved him in the notorious Overbury case; there were people then, and there are still historians now, who believe that James was actually implicated; this belief was naturally strengthened when James pardoned his erstwhile favorite.

For he had long since gone on to another one, George Villiers, the Earl, and later the Duke, of Buckingham. King James had a wife, Anne of Denmark, and a beautiful daughter Elizabeth and a promising son Henry and a delicate son Charles; but, as he frankly said, "You may be sure that I love the Earl of Buckingham more than any one else. . . . Christ had his John, I have my George."

This analogy was bad enough; to make it worse, James, getting his saints mixed up, called his George Steenie, because he reminded him of a certain picture of St. Stephen. Nobody else could see any resemblance between Buckingham and any saint whatsoever.

King James spent plenty of money on these favorites, obviously. He was also very open-handed—generous is hardly the word for him—with less intimate friends and hangers-on at court. He gave presents of money, as well as titles and properties of every kind; apparently he thought this was the only way to make his English subjects love him, and he may have been right.

He also spent plenty of money on himself—foolish though it may seem for him to have bothered with velvets and jewels when he never bothered to wash his hands. Coming from a poor, uncomfortable country, he had the impression some of his "adventurers" had, when they went to Jamestown in 1607 and (fleeing his bigotry) to Plymouth Colony in 1620—that the streets would be paved with gold. He acted as if the streets of London were. He was wildly extravagant.

He also indulged the light-minded, idle Queen in her passion for the new "masques"—expensively produced and costumed extravaganzas with scenery by Inigo Jones. He then employed this remarkable architect more constructively on a new palace for the Queen. The Queen's House, at Greenwich, which is still one of the great London sights, was in the new classical or Italian style and it was a house, not a fortress as palaces had always been. It revolutionized English architecture. King James also had plans for Inigo Jones to replace the old Palace of Whitehall, now grown up into an indiscriminate cluster of buildings which did not, he thought, do him justice. Jones began with the new building we call the Banqueting House.

The result of all this was James's discovery that the streets of London were not, after all, paved with gold. He needed money. And the only way he could get it was to ask Parliament. This went against the grain, for James was an autocrat who reigned without a Parliament (1614–1621) when it suited him. But he summoned Parliament this time because he had to have the money, and in so doing brought about the very last thing he wanted. He made Parliament stronger. That body, which had not felt very powerful before, began now to realize the strength of the hand that holds the purse-strings.

James also weakened the throne itself by his insistence upon its insuperable strength. Just as "It's no good shutting your eyes and saying 'British is best' three times a day after meals"—so the present Duke of Edinburgh told an audience—it was no good for King James to assert that "the state of the monarchy is the supremest thing on earth." His subjects believed in the divine right of kings too, up to a point, but this was overstating it. James could have been more tactful; but why should he, when he was answerable only to God?

He was never very curious about what was going on in his kingdom, or what people thought or felt. He imposed taxes on his own responsibility. Political prisoners were given no trial at all, just shut up in the Tower at the King's or the Privy Council's pleasure. His courts of the Star Chamber and High Commission were in the hollow of his hand. Evidence was of less importance than the King's wishes—and his wishes could include the prisoner's death.

Sir Walter Raleigh was, of course, his most famous victim. This Elizabethan favorite, poet, scientist, seafarer, importer of both tobacco and the Irish potato, was no favorite of the King's. Raleigh knew this; it was not much less than a death-wish that brought this brilliant, morbid adventurer back to London and certain imprisonment when he could have sailed on, and on, and on. He was thirteen years in the Tower. There he had many privileges and amenities—books, a garden, a laboratory, his family with him—but his greatest privilege, as he saw it, was being allowed to tutor the heir to the throne. If it seems strange that a convicted "traitor" should be entrusted with this job, remember that King James I was a very strange man. But actually most of the credit for the arrangement goes to Queen Anne. Perhaps she was not as light-minded and idle as she otherwise seems to be. She recognized genius when she saw it, and she personally brought her son to the Tower to visit Raleigh. This was in 1607 or 1608, when Prince Henry was fourteen or fifteen years old, a highly promising boy. "He was frank, open, and manly, neither like nor liking his father," Raleigh's biographer says.* "No one but my father would keep such a bird in a cage," the Prince said himself, of his new mentor. For him Raleigh wrote essays like "The Prerogatives of Parliament" and "The Cabinet Council," and his monumental *History of the World* was, he says in the preface to the 1614 first edition, undertaken expressly "for the service of that inestimable prince Henry, the successive hope . . ."

But in 1612 the successive hope had died. The heir to the throne

---

* Willard M. Wallace, *Sir Walter Raleigh* (Princeton: Princeton University Press, 1959), p. 237.

became his younger brother Charles. There was no reason to suppose that Charles would make a better king than his father.

James I's greatest fault as a king, the inability or unwillingness to work with Parliament, and his intolerance of the role of the House of Commons—they should not even discuss "matters far above their reach and capacity," he said—redounded, however, to the advantage of England. It kept England out of war. War costs money, and Parliament would not vote money for so intransigent a king. So it was a peaceful reign until the breakup of the Spanish marriage negotiations, which canceled out the peace treaty of 1604.

Much may be forgiven a king who, however indirectly and for whatever reasons, keeps his country in tranquillity. And much can be forgiven a king with James's stormy background. It is easier for us than for the Jacobeans—Lady Raleigh, for instance—to make allowances; and it was not then customary to evaluate people in terms of broken homes and violent bereavements and traumatic episodes.

Almost every one of the ruling Stuarts had died in consequence of war or assassination or beheading. James died in his bed. He is distinguished for that, as for the King James version and for employing Inigo Jones and for introducing the game of golf.

Elizabeth I

1533–1603

S<small>HE</small> succeeded to the throne in 1558, upon the death of her elder half-sister, Mary I.

Speaking of broken homes and violent bereavements and traumatic episodes, consider Queen Elizabeth, the most fascinating of case studies.

Everyone knows her background. Tourists sigh with pleasure and relief when, in the long and obscure narrative of English history, the guide or the guidebook comes to this familiar part. Everyone knows how her father, King Henry VIII, divorced his first wife Catherine of Aragon so he could marry Elizabeth's mother, Anne Boleyn; how, angry because that black-eyed shrew also failed to give him a living son, he trumped up a charge of adultery against her and cut off her head; how Elizabeth as a child was pushed from manor to castle and never knew from day to day whether she was a princess or a bastard, so often did her father change his mind; how following the brief security of her little half-brother's reign she was on even shakier ground with Mary queen; how the violently Catholic Mary actually sent her to the Tower and how only luck, and her enemies' overplaying their hand, had kept her from being another bloody statistic; and how she came to the throne brilliant, beautiful, victorious, happy, and glorious, long to reign, when she was only twenty-five years old.

Beautiful she may not really have been, except as queens go. But she had the assurance and effect of beauty. Tall, pale, red-haired, with long, fine fingers and a fine hook to her slender nose, she was never quenched or outshone by the most fantastic and elaborate clothes a queen ever wore. That she was brilliant does not seem to be in doubt. It is hard to tell out of context, out of the framework of her own times; girls like Elizabeth and her bluestocking cousin Lady Jane Grey did not have books like the Nancy Drews to divert them, so all their reading energy went into Latin and Greek and the Bible and other "improving" books. No wonder they were "learned." Hampered by the long, stiff, complicated costumes which were replicas of adult clothes, girls even when small were channeled into the ladylike diversions of embroidery and lute-playing and stately dancing, rather than outdoor games. No wonder they were "accomplished." And especially for girls who were princesses (even part-time princesses like Elizabeth) there was every incentive to apply oneself and no time to waste, for marriage would come very soon indeed.

For Elizabeth it never came, and this was so unusual that she is, perhaps, more celebrated for being the Virgin Queen than for any of her other achievements.

It was indeed an achievement, a continuing effort that lasted half a lifetime. Constantly there was pressure on the Queen to marry for the good of the realm, for the safety of the succession. From the time she came to the throne until she was many years past childbearing age she was flirting with this alliance or that one. The King of Spain, the Duke of Anjou, the Duke of Alençon, the Duke of Saxony, Prince Eric of Sweden, and the Archduke Charles were some of those she lingeringly considered (or pretended to consider) and dismissed.

Queen Elizabeth remains an enigma in spite of proliferating biographies, so we are still not sure why she was both fascinated and repelled by the idea of marriage. One school of thought holds that she merely hated to give up her freedom and her identity, as indeed she would have done, to some extent, if she had submitted herself to a husband. If she knew or believed, as another school of thought has it, that she could not bear children, that would be an excellent reason. Some people said that she had a great unhealing sore on her leg, like her father's. (His has always been presumed syphilitic.) Other contemporaries went further and said that she "had a membrana on her, which made her incapable of man." Later historians and biographers have speculated on how much she was injured emotionally by her father's cutting off her mother's head. That may have been her handicap, they believe, rather than any physical one.

When she was young she appeared to be much in love with Lord Robert Dudley, whom she made Earl of Leicester, and preserved a great tenderness for him until he died. They were the same age and had been childhood friends. But it was an advantageous foreign marriage that was being considered for and by Elizabeth—her dynasty needed more royal blood—and anyway Robert was married himself, very young, to an heiress, Amy Robsart. It was one of the great scandals of Queen Elizabeth's reign when this inconvenient wife died by falling down a flight of stairs and breaking her neck. Did she fall or was she pushed? It was the most famous instance of the classic question. Her husband was away at the time—he left her often in the country—but had he arranged this to further an ambition, to give himself a chance, perhaps, of marrying the Queen? Or had the Queen herself—?

It appears now that Amy Dudley's death was no one's fault.* But rumor and gossip would have turned to hue and cry if the Queen had married the widower. Probably she never wished to anyway. Even after she made him Earl of Leicester he was still beneath her, and Elizabeth was very conscious of her position. But she was absolutely beside herself when her Robert married, after his first wife's death, somebody else.

This was the first of the royal rages, or more plainly temper tantrums, she had over young men. All Elizabeth's life, though she grew old and ugly, a painted, raddled old hag, there were always young men. They wrote her verses telling her how beautiful she was and perjured themselves with professions of love and adoration; and she rewarded them with money and titles and sinecures and fame. One after another these ambitious young men rose as courtiers do—Christopher Hatton, Sir Walter Raleigh, finally Leicester's stepson the Earl of Essex, and only one of them, Raleigh, ever hated himself for it. It was simply a fact

---

* If she had cancer of the breast, as was said, she would have soon died in any case. Breast cancer is much inclined to metastasize to the spine, weakening it so that it breaks sometimes with no accident at all. Falling downstairs is a very violent accident.

of life that buttering the old Queen was the way for a courtier to rise in the world.

The Elizabeth-and-Essex business was the last romantic comedy in her life. Some historians, such as the Earl's latest biographer, think she played it tongue-in-cheek, and certainly it contradicts her vaunted intelligence to think she could have played it any other way.* She was in her fifties and Essex, at twenty, could have been her grandson. But they went through the high-flown, romantic routine. "Since I was first so happy as to know what love meant, I was never one day nor hour free from hope and jealousy," Essex would write her, and "When I think how I have preferred your beauty to all things . . . I wonder at myself what cause there could be to absent myself one day from you . . . ." Their quarrels, too, were emotional lovers' quarrels, frequent and often severe. After one of them had been happily resolved the Queen gave Essex a ring of special significance. If everything else should fail, he should send it back to her and it would plead for him; she would forgive him no matter what he did.

But finally he did the unforgivable. He committed treason. He actually tried to "surprise the court and the Queen's person," planned to summon a Parliament "and alter the government." Did he really think he could rebel against the Queen successfully in this way? He really did. He counted on the masses of people who considered him a dashing young man; he counted on his few drops of Plantagenet blood. But the fiasco was complete. Essex left his house with two hundred swordsmen and swaggered through the streets calling on other men to join him; and not one single man did.

The story is that from the Tower he sent his ring to the Queen. He could not believe it when there was no reply. But, as Elizabeth said, "I had put up with but too much disrespect to my person, but I warned him that he should not touch my sceptre." There is a story, too, of course, that she never got the ring.

Essex went to the block; Mary Queen of Scots went to the block; men who wrote or talked against the Queen had their right hands cut off or their tongues torn out. Elizabeth could and did take severe action. But

* Robert Lacey, *Robert Earl of Essex* (New York: Atheneum, 1971).

the difference between her and some of her predecessors and some of
her successors was that she minded doing it. Condemning Essex, whom
she loved, brought her to the perilous edge of a nervous breakdown.
Condemning Mary Queen of Scots, whom she never met in her life but
who was a close relation and a queen—to harm any royalty was to harm
the mystique of royalty, and they all knew it—was almost as devastating
an experience. Queen Elizabeth had not the single-minded purpose and
dedication her sister had had. She permitted her feelings to be mixed.
She wavered, she contradicted herself, she changed her mind.

She showed herself to them as a human thing, and it was one of the
reasons her subjects loved her. But there were many reasons. One was
that she was truly an English queen. Except for her father's French
great-grandmother's her blood was English entirely, and she took the
greatest pride in it. The speech she made as her fleet set out to catch the
Spanish Armada has come down to us. Blazing with jewels, riding a
spectacular white horse, she had come to Tilbury to share the fortunes
of her subjects, she told them, to win or die with them as the case might
be: "I know I have the body of a weak feeble woman but I have the
heart and stomach of a king, and a King of England too, and think foul
scorn that Parma or Spain or any prince in Europe should dare to invade
the borders of my realm."

The defeat of the Armada was of course the high point in Elizabeth's
reign. It announced to the world England's coming of age as a world
power. In the early Elizabethan years her seamen had been only
impudent pirates and buccaneers, singeing the King of Spain's beard
over and over again and coming home with his gold, raiding not only his
ships but the New World colonies which (the Pope had said it)
belonged only to Portugal and Spain. The current Pope had excommunicated Queen Elizabeth in 1570 and she was beautifully uncon-
cerned about that, too. Early in her reign she and her great minister
Cecil (later Lord Burghley) had settled upon a religious policy which,
though satisfying neither the Roman Catholics nor the Presbyterians,
worked very well for England as a whole and for its strictly secular
Queen. Internal affairs remained at peace. "There was never any prince
that in so long a reign was less troubled with civil dissension at home,"

Clapham says.* Taxes were raised and raised again, for the Queen's running war with Spain had to be extensively funded, but there was no real outcry. To relieve actual destitution, Elizabeth's reign pioneered in revising the Poor Laws. The great statute which passed in 1601 is substantially like welfare laws today; in fact it is more intelligent in some ways, and what professionals have always considered its weak spot, its failure to respect the privacy and dignity of the poor, is coming into style again as the poor increasingly demand publicity. Children were differentiated from adults, and able-bodied adults from those physically or mentally unfit. It was a giant step forward that government now thought itself responsible, and tax money would be used, for at least the basic maintenance of people who could look to no one else; and there was the corollary implication that their situation was not necessarily all their fault.

At the same time that England was recognizing that some people would always have to be dependent on society, England was producing more vital, exuberant, achieving people than ever before. Talent and energy were in demand. Birth and inherited money no longer mattered as much. It was the glorious age of the climber. A whole new aristocracy was springing up, looked on by the old with as jaundiced an eye as the new religionists were looked on by the old—Roman Catholic—religionists. Henry VIII, in despoiling the monasteries and making himself Supreme Head of the Church (Queen Elizabeth thought Supreme Governor was a better title), had bestowed upon upstart families some very rich properties and the wherewithal to build upon them. Secure under Elizabeth, they burgeoned out with fine, sometimes beautiful, and usually big new-rich houses. Houses in the form of an E, with or without the middle stem, were popular—so popular that on into the next reign they were still being built, Hatfield House, for instance. The countryside was peaceful, so slits were out of style; it seemed safe to experiment with large expanses of window-glass, as at Hardwick Hall. And money was no object, so gilding, painting, carving, and convoluted plastering, like those at Longleat, embellished

* John Clapham, *Elizabeth of England*, edited by Evelyn Plummer Read and Conyers Read (Philadelphia: University of Pennsylvania Press, 1951), p. 58.

everything. It was as if a new-rich woman decked herself with every ring and brooch and necklace and bracelet she possessed. But Elizabethan women often did just that, copying the Queen who was a walking Christmas tree. And, really, the elaborate exuberance in architecture and dress suited the exuberant times.

Literature was burgeoning as lushly as they. Shakespeare was not considered as preeminent then as now; Beaumont and Fletcher, Marlowe, Jonson, Spenser, and Kyd were also of the first rank. Sir Walter Raleigh was too busy sailing his ships and spreading his cloak to have much time for writing—that would come later, when in the Tower he undertook his *History of the World*—but he and Sir Philip Sidney stood for the talented amateur who might have been in the front rank too.

It was a glittering, cruel, effervescent age, and a glittering, cruel, effervescent Queen who can hardly be imagined, much less estimated, outside its context. Within it, she was a very fine one. It is possible to take Queen Elizabeth at her own evaluation when she told her people, toward the end of her reign, ". . . though ye have had, and may have, many princes more mighty and wise sitting in this seat, yet you never had, or shall have, any that will be more careful and loving. . . ."

Mary I

1516–1558

S<small>HE</small> succeeded to the throne in 1553, upon the death of her half-brother, Edward VI.

But it was not quite that simple. Edward had been influenced to will the crown away from both his half-sisters and leave it to his first cousin once removed, Lady Jane Grey.

This was illegal; only Parliament could change the succession; but Edward even as a boy, even dying, was his terrible father's son. He fixed them with a glittering eye, and the Council all signed the Letters Patent. He was quite capable of sending any of them to the block while life yet remained to him.

Lady Jane Grey was the eldest daughter of the Duchess of Suffolk, whose mother had been Henry VIII's younger sister Mary. She did not, frankly, have much claim to the throne. If Edward's half-sisters were to be passed over (and the question of their having been born out of wedlock certainly had been previously raised), the line of Henry VIII's older sister, Margaret of Scotland, would have had precedence. If that line were to be passed over too (because little Mary Queen of Scots was being brought up a Catholic) then Lady Jane's mother would still be the one in line for the throne, not Lady Jane.

The thing was that Lady Jane was married to a son of the Duke of

Northumberland, and it was Northumberland who had persuaded Edward to name her in his will.

Poor Lady Jane knew she should not have the throne and she did not want it. But she was caught in the middle. She was only sixteen, a slight, pale, freckle-faced little girl with a very bright mind who had learned to obey her elders. She had been beaten when, at first, she refused to marry Northumberland's son. In virtual custody out at Syon House, surrounded by her father-in-law and her own father and mother, she was bullied now into a nine-days' "reign" which ended in her imprisonment and death.

So the reign of the queen who would be called Bloody Mary began with the bloodshed of this pathetic child who had not even wanted to be queen.

Mary had, however, no option. What Lady Jane had done, however pushed into it by her relatives, was treason. They died for it too, and Queen Mary, the rightful heir, ascended to her throne with dignified calm.

She was thirty-seven years old. She too was slight, pale, plain, and red-haired, with a very bright mind. She had had a miserable life. Her mother, whom she adored, had been put aside by the King when she herself was only fifteen, in 1531; and she had not been allowed to share her exile. The King specifically ordered that she was not to see her mother. This is not to say that she was always kept at court. Two years later, after the divorce and the King's remarriage, she was indeed sent for—but so that she could act as waiting-maid to her baby half-sister Elizabeth. Elizabeth's mother, the usurper Anne Boleyn, hated her, of course. She behaved exactly like the wicked stepmother of Cinderella. Her own child's legitimacy was predicated on the claim that Catherine of Aragon, the widow of his brother Arthur, had never therefore been legally married to the King; and that meant, of course, that Mary was not legitimate. Anne Boleyn pushed this for all it was worth.

But Mary was very sure that she was indeed legitimate. She knew that her mother Catherine had indeed been Queen. She knew that she was the Princess Mary, not a bastard, and from this position she did not retreat one inch.

Her mother died—not allowed to see her again—when she was twenty, her father when she was thirty-one. There had been no serious attempt to arrange a marriage for her—not since she was young, before the question of her legitimacy had been raised. She grew into the classic image of the old maid, a stiff, sour, plain, hostile, unwanted woman. Actually she was not merely bitter but frightened and wary. At any minute something disastrous could happen, her father could turn on her even more viciously than he had before. Her stepmothers after Anne Boleyn would have liked to make things easier for her; Jane Seymour and Catherine Parr actually did, Anne of Cleves was kind in the brief time allotted to her, even light-minded little Catherine Howard must have tried. But there was a limit to how hard anyone could press the King, and no one knew it better than his daughter Mary.

When he died, and Edward VI came to the throne, Mary was still wary and insecure. Her little half-brother had no hatred for her, but he was a child, under the domination of determined and unscrupulous men. And these men hated Catholics like Mary, and had no idea of letting one come to the throne.

Mary's Catholicism was the one thing nobody had been able to take away from her. Naturally she felt intensely about it. Whether she would have been a fanatical Catholic in other circumstances we do not know. Probably she would. She was after all the granddaughter of Their Most Catholic Majesties Ferdinand and Isabella, who had promoted the Spanish Inquisition and burned heretics without number in the calm certainty that they were doing it to the glory of God. This certainty was Mary's also. Basically she was a kind rather than a vindictive woman; she gave heretics every opportunity to recant and save themselves from the flames; but if they stubbornly refused they left her no choice. The fires that were lighted at Smithfield burned far fewer victims than the fires in Spain and the Spanish Netherlands, but there were perhaps two hundred in three years, quite enough to fix on the English Catholic Queen the enduring name of "Bloody Mary."

Mary's marriage to Philip II had, again, little to do with her burning of heretics. She married him for personal reasons. Mary had always had a *tendresse* for this first cousin once removed—her mother's great-nephew—and in the face of much opposition from her Council and her people pushed through the marriage in the year following her accession, 1554.

Philip for his part was polite and willing. He had already buried one wife, and, as it turned out, would bury three more. He already had an heir, if an unsatisfactory one; with him there was no urgency, as there was with Mary at thirty-eight. He accepted with his usual grave courtesy the title of King of England—a title which set English teeth on edge—but he never showed any tendency to take over and to try to rule instead of or through his wife. Though he too was a firm believer in burning heretics—he burned many in his own country—and though the English disliked him very much, they were not unfair enough to hang the sobriquet "Bloody" on Philip too.

Philip in fact spent very little time in England. Politely, gravely, he made it plain through his actions that though he was the light and center of Mary's life, she was only an incident in his. Nevertheless, in due course Mary's pregnancy was announced.

It came to nothing. Some subsequent authorities have thought that what seemed to be the symptoms of pregnancy were those of ovarian dropsy instead. There is also the possibility of tumor—not the malignant kind that caused the Lady Flora Hastings scandal in Victoria's reign, but a fibroid which, untreated, may later shrink away. This seems less likely, for Queen Mary had two separate and distinct "pregnancies." And rather unlikely, too, seems the diagnosis of false pregnancy which historians so long and so confidently endorsed. There certainly is such a thing, complete with abdominal distention and even lactation, but such patients are psychotic. Queen Mary was a rather peculiar woman who had led a very peculiar life, but she was not insane.

Her disappointment was pathetic; both for herself and for the future of her Catholic dynasty she needed a child. And her unhappiness over her husband's long absences was intense. And both circumstances were embarrassing.

But she dissembled them both. If her heart were opened after her death, she said, the word that would be found written on it was Calais. This last of England's strongholds on the continent was lost in the year of her death—England at war on the side of Spain against France—and England was an island again.

Edward VI

1537–1553

He succeeded to the throne in 1547, upon the death of his father, Henry VIII.

His was a short life and a short reign. Nine at his accession, he was only fifteen when he died. Most royal children who die prematurely are said to be full of promise, but Edward really was. His mother Jane Seymour's only achievement had been to give the King a living son, but she came from a markedly intelligent and energetic family. Two of her brothers, Edward who as the Duke of Somerset was Lord Protector for the young King, and Thomas who had quickly married the Queen Dowager, Catherine Parr (three wives on from poor little Jane), unfortunately pitted their intelligence against each other, their power struggle being one of the chief features of Edward's reign. In this they were ably seconded by their wives, the Duchess of Somerset losing no chance to try to precede and outshine and insult the Queen Dowager (refusing to carry her train, and so on), and that lady, though a very nice woman indeed, refusing in her turn to be pushed around.

Nor would Edward permit her to be. For five years, until her death in 1548, when the young King was ten, she had been an admirable mother to him. Immediately after her marrige she had brought her stepchildren together with their father and given all three a pleasant home life, for the first time, under one roof. She played no favorites and, though a

Protestant herself, left strictly alone the matter of the Princess Mary's religion. Her tact interposed itself between all the children and the King, whose painful leg made him increasingly violent in his tempers and whose experience with her predecessor, Catherine Howard, had left him with an even sorer wound. She made the least impression, of course, on the Princess Mary, who was in her late twenties when this latest stepmother came into the family, her unhappiness and bitterness reflecting the ups and downs of a wretched life, her character firmly set. But the Princess Elizabeth was only ten, and though a sharp child who at the age of four had already noticed there were ups and downs in her life too ("Why, Governor," she tackled Sir Thomas Bryan, "how hap it yesterday Lady Princess, and today but Lady Elizabeth?") was also a very affectionate one. She stayed with Queen Catherine Parr after her father's death and even after her remarriage to a man Elizabeth emphatically did not like. But it was little Edward, of course, on whom his father's sixth wife had the greatest influence.

Edward did not like his stepmother's new husband very much either, though Thomas Seymour was his own uncle. When Seymour complained to him that the other uncle, his brother Somerset, would not let the Queen Dowager keep the jewels Henry VIII had given her on her marriage, Edward replied saying surely not, but he would attend to it, and to any future problem "I shall be a sufficient succour. . . ." And this letter, the first extant which he ever wrote all by himself (in most of his letters, certainly the ones which have been called "priggish," the hand is the hand of Esau but the voice is the voice of Jacob), he sent not to the complaining Seymour but to Catherine herself.

As Edward's biographer says, after he succeeded his father "the King was much more dependent on Catherine than he had been when his father required all her attention" as he did during his long and trying last illness. "She kept her apartments in his palaces, and he was in the habit of walking unaccompanied through galleries and ante-chambers to see her privately." * This was truly remarkable in the light of the stiff court etiquette, which dictated, for instance, that his sisters sit on

* Hester W. Chapman, *The Last Tudor King* (New York: Arrow Books, 1961), p. 111.

benches and cushions, not in armchairs, when they visited his apartments. "I have seen the Lady Elizabeth kneel before her brother five times before she sat down," one foreign visitor said.

Edward had come to the throne a very promising little boy, even a healthy one. Since he died young, hindsight has made him "always delicate," but this biographer denies it. It was not until he had measles and/or smallpox in the last year of his life that his constitution was weakened, leaving him open to "consumption" and surely, from the harrowing symptoms described, another disease as well. He had an excellent mind, and under the direction of highly competent tutors, Sir John Cheke and Roger Ascham, his knowledge and comprehension became impressive. Religion, never an emotional thing with him, was one of his intellectual interests.

You will see, in the British Museum, the prayer book that Lady Jane Grey carried to the scaffold. This prayer book was a landmark of King Edward's reign. In recent years, in their desperate flounderings to attract youth, Church authorities have tinkered with the *Book of Common Prayer;* but for over four hundred years this piece of literature has deservedly stood alongside the works of the great sixteenth-century poets and dramatists. Young Edward VI did not merely sponsor it, he was actively engaged in its composition. This sort of thing—pomp and circumstance—fascinated him. He himself wrote the order of service for the Knights of the Garter. Incidentally, he made three drafts, one in Latin and two in English. Latin was his second language; he spoke as well as wrote it quickly and correctly.

He wrote also (age thirteen) "A Discourse about the Reformation of Many Abuses," detailing the abuses at great length, and then: "These sores must be cured with these medicines or plasters. 1. Good education. 2. Devising of good laws. 3. Executing the laws justly, without respect of persons. 4. Example of rulers. 5. Punishing of vagabonds and idle persons. 6. Encouraging the good. 7. Ordering well the customers. 8. Engendering friendship in all parts of the commonwealth." And he thought it best that all the great noblemen, "except a few that should be with me, went to their countries"—their home counties—"and there should see the statutes fully and duly executed. . . ." *

* Chapman, *The Last Tudor King,* pp. 174-75.

But the great noblemen continued the power game at court. In the course of it, both the King's warring Seymour uncles lost their lives. Thomas, the Lord Admiral, caught red-handed in what must have been an attempt to kidnap the King, was executed in 1549. The Duke of Somerset, losing his influence over Edward to the Duke of Northumberland, was on less evidence convicted of conspiracy. Edward, convinced of his guilt, finally agreed to the execution of this uncle as well.

One member of Somerset's household burst out rashly with what many people must have thought—then as now—about "this unnatural nephew—I wish I had the jerking of him," she cried. It is hard indeed to reconcile Edward the nice little boy, the one who stopped his coronation procession to watch an acrobat sliding down a rope, who loved his stepmother and kept his little dog in a basket in his bedroom, with the Edward who, when he hit a target and Northumberland praised him, "Well aimed, my liege!" answered coolly, "But you aimed better when you cut off the head of my uncle Somerset." The thing is that Edward was not, or not merely, a nice little boy. He was a cold, intelligent, calculating Tudor. Like his half-sister Elizabeth—like everyone—he cannot be fairly judged out of the context of his cold, intelligent, calculating times. He had made a brilliant beginning; he would have made, perhaps, the greatest of all England's kings.

Unfortunately, he died young.

Henry VIII

1491–1547

HE succeeded to the throne in 1509, upon the death of his father Henry VII.

The death of his elder brother, Prince Arthur, had made him the heir apparent. And thereby hangs the tale.

Like Charles II, who is chiefly remembered for his mistresses when much about him, very worthy of mention, is forgotten, Henry VIII is chiefly remembered for his wives.

The first wife was his brother Arthur's widow, Catherine of Aragon. Though she was a very Spanish princess, the daughter of Ferdinand and Isabella, it must be remembered also that she had English blood. Her mother was a great-granddaughter of John of Gaunt, Edward III's son, and it was from this branch of the family that Catherine, usually depicted on stage and screen as very dark, with flashing black eyes, inherited the china-blue eyes and reddish-blond hair that made her strongly resemble her relatives-in-law. She came into their family nevertheless as a stranger and a foreigner, learning English with a strong accent which she never lost, and when her young husband soon died her position was uncomfortable and unhappy. Shunted to one side, she was treated very badly by her penurious father-in-law, who kept her in England only because he could not bear to send back her dowry—not that all of it had been paid; her own father was penurious too. The theory was that she would be married next to the next heir to the throne, young Prince Henry, but nothing happened. Years passed, and Catherine was bitterly poor, bitterly humiliated, and desperate.

From this situation she was rescued by a kind, handsome young man, and she never ceased to be grateful to him. Ascending the throne at seventeen, Henry VIII made it one of his first acts to marry his brother's widow.

With her he lived happily enough for ten or fifteen years. He was not altogether faithful, of course, but he was devoted in his fashion and Catherine bore, or tried to bear, him many children. Unfortunately, sometimes she miscarried and sometimes her babies died at birth or in infancy. Only one, the Princess Mary, survived. She was given the title of Princess of Wales.

By the time Mary was eight years old the King seems to have despaired of Catherine's giving him a male heir. He hurt her feelings then by bringing to court his strong, beautiful, six-year-old illegitimate son Henry Fitzroy, creating him Duke of Richmond amid great pomp and circumstance. The fact that Richmond had been King Henry's own title, when he was a cadet, and also that of his father before Bosworth Field, did not escape notice; but in every way he treated little Richmond like an heir.

This was bluster, though. The Tudor dynasty was not so firmly seated that Henry could expect an illegitimate successor to be well received—or accepted at all. Similarly, he knew there would be no ready acceptance for a girl, even a legitimate heir like the Princess Mary.*

Or was she a legitimate heir? In his desperation, this thought occurred to the King.

There was a passage in the Bible—in Leviticus—that specifically forbade marrying one's brother's widow.† To take the curse off this, there had been a dispensation from the Pope (Julius II, then) at the time

---

* Henry VII's mother had not been even considered for the crown, nor had his wife, Elizabeth of York, who had a much better claim. Matilda (way back) was never fully accepted and never managed to be crowned.

† Leviticus XX:21: "And if a man shall take his brother's wife, it is an unclean thing: he hath uncovered his brother's nakedness; they shall be childless."

Henry had married Catherine. But was the curse really off? Apparently not—though Leviticus did say "they shall be childless," and Henry and Catherine did have children, one of whom, Princess Mary, was still living. Having a child who was only a girl was, however, practically the same as having no child at all.

Henry was a very religious young man, and his conscience began to hurt him badly.

By a strange coincidence, there had appeared at court a black-eyed maid of honor named Anne Boleyn. She was twenty-two years younger than Queen Catherine (at forty-one, approaching the end of her dynastic potentialities), and though she was not beautiful she was charming, irresistible. But she was not willing to become the King's mistress, and anyway what he needed was not another mistress but another wife. One who would give him a legitimate son.

This was in 1526. Within a year after he first noticed Anne, Henry had set in motion "the King's great matter," the divorce from Catherine which would overturn his English and Roman Catholic world.

But it was a long and bitter business. Catherine fought him every step of the way. He sent an emissary to the Pope, but the Pope (Clement VII, by now) had Catherine's side of the story too. And Catherine was the aunt of Emperor Charles V, who had held the Pope as prisoner since the sack of Rome in 1527. Obviously Clement, "cowering in Castel' Sant' Angelo," * needed the goodwill of the Emperor more than he needed the goodwill of the King of faraway England. Back to England, therefore, the emissary came with a noncommittal, worthless document. Two more envoys, bishops this time, were sent. They got the promise that a papal legate, Cardinal Campeggio, would come to England and join Cardinal Wolsey, the English primate, in a court hearing touching a divorce. But many months passed before he procrastinatingly got there, and when he did, Catherine, called into court, beat Henry at his own game.

This was in 1529. Speaking eloquently in her Spanish accent, she appealed directly to the King. She challenged him to deny that she had been still a virgin at her second marriage. This was a debatable point;

* Garrett Mattingly, *Catherine of Aragon* (New York: Vintage Books, 1960), p. 242.

Catherine and fifteen-year-old Prince Arthur had occupied the same bedroom for several months, and many people thought it logical that the first marriage had indeed been consummated; but it was hard to disbelieve what the Queen was saying, and the King himself was visibly abashed. Catherine finished, curtsied, swept out of court, and refused to return.

The court adjourned without a decision. Cardinal Wolsey, under pressure from Henry to act without Cardinal Campeggio and defy Rome, under pressure from Anne who had always hated him and who was frantic now because of his slowness, was suddenly stripped of his offices and riches. He would have gone to the Tower if he had not opportunely died. Better men than he did go to the Tower because they would not rubberstamp Anne Boleyn as the mother of lawful heirs, and later Sir Thomas More and Bishop John Fisher were beheaded for it.

Six years had passed. Six years! Incredibly, Henry, whose attention span had been short before, never ceased to want his Anne. Cleverly, Anne kept him on the string. But she knew, too, when the string was about played out. When she became pregnant, the new Archbishop of Canterbury, the King's faithful man Thomas Cranmer who had replaced Wolsey, by his legal authority divorced Queen Catherine (now called the Princess Dowager) from King Henry VIII.

For some reason Henry and Anne's secret ceremony of marriage was not publicly repeated. But in May 1533 there was a ceremony of coronation for Queen Anne; and in September 1533 there was a royal baby.

But it was not the longed-for boy. It was a girl, Princess Elizabeth. She was the only royal princess, for of course the Princess Mary was a bastard now. And, since Richmond had always been a bastard, she remained the only royal child of either sex. Eventually there was a stillborn boy, but this time the blame could not be laid upon Leviticus.

And even before this the King had begun to notice Jane Seymour.

It was history repeating itself, because Jane like Anne before her was a maid of honor to the Queen. And it was history repeating itself that there were no real grounds for divorce—much less for execution. Of course Anne was not the model of circumspection Catherine had been, and undoubtedly she batted her eyes at this or that young man, and it was a well-known fact that she had once wanted to marry young Thomas Percy. But that was long before her marriage to the King, and there was no shred of evidence that she had misbehaved with Percy since—or with the court musician Mark Smeaton—or with Henry Norris or Francis Weston or William Brereton—or with her own brother George. This charge of incest was based solely on her having spent several hours with her brother alone. The King's men, making up their case against the Queen, did not do things by halves.

All five of the routinely convicted young men were beheaded under Anne's window, where she was imprisoned in the Tower. The next day she herself was beheaded on Tower Green.

One biographer (Henry VIII's dazzling Hackett) points out that legally as well as ethically there was a flaw in the proceedings. Two days after her trial the Archbishop of Canterbury (the same unholy man, Cranmer, who had declared Queen Catherine's marriage null and void) proclaimed Queen Anne's marriage null and void also. If she had never been married to the King, as Cranmer now ruled, she could never have cuckolded him. This is true. The point is well taken. But Anne had been accused and convicted not only of adultery but of an incestuous relationship with her brother, which had no bearing on whether or not she was legally married to the King, and of plotting the King's death, which also had no bearing. So she was executed quite legally, if most disgracefully.

And the King's second daughter, in her turn, was demoted from princess to bastard.

The King waited until he heard the cannon fired on Tower Green. At nine o'clock in the morning, May 19, 1536, the sound came. Anne Boleyn was dead. Her widower set out promptly on a now familiar trip—down river to Jane Seymour's father's house. He married her there next day.

Queen Jane, undoubtedly much prettier than her Holbein portrait, made Henry an excellent wife. She produced promptly, but not too promptly, the wanted heir. Then she died "of childbed fever, Before her looks or his heart could leave her."

Little Prince Edward was a sturdy, handsome child. But in the sixteenth century even the healthiest baby could soon sicken and die.

author's opinion / naughty! [handwritten marginal note]

Nobody planned only one. A Duke of York, to make the succession doubly sure, was needed too.

But succession or not, King Henry was not especially eager to remarry this time. The loss of good little Jane had been sobering. He would never forget her, and when he died he would be buried by her.

The wife who followed this perfect wife might have suffered the comparison in any case. But Anne of Cleves, the sister of a powerful Flemish duke, was hardly Henry's type. A mail-order bride, she had been accepted on the strength of her portrait by Holbein. Most female Holbeins are, to say the least, understated, but this one flattered Anne of Cleves. Henry simply could not "stomach" her; she was, he went on to say, "a great Flanders mare"—and if you go to the Low Countries today you can see exactly what he meant. (There are painfully few pretty women, and even those are handsome in the sense that a Clydesdale or a Percheron is a handsome horse—thick, sturdy bodies, utilitarian legs.) Henry liked racehorses, and he frankly and simply refused to live with Anne of Cleves.

Anne of Cleves did not seem to mind. She was as stolid as she looked. Her proxy marriage had had no emotional impact, and though she did not want to go back to Cleves, she was very willing to be bought off with a nice castle (Hever Castle, Anne Boleyn's family's seat, which seems unnecessarily crude), plenty of money, plenty of obeisances, and the title of "the King's good sister." She was the luckiest of all Henry VIII's wives.

Henry chose his next wife himself, not from a picture. There was a charming little girl at court named Catherine Howard. She was a first cousin of Anne Boleyn, which like Hever Castle would have bothered a more sensitive man, and there was nothing whatever to be said for her except that she was young and pretty and the King wanted her. She was practically brainless, had been badly brought up, and had a reputation for lightness and laxity which nobody dared to mention to the King.

He found out about it later. He also learned that, in addition to the several young men (one in particular) whom she had "lain with" before her marriage, there were several young men (one in particular) who were still admitted to her room when everything was quiet, and either the King was away or Catherine herself was on a "progress." This had required the connivance of her lady-in-waiting, so Lady Rochford was sentenced to be beheaded too. Her name is on the marker on Tower Green along with Queen Catherine Howard's.

On the block, Catherine said, hysterically, "I die a Queen, but I would rather die the wife of Culpepper." Culpepper was the young man—he was executed too, after torture at Tyburn—whom she had loved both before and after her marriage to the King. They were courageous, at least. "It is true," Catherine told the little crowd around the scaffold, "that long before the King took me, I loved Culpepper and . . . he urged me to say that I was pledged to him . . . but sin blinded me and greed of grandeur. . . . Pray hasten with thy office," she said to the executioner. "Good people, I beg you pray for me."

King Henry was never the same after Catherine Howard. He had really believed her what he called her, his "rose without a thorn." As if he had never seen in the mirror the enormously gross, diseased, predatory monster of his later portraits, he really believed that this beautiful young girl had married him for love. His Council, spreading the evidence of her infidelity before him, had been shocked and abashed by his tears.

But the King's resilience was one of the remarkable things about him. His eye fell on Catherine Parr.

This lady, who would become the sixth and last of Henry VIII's wives, had almost the compulsion to marry and remarry that he did. Though only thirty when she came to his attention, she had already been widowed twice, and she would marry again (very promptly) when he died. After his sensational previous marriages—imagine the talk in the courts of Europe—the happy marriage Henry had with this serene and pleasant woman was anticlimax.

Other things besides his personal life had Henry's attention during his thirty-eight-year reign. But the very nature of his reign was shaped by his famous divorce. It changed England's economic, political, and social structure as well as its religion.

When he was younger Henry had been a truly dutiful son of Mother Church. He more than his people, more even than some of his clerics, was inclined to make very sweeping statements about the power and authority of the Papacy. Sir Thomas More, of all people, thought the

King was overstating it when he said, "We will set forth that authority to the uttermost. For we received from that See our Crown Imperial." But when the matter of his own divorce came up it was easy for Henry to see that the Pope was not judging his case on its merits. He knew the Pope was not inexorably opposed to divorce, having just (1527) granted one to Henry's sister Margaret in Scotland. And he knew the situation of the Pope, actually the prisoner of Queen Catherine's own nephew.

His break with Rome over this personal matter was much more of an emotional thing for England's King than it was for England. England was pious enough but not, on the whole, fervently religious. England did not altogether like its clerics, their rapacity, their conduct, or their numerosity. In Henry VIII's time there were ten thousand people in York, for instance, and five hundred clergy to "serve" them. In practice it turned out that the people were serving the clergy, who in such numbers were burdensome to support. Some of the clergy lived high, too, which made them specially expensive—and, of course, unadmirable. Royalty was expected to make a show, but houses like Wolsey's Hampton Court were nobody's idea of how men of God should indulge themselves.

Also it seemed to the English ridiculous that they should have to seek permission for this and that from a Pope who was a stranger in a far-off land, waiting for months and perhaps years for his answer and then finding that he had not really comprehended the distant circumstances on which he had based it.

This last objection was a matter of national temperament. The English have an independent habit of thought. In 1765 Englishmen would object, again, to being told by someone many miles and weeks away how to regulate their local affairs.

So while there will always be people to say that Henry VIII's divorce caused the English Church to splinter off from Rome, it seems more reasonable that the divorce was the impetus, not the cause. It was like a personal tragedy that "causes" a person to lose his mind; this is not what happens, really; the tragedy is the spark that sets off dynamite already piled up and waiting.

The consequences of Henry's break with Rome were tremendous. First, the power and importance of the sovereign were increased. He

was responsible now to no one. He himself was the Head of the Church
as well as State.

Also, he had much more wealth at his disposal. The rich trappings
and appurtenances of the old religion—the gold altar vessels, the silver
reliquaries and statues—could now be melted down and the jewels
picked out. The wide monastery lands were now royal lands.

The King kept some of the property he confiscated—the London
parks, for instance, are old monastery acreage—but much of it went
cheaply, or as outright gifts, to the King's friends and supporters. Such
tourist attractions as Woburn Abbey, which went to an ancestor of the
Duke of Bedford, and Newstead Abbey, which went to an ancestor of
Lord Byron, still reflect their origin in their names. Sometimes the
fortunate new owners remodeled the existing abbeys and lived among
pointed arches and flying buttresses. Sometimes they tore the abbeys
entirely down and used the materials for domestic architecture.

The old Establishment, the old nobility, looked on glumly—and
helplessly. Some of them still kept their old religion and rode out the
storm; but they did it quietly. The noise you heard all over England was
the new landed gentry celebrating.

It was rather like our twentieth century, when the saying is that the
English gentry are no longer landed and the present landholders are
certainly not gentry.

But in the sixteenth century they became a very reasonable facsimile.
They learned fast. What are now the fine old families of England were
hard-headed career people and social climbers, who with their new
lands, their new money, and often their new titles soon acquired the
habit of command. They acquired Oxford and Cambridge educations
for their sons. They learned the ways of the court, but they learned also
that it is good to keep one foot on the land. And having come up the
hard way quite recently, they knew more about the facts of life than the
old entrenched Catholic nobility and gentry had known.

They were the King's men for life, and on down from father to son.
In giving his friends and supporters the confiscated monastery lands, the
King had gained even more committed friends and supporters. Without
divesting themselves of their new possessions, these men could never
turn back, could never decide to return to the old religion, decide that

the Pope was, after all, the true Head of the Church and holder of the only keys to heaven, decide that the King's divorce was therefore worthless. Henry's dynasty was assured of the future, as well as the present, backing of this whole new powerful block.

To be on the safe side, however, the King proceeded to wipe out any remaining Plantagenets whom any disaffected old families might be tempted to get behind. He even beheaded the poor old Countess of Salisbury, Margaret Pole, who in her seventies was likely neither to seize the throne nor produce a new heir who might. He also cut down some of the more powerful or popular old nobility. The Earl of Surrey, the Duke of Norfolk's son, was beheaded; Norfolk himself was saved only by the King's death the day before the day appointed for his own. Enemies as well as fancied enemies, whole towns as well as individuals, were dealt with savagely. The commander of the King's army invading Scotland (1544) was ordered to "sack Leith and burn and subvert it and all the rest, putting man woman and child to fire and sword, without exception . . . turn upside down the Cardinal's town of St. Andrews, as the upper stone may be the nether, and not one stick stand by another, sparing no creature alive within the same. . . ." It sounds very modern; more properly it was timeless; it was simply war.

But the King Henry who gave these orders had come a long way. He was changed as much as he had changed England. This cruel, vindictive man had no resemblance to the kind, gay, studious young one who had married the first Catherine. This enormous, repulsive, bloated hulk could not be the beautiful, spectacular athlete his oldest subjects remembered—"St. George in person," someone had said, watching him jousting in a tournament. For some time it had been necessary to get him up and down the stairs with a "hoisting device." His leg was a solid flaming sore. It was the unbearable pain in his leg that caused the black-faced, murderous rages; his court knew that, tried to believe that. But it was awful to see him, in the last few days, trying to sign the old Duke of Norfolk's death-warrant. He could not do it. He simply could not move his hand.

Henry VII

1457–1509

HE ascended the throne in 1485, having defeated and killed King Richard III in battle at Bosworth Field.

Kings wore their crowns into battle in those days, and when Richard was killed the crown of England fell into a hawthorn bush. Somebody picked it out and the new King was crowned then and there—Henry, by the grace of God . . .

God that day was on the side of the strongest battalions.

Henry VII had a family claim to the throne too, but of itself it would not have put him there. He was the great-great-great-grandson of Edward III. Six generations removed—more than a hundred years since Edward III had sat on the English throne; and not only was Henry's a female line of descent, it was a born-out-of-wedlock line. It was true that his great-great-grandfather (John of Gaunt) had belatedly married his mistress and Parliament had legitimated all the children; but at the same time Parliament had expressly excluded them and their descendants from inheriting the throne.

Also, there were eight or ten people—literally—who had much better claims than Henry. One was the Princess Elizabeth of York, the eldest daughter of Edward IV, the sister of the Little Princes of the Tower, and the niece of the Richard III dead on Bosworth Field. The new King married her, so that took care of that. Elizabeth's motivations and sentiments are not recorded.

Another person with a good claim to the throne (assuming a woman was not acceptable) was the Earl of Warwick, Edward Plantagenet. King Henry had him imprisoned and finally executed.

There remained other persons with claims (all better than the new King's), but Henry had made his point at Bosworth Field and they did not trouble him. He did have trouble with various imposters; Lambert Simnel appeared promptly after his coronation, and there were several other "feigned boys"; but after he hanged Perkin Warbeck the pretenders got the point too.

Henry settled down then to make England a very good king indeed. He had wanted the throne and—this is not always the case—knew exactly what to do with it when he got it. He was a cautious, prudent, constructive man—the circumstances of his accession make him sound dashing, but he was not—and he took hold of the affairs of England as a competent businessman would. Its finances were his first concern. He was a penny-watching, pound-pinching sovereign. Some contemporaries and historians have sneered at him for this but it was exactly what England needed. The country was heavily in debt. In very few years Henry got it out. He doubled the revenues from crown lands and customs and tripled his own. Soon he was saving money and was able to buy—as an investment, of course, not to indulge himself or anybody else—over £100,000 worth of jewels. Some of his business practices were commendably sound, some merely sharp, but they all contributed toward making England solvent and the King rich.

Henry encouraged trade, taking a cut. An absolutely great tax-collector, he believed in strict courts to back him up. They soon became strict in every way, and his Star Chamber—part of his Council sitting as a court—was hated and feared and respected. People were fined for some very strange things, as well as the usual ones. Henry had a prejudice against the "over-mighty subject," and one may imagine the Earl of Oxford's rage when, after entertaining the King, he was fined £10,000 for doing the thing too splendidly.

Another way the King helped the economy was by staying out of war. In the matter of courage as well as ancestry, he had made his point at Bosworth Field. Nobody accused him of cowardice because he stayed at home and built up his country. When it was absolutely necessary to fight—the Scots along the border were troublesome—he did it on half the money that had been voted for his military expenses, and pocketed the rest. But his finest hour came when (1492) he got money from Parliament to fight France and then not only did not fight France at all but blackmailed the French king into paying him not to.

He was too clever by half, as the English say. But he knew how to get along in the world. He was a wise and far-seeing executive. With solvency he had brought peace and prosperity and law and order to England, and in this atmosphere the arts and trades and crafts flourished.

He also was carefully building up his dynasty, the great Tudor dynasty, making his bricks with a minimum of straw.

Tudor was a Welsh name, virtually unknown in England. (It was not even very important in Wales.) Henry's father, Edmund Tudor, whom Henry VI had created Earl of Richmond, had married Lady Margaret Beaufort, and Beaufort was the family name of the out-of-wedlock pseudo-Plantagenets whom Parliament had legitimated but expressly excluded from the succession. This line was Henry VII's only shadow of a claim to the English throne.

He did have another royal line, but it was French, not English. Edmund Tudor's father, Owen Tudor, had married the Queen Dowager of England, the widow of Henry V. She had been born a Valois, the French King Charles VI's daughter. So King Henry VII of England, the first royal Tudor, was King Charles of France's great-grandson. He was also a half-nephew of a recent King of England, Henry VI, who had been the son of Henry V and Catherine of Valois. His father was, as contemporary genealogists delicately put it, uterine brother to Henry VI—half-brother on the mother's side. This was why, of course, Henry VI had made Edmund Tudor Earl of Richmond.

All this was irrelevant and immaterial, in a way, because it certainly had no bearing on Henry VII's claim to the English throne. As to that, the Beaufort line was all he had. But by crediting him with more royal blood it did take some of the curse off the upstart Tudor blood. It gave him dignity and prestige.

The Tudors claimed to be descended from King Arthur, though, and King Henry and Queen Elizabeth emphasized this creditable connection by giving his name to their oldest son and heir.

Prince Arthur's death, at fifteen, affords us one of few glimpses into his parents' relationship. It could have been anything, for obviously they had married for dynastic reasons. But Henry hurried to comfort his Queen when Arthur died, and part of what she said, comforting in her turn, was written down. She reminded him "that God had left him yet a fair Prince, two fair Princesses, and that God is where He was, and that we are both young enough." If that was her philosophy, "that God is where he was," Elizabeth of York had remarkably surmounted a tragic early life. She looks, indeed, beautifully serene as she lies in bronze beside her husband, in the Henry VII Chapel which he soon built in Westminster Abbey to receive her body. She proved not, after all, young enough to recover from bearing another child.

Many historians have thought that her widower's promptness in putting himself back into matrimonial circulation, very soon after Elizabeth died, showed he cared nothing about her. But this is not true. It is not necessarily true even of a private citizen, and in Henry VII's case it was a logical part of a long-term plan. He had used Arthur, and he intended to use young Henry and Margaret and Mary, to strengthen his Tudor dynasty by useful foreign alliances; being now available, he would use himself too.

But fortunately his plans came to nothing—fortunately, because the queen he really wanted to marry, the greatest heiress in Europe, Joanna of Castile, was quite insane. Crazy Jane—the name still survives. Passionately in love with her handsome, unfaithful husband, Philip of Austria, Joanna had never recovered from his death. (Here is a prime example of a personal tragedy that was a trigger rather than a cause. Insanity ran—galloped—in Joanna's family.) For a long time King Henry persisted, his mouth still watering for "la Loca"'s money, that a kind new husband was all she needed to make her well again; but even he wavered from his purpose when he realized that Queen Joanna really would not be separated from the embalmed body of her first husband, which she carried with her everywhere and would undoubtedly have brought to England.

So Henry VII died still a widower. But Joanna was just about the only opportunity to enrich and establish England that he had let go by, and his imprint would be on England always.

Study if you can the face of Henry VII—not the stylized bronze on his beautiful tomb, or the young picture holding the gillyflower, or the older picture with the Tudor rose. In the crypt of Westminster Abbey is the effigy that was carried in his funeral procession, made unquestionably from his death-mask. Look at this. You are looking at England's first modern king.

Richard III

1452–1485

H<small>E</small> usurped the throne in 1483, upon the death of his elder brother, Edward IV, and the mysterious disappearance of Edward's two little boys. Yes, these were the Little Princes of the Tower, and Richard III, formerly Richard Duke of Gloucester, was the Wicked Uncle of history and legend.

He was the last member of the Plantagenet family to reign in England, but he looked nothing at all like them. The Plantagenets tended to be tall, blond, godlike, with blazing blue eyes; Richard was small, dark, unprepossessing. He may or may not have been slightly deformed, with one shoulder higher than the other; the controversy which rages over his character extends to this physical flaw. Shakespeare, of course, is played with Richard looking like the Hunchback of Notre Dame and exuding waves of pure evil, but historically one must pay no attention to Shakespeare. Unfortunately the so-called serious historians have written less than objectively, too, the earlier ones as Tudor propagandists, some later ones as zealous unblackeners of Richard III.

Did Richard III really have the Little Princes in the Tower, his nephews, put to death? Everyone will have to make up his own mind.

King Edward IV, his elder brother, left seven children, all technically capable of inheriting the throne, though five of them were girls. There was no law in England forbidding female succession. But it was one of those theoretical female rights that from Matilda on down had somehow never materialized, and for all practical purposes the heirs to the throne were Edward's two boys.

The elder, Edward also, automatically became Edward V. The younger, Richard the Duke of York, automatically became next in line.

The new King, aged twelve, had as Prince of Wales been living in Ludlow Castle up near the Welsh border. Some of his mother's relatives were with him there and when his father died they set out with him for London. But they were "intercepted" by one of his father's relatives— the Wicked Uncle, Richard Duke of Gloucester. Intercepted is a very polite word for the holdup and abduction that took place on the Ludlow/London road. Richard captured little Edward's uncle and older half-brother, thrust them into prison, and subsequently put them to death. Edward he shut up in the Tower.

This part was not quite as bad as it sounds. The Tower of London was a palace then as well as a prison. In fact, up to the time of Charles II it was customary for kings to spend at least the night before coronation there.

But little Edward V was not about to be crowned.

His mother the widowed queen, hearing that he had been abducted by his uncle Richard Duke of Gloucester, could not have been too surprised. Competition for the control of a young king was customary between different branches of a royal family. But she was alarmed. The formal, detailed story of Richard III as a murderer may not have been written till after the Tudor dynasty came in, and it may have been used as Tudor propaganda, but Richard's contemporaries were afraid of him. The Queen trembled for her elder son.

With her younger son, the Duke of York, aged ten, and her little daughters she took sanctuary in Westminster Abbey. This had worked for her before, but it did not always work; Thomas à Becket, for instance, had been murdered in Canterbury Cathedral; but generally it was pretty safe, and petty criminals made quite a career out of darting into churches when they were hotly pursued. Most people hesitated to violate sanctuary.

Richard Duke of Gloucester hesitated. But he wanted to get the second little boy, too, in his custody, and he opened negotiations with the Dowager Queen.

"Negotiations" probably meant blackmail, threats against her elder son who was already in Richard's power. But even so it is hard to excuse the Queen for yielding. She could not huddle in the Abbey precincts forever, of course, but she could have stayed a long time, and maybe there would have been a popular uprising against this so obviously wicked uncle. But she was afraid, she was perhaps badly advised, and she gave in.

So the little ten-year-old was shut up in the Tower with his brother, and like his brother never came out again.

Their deaths—if they had occurred—were not announced. There was no news about them whatever. Their uncle Richard, who had been named Protector, within a few weeks was named king. He was crowned—crowned and anointed in the Abbey, which seems much worse than merely violating its sanctuary would have been—on July 6, 1483.

But though he did not indicate what had happened to the children, he did indicate why he had felt justified in usurping the throne. It was because they, and all of Edward's children, were illegitimate. Edward had been betrothed—so Richard's sycophantic priest announced at Paul's Cross—to someone else before he married Elizabeth Woodville and the marriage was not, therefore, valid. This was a thin story indeed—in-and-out, off-and-on betrothals were the rule rather than the exception among royalty, and anyway Warwick the Kingmaker would probably have found the flaw, if there had been one, in Edward's marriage. His motivation to do this had been as strong as Richard's was now. In any case, Richard should not have made the Little Princes disappear, whether they were illegitimate or not. He had promised his brother Edward to take care of them, he had put them in the Tower, and he was obviously responsible for producing them again. Even his most zealous supporters cannot deny this. They would like us to believe, though, that Richard was merely keeping them in protective custody—and in silence—and would have produced them some day if, within two years' time, he himself had not died fighting at Bosworth Field. They would like us to believe that Henry VII, Richard's successor on the throne, a Tudor, found the boys still shut up in the Tower when he came victorious into London, and had them murdered himself.

This is possible. Henry was quite capable of murdering the boys. He put to death other persons who had better rights to the throne than he did. He would not have failed to put these two little princes, who had the best rights of all, to death if they had still been around waiting for him to do it. And it is quite true that the case against Richard III was spelled out after his, Richard's, death, after Henry's new Tudor dynasty had come in, and some excellent people, both conscientious historians and one very persuasive writer of murder mysteries,* think it was Tudor propaganda, covering up Tudor murder by blaming it on the Plantagenet.

But do they really think anybody would have spelled out the case against Richard III *before* Richard's death? Anybody who did that would have been spelling it out before his own death, too. Very shortly before.

It is not possible to go into the matter of the disappearance of the two Little Princes, which is undeniable, and the matter of whether or not they were murdered by Richard III, without taking sides and coming to some conclusion. My conclusion is that the detailed account of it is fictitious, but that Richard did indeed kill them.

Enough to say here that only a stupid man would have failed to do so, and Richard III was not a stupid man.

Being intelligent, he made a very good king. He concluded a truce with Scotland, convened a progressive Parliament, patronized the publication of Malory's *Morte d'Arthur*, put down an insurrection led by his cousin and former friend Buckingham, and had King Henry VI's body moved to a more splendid burial place at Windsor Castle.

This last has been interpreted as a good sign that Richard had not murdered the unfortunate Henry. Richard does not, however, need this good sign; he seems to have been far away when Henry was murdered. More probably, it was a gesture toward his Queen, who in her first marriage had been Henry VI's daughter-in-law.

The relationships of the Plantagenets, as among other royal houses, have the fascination of horror. One keeps wondering what was going on in their minds as they broke bread together, at home and in church.

---

* Josephine Tey, *The Daughter of Time* (New York: Macmillan, 1952).

Anne Neville, Richard III's queen, was his first cousin once removed. His mother was Cecily Neville; Anne was her great-niece. Anne's father was that Earl of Warwick, Richard Neville, Warwick the Kingmaker, who had turned his coat halfway through the Wars of the Roses and, having labored mightily to put Edward IV on Henry VI's throne, fell out with him and made a deal with his enemy, Margaret of Anjou, Henry VI's queen, to restore poor simple-minded Henry. Part of the deal, it was thought, was marrying his daughter to Margaret's and Henry's son, in return for his, Warwick's, changing to fight on their side. If so, this may have been one reason Margaret hesitated. This traitor's daughter a wife for her son, her lovely Edward, as she called him, the Prince of Wales? But the match was made. Soon afterward, Edward was killed at the Battle of Tewkesbury and Anne was a widow.

Richard (who would be Anne's second husband) fought in this battle on the other side. But it is overdoing it to say, as some historians have, that he was personally responsible for the death of Prince Edward. Because he probably did have the Little Princes of the Tower killed, there has been an enthusiastic tendency to make a mass murderer of him, responsible for every death mentioned. Richard was a violent man and, in ruthlessness, a true Plantagenet, but he was surrounded by many other ruthless and violent men and they were doing their fair share of killing, too.

Anne's father had, meantime, been killed at the Battle of Barnet. This was just as well. It would have been distinctly awkward, even in Plantagenet circles, for him to have been around after the final triumph of the White Rose. But when the Prince of Wales died and Anne married Richard, it was less awkward than it might have been because, after all, she was his first cousin once removed and blood in the veins is thicker than blood on the ground.

Because they were so closely related, Richard probably should have got a dispensation to marry Anne. He laid his heir wide open to the charge of illegitimacy. But at that time, of course, he was not thinking that he would ever become king.

Richard and Anne were married in 1472, more than a decent year after the death of her first husband; more than a decent year after that their only son, Edward, was born. He was ten years old when Edward

IV died and his youngest brother Richard decided to seize the person of little Edward V and make himself King and his own little Edward Prince of Wales.

Again, *what* could have been going on in Anne Neville's mind? We do not know much about her but we can certainly say that she was flexible.

We may also, though not without fear of contradiction, say that Richard was devoted to her. The story was actually spread, when the year after his usurpation of the throne his only son died, that he wanted to get rid of his Queen so that he could marry again and have another heir. When Queen Anne herself died, the year after that, it was said that Richard (the mass-murderer at work again) had poisoned her. It was said that he was not only going to remarry, but that he was going to marry his own niece, Princess Elizabeth of York, the sister of the two Little Princes done to death in the Tower.

Of course he did not. Kings have married their nieces in Portugal and Spain, and in ancient Egypt they even married their sisters, but England has always, at its most uncivilized, been more civilized than that. But the death of his heir certainly did place Richard in a bad position. No matter if he married, no matter whom he married, he did not have time, he could not hold on, to breed up a new son to take his place. He faced the fact that he might be only an interim king, with the succession wide open again. Richard made a gesture; he settled the succession on John de la Pole, who was the son of one of his older sisters. He went before Parliament to make this nomination. But he went knowing it was utterly futile. Across the channel, a much more likely claimant than John de la Pole was biding his time.

Richard had put down, in 1483, the insurrection masterminded by the Duke of Buckingham. (This cousin and former friend had been with Richard when he kidnapped little Edward V on the Ludlow/London road, but later he thought he had better change sides.) Buckingham had been captured, tried, and executed. But the plotting still went on without him.

The crux of it was the invasion of England by young Henry Tudor, the Earl of Richmond. His family claim to the throne was slight, but he

did have a Lancastrian line and Richard's own claim to the throne had
been slight, too. Henry had actually sailed from France once before, but
when Buckingham's part of the scheme failed he went back again. Now
with Richard's heir dead he was ready to try again. He landed
dramatically at Milford Haven—featuring his Welsh background,
hoping that Welshmen as well as Englishmen would rally to his
standard. But his main reliance was in the French mercenaries, about
three thousand of them, he brought along. Richard may well have hoped
that men would flock to *his* standard to repulse these foreigners, and
indeed he did gather a much larger army than Henry Tudor's. But his
men were not enthusiastic. They were tired of fighting the Wars of the
Roses, which had been going on since most of them could remember.
What did it really matter, Lancaster or York? Why should they fight
and die for this man who had been king for only two years, who had
surely seized the throne even if he had not murdered King Edward's
heirs, who had no heir of his own body to succeed him?

The Stanley family, in particular, was thinking along these lines.
Stanley had raised five thousand men, but he was not clear in his mind
whether he was going to fight for Richard or for Henry. (He was
married to Henry's mother by this time, but that was only one factor.)
He had been negotiating with Henry, however, and finally he decided
to throw his strength that way. (He got the Earldom of Derby for his
services, incidentally.) Like all the famous turncoats in English history,
Buckingham, Marlborough, Warwick, he knew a rising from a setting
sun.

Richard and Henry met on Bosworth Field. With Stanley's defec-
tion, Richard's army was outnumbered. But there still remained the old
chivalric tradition of hand-to-hand fighting between the leaders. Richard
thought he knew himself to be a better fighter than Henry Tudor. If he
could only cut his way back through the lines to Henry—and, swinging
a battle-ax, he tried. He cut down men right and left, even Henry's
standard-bearer. He was almost upon Henry when he was cut down
himself.

"A horse! A horse! My kingdom for a horse!"

It is wrong to discredit Shakespeare as a serious historian and then quote him, for Richard's cry for a horse may be as fictional as anything Shakespeare wrote about him. But it will always be remembered whenever Richard III is.

The Plantagenet dynasty had ended on a high note. The Wars of the Roses were finally over. Stanley—who else?—plucked the crown of England out of a hawthorn bush and set it on the first Tudor king's head.

Edward V

1470–1483

HE succeeded to the throne in 1483, upon the death of his father, Edward IV. He probably died in that same year. Certainly that is when he disappeared.

The bones of two children, buried together in a wooden chest, were found in the Tower in the reign of Charles II. Everyone believed at once that they belonged to the almost legendary Little Princes, twelve-year-old Edward V and his brother Richard, and King Charles ordered them reburied in Westminster Abbey, in an urn inscribed with their names.

Nobody since has seriously questioned the identification of these bones. Everybody still believes they are the Little Princes'. Examination by an eminent physician and an eminent dentist, in 1933, and, a generation later, the review of this evidence by equally distinguished anthropologists and orthodontists, give no reason to dispute the obvious conclusion. There is not, of course, absolutely positive identification—no dental charts, for instance, to corroborate the shape and position of fillings these fifteenth-century children did not have.

But the probability is overwhelming. The two little boys are known to have been in the Tower; they disappeared from it; they were not seen again elsewhere. No story about their fate was given out. If they had died natural deaths in the Tower (which is possible—it was an unhealthy place) they would have had a proper funeral. Their uncle King Richard had everything to gain by this, nothing to lose. If they were living in safety somewhere else—and this too is a possibility—their mother would have been glad to hear it. On this point, too, their uncle King Richard had everything to gain and nothing to lose. He was the rightful king after these children were declared illegitimate; the flaw (if there was a flaw) in their parents' marriage left him, Richard, next in line, for the children of George Duke of Clarence had already been eliminated by his attainder. So the Little Princes could have lived out peaceful lives as harmless bastards; but not without somebody's knowing about it. If they had been still alive, somebody would have come forward, after Richard died, to assert the right of Edward IV's son to his throne. Even if he were an illegitimate son, he was the illegitimate son of a king, and Henry VII, we are reminded, was merely the great-grandson of the illegitimate son of a king's son.

But the main reason to believe the Tower bones are correctly identified is a negative one. If not the bones of the Little Princes, whose were they? The Tower was not only a hard place to get out of, it was a hard place to get into. It is possible, of course, that two other boys of the right ages, alive or already dead, were smuggled into the Tower so that their bodies might be mistaken for those of the two Little Princes who were being spirited away. (This is of course pure fantasizing à la More; nobody has ever suggested that such a thing really happened.) But in that case the bodies would not have been so extremely well concealed. They would be buried where they would soon be found.

In point of fact they were buried ten feet underground and under a flight of stone steps. It was not until the steps happened to be torn down, nearly two hundred years later, that they were revealed. Whoever buried the bones there did not want them found.

But though no question has been raised about these being the Little Princes' bones, there is considerable question about who the Little Princes' murderer was.

Under the Tudors, he was firmly identified as King Richard III, who had put his nephews in the Tower, never produced them again, and owed his crown to their being out of the way. Tudor propaganda-historians—Polydore Vergil and Sir Thomas More—elaborated on this theme and Richard emerged a real monster, very justifiably overthrown by Henry VII. His reputation historically went from bad to worse, worse even than King John's. But then finally the pendulum swung.

For two hundred years now Richard has had a party of friends and admirers unable to believe that he murdered his two little nephews. They are like the people unable to believe that William Shakespeare, briefly educated in a provincial town, never at court except as an actor, never out of England, could have written those sophisticated plays. These people have always felt that some far more impressive person— Sir Francis Bacon, for instance—must have written Shakespeare's plays and used his name to hide the fact.

Similarly, the people who feel that Richard III is innocent of murder have someone else to suggest. Most of them have theorized that Henry VII, coming to the throne in 1485 after killing Richard III in battle, found the two Little Princes still (since 1483) languishing in the Tower and had them murdered because he wanted a clear title.

From the physical findings, though, it appears now that the bones could not be those of boys fourteen and twelve years old. They were the bones of boys twelve and ten.

So this seems to wash out Henry VII. He was still in France, still in every way far from the throne, when this twelve-year-old and this ten-year-old were murdered. The year was 1483.

A more recent theory is that the murderer was the Duke of Buckingham. This is the friend and cousin who had helped Richard intercept little Edward V on the Ludlow/London road. Descended from Edward III's youngest son, Buckingham too coveted (of course) the throne. He had opportunity as well as motive. He was fomenting a rebellion against Richard III. The theory is that he hoped to frame Richard, do the murders himself (or have them done) and hang them on the King. Then with any luck the King would lose his throne and Buckingham could step forward.

This theory has its points, and it has some very distinguished proponents. But a plot to discredit Richard would have to be predicated on finding the bodies—murder needs good evidence—and these bodies were not buried with the idea of their being found. They were buried, remember, ten feet deep underneath a flight of stone stairs.

It is rather questionable too whether denouncing Richard as a murderer would be very effective or dramatic. He had already demonstrated that he did not mind killing people who got in his way—Lord Hastings, for instance. During his brief Protectorate, little Edward V still alive in the Tower, Richard presided at a Council meeting there and Lord Hastings, among others, crossed him. The others Richard merely had arrested. Lord Hastings (the Lord Chamberlain) he ordered beheaded immediately—"before dinner." It was done on Tower Green, on a log or a carpenter's chunk of wood.

No—to get back to the Duke of Buckingham—he is not too convincing as the murderer of the Little Princes.

But whom does that leave?

Well, it leaves John Doe, and Richard Roe, and all the other loyal followers of Richard III, the counterparts of those four loyal followers of Henry II who heard him say "Will no one rid me of this lowborn priest?" and forthwith rode to Canterbury and murdered Thomas à Becket. We certainly cannot dismiss the possibility that some person or persons unknown to us served King Richard in this way. But this possibility is, like the Duke of Buckingham, not too convincing.

But if not the Duke of Buckingham, or the unknown loyalist, or the Tudor king who got there two years too late, who is left for the part of murderer?

Richard III is left.

But the case against Richard III has been demolished. All that "evidence"—Tudor propaganda! Thomas More, the sainted Sir Thomas, has been shown as either the most credulous or the most unscrupulous of historians. Polydore Vergil has been shown to have written what King Henry VII wanted written. And as for William Shakespeare, he made it up as he went along.

This is true. The classical evidence against Richard III is plainly spurious. But it is the evidence against Richard III which has been demolished, the elaborate circumstantial fictions about how the Constable of the Tower, Sir Robert Brackenbury, refused to murder the Little Princes for him; how Richard, in a rage, sent him a letter ordering him to turn over his keys, for one night, to Sir James Tyrell; how Sir James and his hired assassins, Miles Forest, "a fellow fleshed in murder beforetime," and John Dighton, "a big broad square strong knave," went by dark to the Tower; and how about midnight (midnight of course, that storied hour) the two ruffians stole into the room of the sleeping children and forced the "featherbed and pillows hard into their mouths" until they died. See it by all means in the tableau at Madame Tussaud's, but don't believe a word of it.

The evidence the Tudor historians manufactured against Richard III has been demolished, but the real case against Richard remains.

Nothing else makes complete, four-star common sense.

He put the Little Princes in the Tower.

He did not produce them again.

He was the only person who profited directly by their death.

It was conventional procedure to dispose of competition by murder.

"It is not surprising that even before Richard's coronation some men suspected that the Princes might soon be killed," Richard's biographer Paul Murray Kendall says. "What, at that time, was the accustomed fate of deposed monarchs . . . ? Edward the Second . . . Richard the Second . . . Henry the Sixth . . ."

Richard would have been foolish indeed to leave Edward V alive.

Professor Kendall likes and admires Richard, and is not at all sure that he murdered the Little Princes. But he calls him "the Protector who usurped the throne, the brother who thus doomed, if he did not murder, the boy king who was Edward's son." He says again, "his assumption of power contained the death of the Princes within it. Horrible as their fate was, it was not a gratuitous or even an additional deed of violence; the push from the dais was itself the mortal stroke. In this sense it can be said that Richard undoubtedly doomed the Princes." *

Why stick, then, at finishing the job?

But it is like the positive identification of the bones found in the Tower. We cannot be absolutely sure.

There had been much blood shed before this in efforts to get or keep the English throne, and there would be much shed after it. Henry VII and Henry VIII did their best to wipe out a whole family of possible

---

* Paul Murray Kendall, *Richard the Third* (New York: Anchor Books, 1965), pp. 440, 468. Appendices I and II, pp. 438–87, should be read for the argument pro and con.

claimants. But there was something about the murder of the two Little Princes in the Tower that has transfixed imagination. It was not just that they were young and helpless; other victims of the system were young and helpless too. But this is the point in English history when it is customary to stop and give thanks that times have changed and that the horrible, wicked, cruel people of the Middle Ages and the Reformation have been civilized and refined. We cannot, we say, simply cannot understand people like that.

Actually there is much less difference between us and them than we like to believe, and we can understand them very well. The expressions on the faces below the gallows are the same expressions we can see at ringside today. Actual physical murder is not done so often in the best circles, but there is the same necessity to clear the field, to remove the obstacles human and otherwise, before a man with a real determination to rise and rule may do so; and this takes place in very upper circles indeed.

The comparison with modern politics, as in a presidential election, is of course obvious. But many historians have also noticed the resemblance between the historical struggle for control of the throne, by two persons or parties both professing interest in the welfare of the country, and the contemporary struggle for control of the voting stock, by two persons or parties both professing interest in the welfare of the company. In one book the author divides his seventeenth-century history into sections with twentieth-century headings: "I. The Power Structure. II. The Power Struggle. . . ."

And if you have trouble grasping the Wars of the Roses, read (for instance) the very different accounts of the Curtis Publishing Company's failure, by several of its former executives. These books will bring insight which is practically revelation. You will not only be able to tell the modern Yorkists from the modern Lancastrians, you will notice resemblances between fifteenth and twentieth century individuals.

The image of disinterested benevolence (royal, really) comes down to us specially unchanged—this is in top management—and there is the same substratum of insensitive and unscrupulous men, "hatchet men" in the corporate jargon, who are available for the actual deeds of violence and, in fact, often love their work. Such a man used a very real hatchet or sword on Lord Hastings on Tower Green. And someone actually, physically, murdered the Little Princes, not just doomed them.

Scarcely anything is known about the character of little Edward V or of his younger brother. There are one or two interesting points about them. Edward V—as Prince of Wales sent to live there, aged three—was the child born in Sanctuary in Westminster Abbey. His mother, Queen Elizabeth Woodville, had been left in London, in the last stages of her pregnancy, when her husband Edward IV fled to France. He was saving his own skin from the oncoming army of Margaret of Anjou, the Queen of Henry VI whose throne he had usurped. Elizabeth took refuge in the Abbey and King Henry, restored to his throne, sent her a lady-in-waiting and things to eat. He was anxious for her to be comfortable. She stayed in Sanctuary till she had had her baby, her first boy after all those girls, and by the time she was ready to leave it her husband had come back, defeated Queen Margaret of Anjou, and put poor Henry VI back in the Tower. There is no record of Queen Elizabeth's sending him anything at all to make him comfortable.

Her second son, Richard the little Duke of York, was born more conventionally, at Shrewsbury, but he married at an age unconventional even for a royal child. He was married, not just betrothed, to the Duke of Norfolk's little daughter, Anne Mowbray, when he was less than five. And he became a widower at the age of eight, when Anne died.

He may have been a king. We do not know—there is so much we do not know—whether Edward V or his little brother died first. If Edward did, then Richard Duke of York, as next in line, automatically succeeded him—succeeded him as King Richard III. So it would have been not only his throne which the Wicked Uncle stole, but his name.

Edward IV

1442–1483

H E was put on the throne in 1461, after his distant cousin Henry VI was defeated in battle and fled to Scotland. But Henry returned, and then there were two crowned and anointed kings in England—until Henry was murdered in 1471. After that Edward was the only one.

This King Edward IV was an episode in the Wars of the Roses. (We are obliged to call them that, though the charming name is sixteenth century, not contemporary, and the white-rose–red-rose business in Temple Garden is pure Shakespeare.) Edward was a Yorkist—White Rose. King Henry had been a Lancastrian—Red Rose. Edward was the son of Richard Duke of York, who had wanted the crown for himself and spent six violent years trying to wrest it from Henry VI. Henry was so simple-minded and/or saintly (and sometimes actually crazy, like his French grandfather) that he would have handed the crown over without a struggle; but his queen, Margaret of Anjou, gave the Yorkists blow for blow. For thirty years altogether the contest would go on, one side up first, then the other. But the Lancastrians'—Margaret's—side was up in 1460, when she personally defeated Richard Duke of York at the Battle of Wakefield.

The Duke of York was killed. His son Edward, seventeen years old, succeeded him in this title and as head of the Yorkist movement to seize the throne.

Left to himself, Edward would not have seized anything. He had some points of ability but they were in other fields. But he had inherited also his father's right-hand man the Earl of Warwick. There are other Warwicks, as you know to your sorrow—the index will show by dates and first names which is which—but this is the one history always calls "Warwick the Kingmaker."

He made young Edward of York King Edward IV.

The ups and downs of the Wars of the Roses had given the White Rose of York victory in its turn. Though Margaret had consolidated Wakefield with another triumph (the second Battle of St. Albans), this time she got chased all the way to the Scottish border.

She had the King with her—poor Henry VI, that is. In London, Warwick was having another King, Edward IV, crowned.

Edward wore the crown unsteadily for four years, because Queen Margaret was known to be raising another army. In 1464, at Hedgeley Moor and Hexham, she thought she was ready. But Warwick beat her soundly. She was lucky to slip away from him, with the little Prince of Wales, to France. Henry VI was not so lucky. He was run to earth finally in Lancashire and shut up in the Tower of London.

It still could not have been a very easy situation for Edward IV—he was an anointed and crowned king, true, but with another anointed and crowned king almost underfoot. The solution would have been simple, and no doubt Warwick often thought of it. But the Yorkists' whole cause and crusade had been based on their righteous horror at the Lancastrians' having murdered Richard II, back in 1400, to get the throne. Now if they in turn murdered Henry VI to get (or consolidate) the throne, would they be any better than the Lancastrians?

Actually they were no better than the Lancastrians anyway. Both sides were murderers, confidence men, kidnappers, blackmailers, and thieves.

But the Lancastrians had been ruling for three generations of kings—Henry IV, Henry V, and poor Henry VI—and so as far as Europe was concerned they were considerably more respectable than the upstart Yorkist Edward IV.

Still, Warwick kept trying to make a good royal marriage for him. If the King of France, say, or the King of Spain were to give a daughter to the new King of England, prestige and stability would accrue to the Yorkist throne. The problem was not easy and years passed—Edward was twenty-two—but finally Warwick thought he had found a princess.

Unfortunately, Edward had found somebody too.

He had fallen in love, inexcusably, with Elizabeth Lady Ferrers, a young widow with two little boys. She came from an excellent English family (Woodville) and she was beautiful (naturally) and virtuous (regrettably). She was not about to become the King's mistress. If anything, she was going to marry him. And she did. They were already married when Warwick heard about it.

Queen Elizabeth made King Edward very happy and Warwick furious. Not only had he to give up the idea of an advantageous royal alliance, but the Woodville family (hundreds of them, it seemed, actually only dozens) followed Elizabeth to court and were picking up titles and sinecures and emoluments on all sides. Edward could deny them nothing, because they were Elizabeth's kin. Warwick was only the military expert who had brought Yorkist victory out of defeat, only the kingmaker who had personally had Edward IV crowned.

Warwick could not stand it. He had been, as kingmaker, almost king himself. Now he was nobody. Conspiring with his son-in-law the Duke of Clarence, the King's brother who had also had enough of Woodvilles, he shut the King up at Middleham while he wiped out some of them. But then he made the mistake of releasing Edward. Had he really thought the King would take the murder of the Queen's relatives lying down? Apparently he really did. He had to get out of England quickly, but he still had ideas. He went to France to talk to Margaret of Anjou.

Margaret was a no-holds-barred fighter; there was nothing gentle about her; but she was about the only upright character in the whole Wars of the Roses, on either side. Obviously she felt contempt for this turncoat Englishman. She also had a personal reason for hating him. Warwick had taken the trouble to announce at Paul's Cross that her son was the Duke of Somerset's and not King Henry's. Now here was this man professing friendship and offering support and asking her to be his ally. Of all the hard things that had been expected of her as Queen of England none could have been more repugnant than this. For, of course, she could not turn Warwick down. She knew his value as a general. Together, they could take England again.

And so they did. Warwick, landing, the Duke of Clarence with him, practically passed King Edward on the way out. Thoroughly frightened, Edward was fleeing to the Continent. Margaret of Anjou marched on London and liberated her husband from the Tower.

With her, of course, was the Prince of Wales. It was the first time the English nobles in Parliament assembled had ever really seen the heir to the throne. He was seventeen. He had always been strong and beautiful—one of the tall, golden Plantagenets—and the advantages of maternal handraising, so seldom the upper-class way in the fifteenth century, were apparent. And he was much brighter than his father the reinstated king. Poor Henry—he seemed scarcely to know or care whether he was chained in the Tower or enthroned at Westminster.

He was still saintly and forgiving in spite of his hardships. Hearing that Elizabeth Woodville, in Sanctuary at the Abbey, was undergoing hardships in her turn—Edward IV had saved his own skin, deserting his pregnant wife—he moved at once to relieve her distresses. The story is that King Henry himself sent her a lady-in-waiting, paying the expenses, allowing her food, and so on, while Elizabeth, who had previously borne King Edward only girls, lay in with a boy, an heir to the contested throne.

Elizabeth Woodville is supposed to have had so much influence over her husband (the Earl of Warwick certainly thought so) that we must conclude she did not ask him to repay King Henry's kindness. For the opportunity soon arose. King Edward, joined by his brother the Duke of Clarence (who had just turned his coat back again) landed on English soil in February 1471 and marched south. Warwick was out of London. So was Margaret of Anjou. Edward walked into the palace and straight into King Henry's presence.

The ex-King's, rather, because now Henry VI was out again, Edward IV was in again, "the King enjoys his own again," as they sang later about Charles II. Henry did not mind at all. He actually offered to embrace his "cousin of York—you are very welcome," he told Edward, "I know that in your hands my life will not be in danger." You can see why people said he was simpleminded.

Edward's reply is not recorded. He merely sent Henry back to the Tower, and himself proceeded to the Abbey, where the crown of England was (again) put on his head.

He had to fight to keep it there, of course. Warwick met him at the Battle of Barnet, a bloody one, fifteen hundred killed. And Warwick was among them, which decided it.

There remained Margaret of Anjou. She had lingered awhile in France, with her son. It has been suggested that she did not trust Warwick. (Why should she?) But finally, on the very day of the Battle of Barnet, she landed at Weymouth, and had the news of Warwick's death.

Of course it took more than this to discourage that stout campaigner. Margaret had won battles without Warwick before, her husband the king had been imprisoned in the Tower before and she had rescued him. She quickly raised another army; Margaret could always raise an army.

But at Tewkesbury her army was defeated and Margaret was taken prisoner.

Her son was killed as well. There is controversy over the exact spot and manner of his death. Persistent tradition has it that it was Richard Duke of Gloucester, King Edward's youngest brother, who killed him, stabbing again and again. There is also a persistent tradition that Richard Duke of Gloucester went from Tewkesbury, on the King's service, to the Tower of London. What is not tradition, but history, is that Henry VI was murdered, there and then, at his prayers.

They took Margaret of Anjou, when she had seen the body of her "lovely Edward" and knew that it was really all over, to the Tower also, to wait ransom by her family in France. The Yorkists read her character correctly. There was no reason not to let her go home. Margaret had waged war according to its rules and she knew the rules, too, of the power game. She could be as ruthless as anyone. When she had defeated and killed Richard of York in battle she had not hesitated to impale his head and set a paper crown on it. And she had ruthlessly put other enemies to death. But Margaret had not been fighting just for the sake of fighting. She was no vengeful Plantagenet; she had merely been taking care of the interests of her husband and son, and now she had neither husband nor son.

Still, the Wars of the Roses went on. Sporadically, of course. But it was not till 1485 that the last blood was shed, the last disaffected Yorkist had at the last disaffected Lancastrian, and the age of feudalism was over. The barons would never again be a real power in England. They had seen to that themselves. Fighting among themselves, they had been like the gingham dog and the calico cat—they ate each other up. Between the nobles that were killed and the nobles that were attainted—that had lost their inheritances because they chose the wrong side—there were not enough nobles left to make a good showing in Parliament. And those nobles that were there, in 1485, were impoverished men. Across from them, on the other side of the Hall, the clerical nobles were far more numerous and prosperous-looking—but that is another story.

Edward IV had twelve years from the time he finally got back the throne, in 1471, to the time he died, in 1483. (And in his bed, which must have surprised everyone including himself.) He turned it into a fairly good reign. He had his traitorous brother the Duke of Clarence put to death—whether in a butt of malmsey, by drowning, is less certain—and put more and more confidence in his youngest brother, Richard the Duke of Gloucester, who had ably represented him in the north of England. Richard had during that time been far away from the throne, however; George Duke of Clarence, the middle brother, and his children had come before him, directly after Edward, King of England, and his. But after Clarence's death, and his being attainted, so that his children could not be in line for the throne, Richard began to have the first symptoms of the royal malady which we call, in this democratic country, presidential fever. King Edward named Richard Duke of Gloucester Protector to act in the interests of his country and his children, in case he should prematurely die, and this turned out to be a mistake.

Edward did prematurely die. He was only forty when, worn out with his excesses, he gave up what he had struggled so long to secure. Like so many of his predecessors and successors, he could have made England a much better king. He was extravagant, self-indulgent, and much ruled by his mistresses in the wake of his wife; three he had concurrently were "the merriest, . . . the wiliest, . . . the holiest harlot[s] in the realm," he said; but he was also a canny businessman who made enormous profits in wool. The country prospered along with the king. By sequestering the estates of Lancastrian nobles he also greatly enriched the crown, for he did not turn around and give the estates to Yorkist nobles. He kept them. He made profitable treaties. If not exactly a friend of education, he patronized the new invention called printing—possibly because his brother-in-law Earl Rivers wanted to publish his first book—and let himself be talked out of abolishing Eton. (He disliked Eton because his rival Henry VI had founded it. His Queen also apparently disliked the idea of Margaret of Anjou's having founded the Cambridge college Queen's—she refounded it and now it is Queens', for both of them.) He was strong on forced loans and high customs, did not scruple to interfere with the courts, bribing juries as well as removing judges (the bribes are a matter of record), and he was a religious bigot. He may have been a bigamist. He had no more people put to death than the average Plantagenet king did, but the first documented use of torture was in his reign.

His grandson, King Henry VIII, was said by people who knew them both to resemble him greatly.

Henry VI

1421–1471

H<small>E</small> succeeded to the throne in 1422, upon the death of his father, Henry V.

He was one year old, so his chances were not good. It was always bad to be a helpless infant in the Middle Ages, and infant mortality was markedly higher when the infant was a king. He was subject to murder as well as to injury and disease. There was not just one Wicked Uncle in English history, though Richard III is always spoken of that way, in capitals. There were fully a dozen, and sometimes they had the active backing of their wives.

In little Henry VI's case it was shown in court that Eleanor Cobham, the duchess of his guardian-uncle Humphrey of Gloucester, had employed several people including "a woman . . . surnamed the witch of Eye [to] devise an image of wax like unto the King . . . [and] by their devilish incantations . . . make the King's life dwindle away . . . as they little and little consumed that image."

Humphrey Duke of Gloucester was one of Henry VI's two regents. He was supposed to handle England for him during his minority, and another uncle, John Duke of Bedford, was in charge of the English armies in France, where the Hundred Years' War still went on. France had, more theoretically than actually, come to Henry VI on the death of his French mother's father, the mad King Charles VI. (He would soon lose it, thanks to Joan of Arc, who fought for a weak dauphin and crowned him in the cathedral at Rheims.) But the power struggle was dependent on nothing more or less than the King's minority, and it went ceaselessly on. Gloucester, Bedford, and the Beauforts sparred and sniped and jockeyed for position with unflagging relish.

The little King's mother seems to have had no authority or standing whatsoever. Soon she married—at least we hope she married—a man named Tudor, who had been her master of the wardrobe, and had other children. Later on Henry VI would give his half-brothers titles and much affection—everything, as someone said, except the legitimacy he could not give. As it turned out, they got along very well without it.

Henry VI grew up to the accompaniment of much talk about how delicate he was, but he survived everything, even the Duchess of Gloucester's witchly efforts. And his body would withstand all kinds of exposure and abuses for fifty years. But it was soon apparent that his mind was not quite bright. This was not surprising, his French grandfather having been insane. Later he would have spells of definite insanity himself, but till he was almost thirty he seemed to be merely feebleminded. Since the story continued to circulate that he was also frail in body, there was great hope in other branches of the family that he would die without issue. His own branch (the Lancastrian) felt strongly, of course, that he should marry and beget as soon as possible.

Their choice fell on a fifteen-year-old French princess, Margaret of Anjou. Henry was married to her (the passive case is used here deliberately) in 1445. Eight years passed without an heir to the throne. But in 1453 Edward, Prince of Wales, was born, strong and beautiful, and now Margaret had a better cause than Henry VI to fight for. She was about to emerge as one of the greatest fighters in English history.

Of that there is no manner of doubt; but there is considerable controversy about Margaret's character and motivations. Yorkist sympathizers then and now have thought her a strident Woman's Lib type; other people find her purely maternal and protective. My own feeling is that these others are more nearly right, but that Margaret loved the fighting. I also consider her far more moral and ethical than the rest of her friends and foes. This little French girl, no serious student of English history, was not concerned with how her husband's branch of the family got the English throne three generations back. They had it. That was enough for her. Her father had given her in marriage to the reigning, the crowned and anointed, King of England and she tried to make him a good queen, suiting her actions to his needs. Married to a childlike man who needed all the help he could get, she protected his interests until he died, as she protected those of her young son. She was a dynast first and last. She saw her duty and she did it.

But the daughter of King René of Anjou, brought up in his artistic, poetry-writing, romantic court, must have been surprised to find her duty chiefly of a military nature.

During her husband's minority there had been the usual intrigues and power struggles that attend an infant king. Rapacious relatives surrounded him. His uncle John Duke of Bedford, the best of the lot, had died in France and his other uncle Humphrey Duke of Gloucester was still and chronically at odds with his cousin the Duke of Somerset (Edmond Beaufort) and the Duke of Suffolk (William de la Pole) for control of the King. Grown up, he was no more able to manage his elders than he had been as a child. But now there was a very able and executive queen. There was also Cardinal Beaufort, another cousin whose mind was fixed on something besides the next world.

In 1447 Humphrey of Gloucester was suddenly arrested for treason. Had he plotted the King's death? Probably not. In any case his arraignment was a severe shock to him and it may well be that he died naturally of a stroke—this was the story given out—soon thereafter. But of course the cry of foul play was immediately raised. Duke Humphrey's body lay in Parliament and it was admitted that he *looked* peaceful, but the question of whether he had met a violent end was never settled, and his death was a major issue in the Wars of the Roses.

This left the dukes of Somerset and Suffolk in charge of affairs— Henry Beaufort, the Cardinal, had died soon after the Duke of Gloucester—and for a few years they seemed to go smoothly. But then the murders which in Plantagenet circles were only natural attrition began again.

There was no question about the violence of Suffolk's death. Banished for five years, he was arrested and executed at sea. Only the Duke of Somerset, Edmund Beaufort, was left.

The Beauforts were the ablest of the descendants of Edward III but (the English were snobbish about illegitimacy) never "top drawer." They were hardly ever liked. But Somerset and Margaret of Anjou, though they may not have liked each other either, were forced into an alliance by the rise of another aspirant to power, who was carrying on where Humphrey Duke of Gloucester left off. This was Richard Duke of York, the cousin—third cousin once removed—of King Henry VI.

In many people's minds, including his own, Richard of York had a better right to be king than Henry did. He was descended from the Plantagenets on both his mother's and his father's sides; he was twice the great-grandson of Edward III; both of his lines were legitimate, and one of them was elder than Henry VI's one line. Henry VI's line had been on the throne for three generations, however unjustifiably, and would not easily be dislodged, but Richard of York never gave up hope that the feebleminded young king would die—without issue, of course. It was a blow when he grew up instead and was married to Margaret of Anjou, but it was heartening when years passed, after the marriage, without the sign of a child.

Richard of York may have masterminded Jack Cade's peasant rebellion. If not, he certainly took advantage of it to come sniffing around London. This was in 1450. He was not alone. He had an army with him. This was not quite as menacing as it sounds, because noblemen with vast estates, like Richard York's, could command the services of the men who lived and worked on them, but their appearances with all these men lined up behind them could make even crowned and anointed monarchs nervous. Richard, however, on this occasion apparently wanted nothing except the assurance that he would be King Henry VI's heir. Queen Margaret of Anjou gave him this assurance. She did not seem able to produce Henry's natural heir, and everybody still seemed to think, as everybody had during his precarious if not delicate childhood, that Henry was likely to die any minute.

Actually he lived to be fifty years old and the cause of his death was murder.

But meantime, in 1453, he definitely lost his mind, and his cousin Richard of York returned to London to take over. As heir to the throne he was obviously, he thought, the person to be Protector. But the situation was complicated by the fact that Queen Margaret, after eight years of barren marriage, was about to give birth. In this same year, 1453, she brought forth her strong and beautiful son, Edward, the Prince of Wales. For Richard of York to be Protector to this baby was like expecting a lion to protect and watch over a newborn lamb.

Margaret was beside herself. Her husband, never much help at best, was abysmally insane. The Duke of Somerset, her colleague, had been arrested and put in the Tower. Her personal attendants had been dismissed and replaced with watchful Yorkists. Everybody was watching. Richard the Protector watched the baby, but Margaret watched Richard. She also watched King Henry for signs of returning sanity, and when they came, in 1454, she propped him up and had him declared sane and competent to rule again.

It followed that the realm would no longer need a Protector. Richard of York was ousted. Margaret and the Duke of Somerset, released from the Tower, were appointed regents, to serve in case of future need.

This precipitated the Wars of the Roses. Richard, enraged, plainly showed his hand. No longer did he pose as a benign defender of the little prince. His army met Margaret's at the Battle of St. Albans (1455). She lost, and the Duke of Somerset was killed.

Now Margaret of Anjou was quite alone, and her husband had lost his mind again. Richard of York, needless to say, made himself Protector again. Again, Margaret took up her watch over her little son.

Something could have "happened" to him very easily during this period; something could also have "happened" to poor mindless Henry VI. Margaret for all her passionate vigilance could not have prevented it. Again, all the positions at court had been filled with Yorkists replacing Lancastrians. The only conclusion possible to draw is that the Yorkists did not want to get the throne by murderous violence if they could avoid it, and they still thought of Henry VI as a frail invalid who would soon die.

Actually he must have had a constitution of solid iron.

Four years passed before he came to his senses—or what passed for his senses. At any rate he recovered from his spell of insanity. Queen Margaret was ready and waiting for this. Her plans were all made. She had an army all ready to throw together.

In 1459 she soundly defeated Richard of York and he fled to France. A year later he came back and soundly defeated her.

So the Wars of the Roses went, first Yorkists and then Lancastrians in the ascendent. Richard Duke of York was killed, and his remarkable second-in-command the Earl of Warwick ("Warwick the Kingmaker") put Richard's son Edward the new Duke of York on the throne as Edward IV. Then it was the Lancastrians' turn again and Edward IV fled to France. He returned; Henry VI went to the Tower; Warwick turned his coat and joined Margaret of Anjou in a new invasion from France; Warwick was killed fighting on what must still have been, for him, the wrong side. Then in the bloody twilight of it all Margaret herself was captured, her son killed, her husband murdered. It had been a long, cruel, wasteful war. It had accomplished nothing.

It was a thirty-year struggle to dislodge and reinstate, dislodge and reinstate, a king who cared nothing about being king. Henry VI had, he explained in one of his rare moments of simple reasonableness, worn the crown for forty years, his father had worn it without question or dispute before that, and his grandfather had been king as well. He thought he was entitled to keep the crown. But he never really thought it was worth fighting for, and his kingdom was never really of this world.

Henry's memory is honored chiefly for two foundations—Eton College, where there is a statue of him out in front, and King's College, Cambridge. His Queen, the daughter of that King René of Anjou who was poet and painter and musician all three, was more suitably the first foundress of Queens' College, Cambridge, but she gets much less credit for hers. Henry, to be candid, probably did no more than agree to somebody else's idea about establishing Eton and King's—he was as agreeable and ductile as he was simpleminded—but no doubt he was mildly interested, and would consider very kind the attention they pay him every year. On his birthday, there are always Etonian white lilies with light-blue ribbon, and Lancastrian red roses tied with mauve, laid by the provosts themselves on the spot in the Tower where he was murdered at his prayers.

Henry V

1387–1422

H E succeeded to the throne in 1413, upon the death of his father, Henry IV.

Because multiple Henrys in the same family were confusing then as now, his father had been called Henry of Bolingbroke (or simply Bolingbroke) after the castle where he was born. This younger Henry was born in the Castle of Monmouth, so he was often called Monmouth—Henry or Harry of Monmouth. Shakespeare called him "Prince Hal," but that was long afterward.

He was not born heir to the throne. He was in his teens when his father, as dashing as unscrupulous, took it away from his cousin Richard II. So he never believed much in the divine right of kings. Kingdoms were won by the sword. He had seen it happen. Kings lived by the sword and died by the sword.

Young Monmouth had known King Richard well. About to go on the Irish campaign, Richard had required him from his father as a hostage for Bolingbroke's good behavior. They went to Ireland together. Bolingbroke had from earliest years coveted the throne; King Richard knew this, knew he had actually conspired with Gloucester and others to capture and depose him. And he knew that Bolingbroke bore him an active, personal grudge. It was something the King had to keep in mind; and yet he liked young Harry of Monmouth, treated him more like a favorite cousin than a hostage, and took the opportunity to knight him.

Bolingbroke's story was that he wanted only to be reinstated in his own lands, which King Richard had confiscated after John of Gaunt died; but he had twenty thousand men under arms, surely more than were needed for this small matter. (It really looked more as if Bolingbroke were finagling for the throne.) Still Richard did not threaten or demonstrate what he would do with Bolingbroke's son, his hostage, Monmouth. He merely transferred the boy to another castle. It was not till after the coup was completed, not till after Richard was actually his father's prisoner, that young Henry of Monmouth seemed to realize what was going on. He was unhappy and amazed.

But Bolingbroke was not a man to be told by his teen-age son how to manage his affairs. Undoubtedly young Henry told him how kind King Richard had been to him as a hostage. But Bolingbroke did not depose Richard in a very kind manner, and though his death may have been necessary, there is no question that Bolingbroke encompassed that death.

Young Henry, no longer called Monmouth once he was heir to the throne, grew up into one of the tall, handsome, swashbuckling Plantagenets. He had the Plantagenet tendency to fall in love at first sight. He wanted to marry the beautiful "little Queen," who had become Richard II's widow at twelve. But Isabella of Valois was horrified at the idea and it was, indeed, a bit crude. Henry, however, knew what he wanted and veered from it only slightly; he professed himself willing to marry one of her younger sisters. But they were both young indeed so he had to wait. Strangely enough his father did not force him to marry elsewhere, and when his father died, Henry being twenty-five, the new king was still unmarried.

For several years he was busy enough with war. On top of a Lollard uprising and a conspiracy on behalf of the Earl of March (whose claim to the throne was far better than his own), negotiations had been broken off with the French. The Plantagenet kings of England were French themselves, Angevins, and they had no idea of giving up to France the French lands they thought belonged to them. Up until Henry IV's time the Plantagenets had not even spoken English, and Henry V was the first king to speak it in the vernacular.* Aquitaine was firmly theirs,

* This claim is also made for Henry IV, who had "challenged the crown of

France had acknowledged by the Treaty of Calais in 1360, but they also wanted Normandy, Touraine, and Maine, the former Angevin empire.

Young Henry V announced these demands to the French king and added a demand for his daughter in marriage, with a dowry of two million crowns.

Such terms were outrageous. The King of France suffered from periods of insanity and the King of England must have been hoping to catch him in one of them. But he did not; the terms were refused; and it was these negotiations which, breaking off, now sent Henry to reopen the Hundred Years' War.

It was soon apparent that war was his element. He was tremendously talented in it. He had a strategic mind, could lead men, could press forward with total coolness and ruthlessness. In 1415 he took Harfleur, where Shakespeare tells us he said, not exactly in the vernacular:

> Once more into the breach, dear friends, once more;
> Or close the wall up with our English dead!
> In peace there's nothing so becomes a man
> As modest stillness and humility;
> But when the blast of war blows in our ears,
> Then imitate the action of the tiger:
> Stiffen the sinews, summon up the blood—

Then he pressed on to Agincourt. There he fought in October one of the decisive battles of the world.

King Henry had embarked with 10,000 men, had lost some at Harfleur, and at Agincourt confronted with no more than 8,000 a French force of over 50,000. (These figures are, of course, disputed; there are several versions; but all convey the same idea of a big force challenged by a little one.) Henry's knights did their fighting on foot, which the French knights thought beneath their dignity; the English used the longbow and the French still did not, though it had been amply demonstrated to them (on them, actually) how superior a weapon it was. Nor were the French strong in archers. Still, 50,000 of them against 8,000 English— If the French felt confident, one could hardly call them overconfident.

England . . . in plain English." But Henry V "owed a great deal of his popularity to his mastery of the pithy, salty, forthright language of the common people."

But King Henry beat them. Trounced them. And came back to the kind of victory celebration London would naturally give a handsome young king who had done the impossible.

The mayor and aldermen met him at Blackheath, the houses were hung with tapestries and flags, and there were literally fountains of wine to sustain the enthusiasm of the cheering crowds. Henry, riding through the streets to give thanks at St. Paul's, proceeded to the Palace of Westminster; it took him five hours. In his train were most of the men who had fought with him—for the English had lost only hundreds (the French thousands) at Agincourt—and such eminent prisoners as the Duke of Orléans. That memorable poet Charles d'Orléans would be shut up in prisons, beginning with the Tower of London, for twenty-five years; if *"Le temps a laissié son manteau"* describes an English spring, it was one he saw through little slit windows.

Back to France for the mopping up, and then at Troyes in May 1420, King Henry dictated the provisions of the treaty.

The French king's son, rather retarded anyhow, was disinherited. Henry was recognized as heir to the French throne and regent of France, and he would marry, with a dowry of two million crowns as above mentioned, the charming French princess Catherine of Valois.

This was a younger sister of the "little Queen," Richard II's widow Isabella, who had refused to marry Henry earlier. He had thought then that he would like to wait for one of the smaller girls; now that he saw young Catherine (though this did not happen exactly the way Shakespeare imagined it) it seemed an even better idea. Someone suggested to King Henry that, since he had apparently fallen in love at sight, he might want to reduce the amount of the dowry he would expect with Catherine.

But no, the king answered, surprised. He saw no reason to settle for less than the two million crowns he had first demanded.

They were married romantically in St. Jean's, which was not the biggest or finest church in Troyes but had merely appealed to the sightseeing king, and he took Catherine home for a splendid coronation. The year after the wedding, they had a little boy, another Henry. Everything was wonderful, but it was not to last long.

Henry was not done fighting. The year of his son's birth he had to go back to France to avenge his brother, Thomas the Duke of Clarence, whom the French had killed in an engagement at Beaugé. The French were like the English; their kings could make treaties all they liked, but the nobles had minds of their own.

Again, King Henry was brilliantly successful in the field; he won Normandy, Brittany, Maine, Guienne, and Champagne. But then he fell ill before he could get back to England. Dysentery, the old army disease, is thought to be the enemy that, finally, was able to overcome this strong, handsome, brilliant young man. Perhaps because he died so young, and at the apogee of his shining fame, he has remained the English people's favorite among all their kings. They have endowed him with all their English virtues, many of which indeed he had. He captures the public imagination, too, because it is sad that he fought so hard, triumphed so splendidly, bargained so well that he doubled England by gaining France, and then died so prematurely that all was afterwards lost. Whether it would have been lost if he had lived is a question no Englishman wants raised. Whether it is regrettable that he studied war instead of peace is another such question. Henry V was superbly fitted for war; in a reign of only nine years it is doubtful he could have done as much for England in any other way. Certainly he could not have done as much for his own image, which is unrivalled.

Henry IV

1367–1413

HE usurped the throne in 1399, forcing the abdication of his first cousin Richard II.

Before that he had been called, most often, "Bolingbroke," after the castle where he was born, but also Hereford and Derby, because he was Duke of Hereford and Earl of Derby; and this Plantagenet was also Duke of Lancaster, so in reading the history of his period one has to be alert for him under many names. He was John of Gaunt's only son by his first wife, Blanche of Lancaster, and John used the title Duke of Lancaster in right of his wife; this is the origin of the Lancastrian branch of the family. Henry when this title came to him signed his name "Henry de l'ancastre," for remember that English royalty was still very French.

But as Henry IV he was "the first king," we are told, "to speak English as his native language." *

He had to talk fast in English as well as French to justify his usurpation of the throne. Of course he claimed that it was rightfully his and he was not usurping it at all. He was descended from Edmund Earl of Lancaster, called Crouchback, a brother (he said an elder brother) of

* Ronald Hamilton, *The Visitor's History of Britain* (Boston: Houghton Mifflin, 1964), p. 75.

Edward I, who should by rights (he said) have succeeded to the throne when Henry III died in 1272. So his other relatives Edwards I, II, and III should never have reigned at all—and if all this sounds bewildering and confusing to you, it also sounded bewildering and confusing to the average Englishman who was being asked to transfer his loyalty from Richard II to Henry IV. Henry IV went on to say that he had confirmed his claim to the throne by right of conquest, and this was something more easily understood.

Shutting the deposed king in the Tower of London, Henry made plans for his own coronation in the Abbey.

From this he went on to a coronation banquet in Westminster Hall, as English rulers after him would do. He had no queen beside him. Mary de Bohun, an English lady of the Norman-descended aristocracy, had died some years before, and though eventually he did remarry (Joanna of Navarre) there was no dynastic need for it. Mary's handsome children surrounded him. Unlike Richard, he had heirs.

King Henry may not have intended, originally, to murder his cousin Richard. He had reason indeed for revenge; Richard had treated him very unjustly in 1398, banishing him because of a quarrel with the Duke of Norfolk and, when his father died, confiscating the great estates he should have inherited. But surely in forcing King Richard to abdicate, and in replacing him, he had made his point.

At any rate, he did nothing hastily. He moved Richard, a few days or weeks after his own coronation, to John of Gaunt's strong castle in Yorkshire, Pontefract. (Pronounce it Pumfret.) In the dungeon there, a man who had never been robust might in due time naturally die, leaving no blood on anyone's soul. Henry had a workable, if frequently latent, conscience.

But with Richard alive he had, foreseeably, no peace. In the first months of his reign he escaped narrowly from Windsor Castle before its seizure by Richard's friends. They claimed Richard was out of prison. He was not, but the new King had a nasty scare. He put down the rebellion personally, and brought the "traitors'" heads back to London to impale in public view. It was not enough. There had to be a more permanent solution.

In February 1400 the death of former King Richard II was

announced. No details came out then or later. He too was brought back to London, and King Henry IV himself attended a service in St. Paul's, where the body lay in state and people were encouraged to file past it and see how peaceful he looked and how peacefully, therefore, he must have died.

But Richard's death did not end all King Henry's troubles, though now he was undoubted king. He found himself unpopular. He had been well liked as Bolingbroke, but he did not go down so well as king. He feared assassins. He had trouble with Parliament and along the Welsh and Scottish borders. There were more uprisings, chiefly Owen Glendower's in Wales, and there were still factions that had no confidence in his claim through Edmund Crouchback and mentioned the Earl of March, Edward III's descendant with right of primogeniture. He had to fight the powerful Percy family, killing Sir Henry ("Hotspur") at Shrewsbury and executing Thomas Percy, the Earl of Worcester, afterwards. Then he executed Richard Scrope the Archbishop of York and Thomas Mowbray the Duke of Norfolk after another rebellion failed—yes, an archbishop; times had changed since the commotion after Becket's death; but the credulous and the superstitious (in other words, most of the people in England) believed firmly that the King's skin disease was visited on him the day the Archbishop was executed. They called it, thinking wishfully, leprosy. It was not, but it was not the least of King Henry's troubles that he itched until he died.

Still his rebellious subjects did not learn. There was another actual battle, this time at Branham, where Northumberland, the head of the Percy family, and Thomas Lord Bardolf were killed fighting against him. The King was always victorious—it would be easy to see where his son got his military talents—but it was wearisome and discouraging to be still defending a *fait accompli*.

Perhaps the worst worry was a party that thought the King's son, Prince Harry of Monmouth, would make a better king than he, and why wait? He did not really believe that Harry was conspiring actively with these people, but knowing Harry's heredity—himself!—King Henry could hardly put usurpation out of his mind.

Also, he had his private horrors. Incredibly—for a Plantagenet—his conscience hurt him more and more. Not enough to make him give up the throne, call in the Earl of March—but he thought that if he went on a Crusade all might be forgiven. It was reasoning typical of his times. Henry had always been crusade-minded; he had got as far as Lithuania in 1390 and Prussia in 1392, but he wanted to get all the way to Jerusalem. He was in increasingly bad health, and he had a premonition, he said, that he would die in Jerusalem.

Instead he merely died in the Jerusalem Chamber in Westminster Abbey, the room off Dean's Court which you may not see unless you are specially interested in King Henry IV and specially ask.

He had been seized by some kind of fit while praying in the church, and they had carried him in there. So in his death as in his life he had the name but not really the game. Nothing in his life was as good as he had thought it would be.

Richard II

1367–1400

H E succeeded to the throne in 1377, upon the death of his grandfather, Edward III.

He was only ten years old; his father, the decisive and dashing Black Prince, had died not long before, leaving him a heritage he could not live up to. His mother, the "Fair Maid of Kent"—this sounds bucolic, like Maud Muller or King Cophetua's Beggar Maid, but she was actually Joan Countess of Kent—and his oldest uncle John of Gaunt undertook to guide him during his minority.

Being the oldest uncle, John of Gaunt would have, except for little Richard II, been king himself. A highly competent and ambitious man, he had only to look at Richard, pretty, delicate, unpromising Richard, to know at once who would make the better king.

But to John's credit (and this was no negative virtue in the Middle Ages and among the Plantagenets), little Richard lived to grow up. If John of Gaunt had not been necessarily away in Spain, Radcot Bridge would never have happened. It had been building up since Richard, seventeen, chafing under the restrictions of his much more officious and overbearing uncle Thomas of Woodstock, the Duke of Gloucester, tried to take over his own government. Or, rather, he tried to exchange Gloucester for another ruler, his own favorite Robert de Vere. This Robert was already Earl of Oxford by inheritance, but Richard did not think this was enough. He created him first Marquess of Dublin and then Duke of Ireland, and if Robert "had said black was white, Richard would not have contradicted him." * But Gloucester soon mustered an army which defeated the favorite's at Radcot Bridge, and then firmly established the King's dependency by setting up a five-man board, the Lords Appellant. Under their control the Merciless Parliament, next year, ordered the execution of all Richard's friends they could catch. It was said that Richard and his young Queen both pleaded vainly, the Queen in tears, actually on her knees, for the life of Sir Simon Burley, an old army friend of the Black Prince's who had been Richard's tutor as a boy.

Thomas of Woodstock does not seem to have been aiming at the throne for himself. Though John of Gaunt was safely out of the country, Thomas acknowledged this elder brother as heir presumptive by including his eldest son in the five Lords Appellant. No, Thomas's aim was simply to rule England through a puppet nephew, whom he manipulated as if he were a puppet indeed, with no mind or will or feelings or thoughts of revenge.

He was completely contemptuous of Richard. He was completely careless of what he said about or to the King. He even threatened him to his face with deposition unless he did as told. Apparently he thought Richard could not hear or did not remember.

He was mistaken. His nephew King Richard was remembering it all and thinking very much of revenge. He was merely biding his time.

On May 3, 1389, he took his council by surprise. "My lords," he asked, suddenly, "what is the number of my years?"

And the lords had to say that he was over twenty-one.

"Then," said the King, "I am old enough to manage my own affairs."

And the government of the five Lords Appellant had been quietly overthrown.

Just like this, it makes incredible reading. Surely the account is oversimplified.† Surely the Lords Appellant could have foreseen this. Could they really have believed that Richard, who though not their idea

---

* Quoted from Froissart, xii, 239, in *Dictionary of National Biography*, xx, 244–45.

† Thomas B. Costain, *The Last Plantagenets* (New York: Popular Library, 1963), pp. 149–50.

of a godlike Plantagenet was far from feebleminded, would always sit silent and let them rule England and him? He let them till he was twenty-one. It was plain that he had been waiting until there was no question at all of his being old enough to rule. He received then and there the Great Seal from the chancellor. He replaced the chancellor, and the chancellor among others (such as Thomas of Woodstock) must have been surprised that nothing worse happened, for the script really called for five prompt executions. But John of Gaunt, returning, was advising the young king, and he was also restrained by the excellent influence of the Queen.

Never had a ruler of England a more successful consort. Though in twelve years of marriage she gave him no child, though she was good and gentle and charming rather than beautiful, Anne of Bohemia was everything her husband needed or desired.

But in 1394 Queen Anne died, and Richard was, literally, never the same thereafter. His character appeared to change. In his immoderate grief, he ordered the Palace of Shene, where Anne had died, razed to the ground. He found himself without friends; his favorite Robert de Vere had died in exile; and certainly there was no one in his family he could trust. His mother had died, and though his uncle John of Gaunt had never taken advantage of him, in a family like this it was prudent to watch one's heir, especially when *his* heir (in this case Henry of Bolingbroke) was so blatantly ambitious. And though for reasons of state King Richard remarried in 1396, his bride was a seven- or eight-year-old child, Isabella of Valois. She was sent to England to be brought up in English ways, and the King became fond of her, as one becomes fond of any nice little girl, but it was years too soon for either consummation or companionship. Perhaps this was why he had been willing to accept the "little Queen" as a successor to his beloved Anne—she was not really a successor at all.

At any rate, King Richard was very alone. He brooded over this and over his wrongs. He remembered what the five Lords Appellant had done to him and to his friends. He remembered particularly, perhaps, Queen Anne in tears before one of them (a subject, *his* subject, who should have been kneeling to *her*), begging vainly for his old tutor's life.

In 1397—ten years after Radcot Bridge—Richard acted. He arrested, imprisoned, and had murdered his uncle Thomas of Woodstock, the Duke of Gloucester. He arrested and had tried before Parliament—himself sitting crowned to listen, his uncle John of Gaunt prosecuting the case—the Earl of Arundel; the sentence was beheading and this was carried out immediately on Tower Hill. He had the Earl of Warwick similarly arrested and tried, but because he at once pleaded guilty let his sentence be merely life imprisonment and the forfeiture of his property.

This took care of three of the five Lords Appellant.

The two that were left by some strange chance got into an argument with each other. There can be, of course, no real proof that the King set this up somehow, but he must have. It is otherwise just too good to be true. The King had perhaps been a little lenient with one of the disputants, Bolingbroke, because of the continuing services of John of Gaunt, Bolingbroke's father, and because he rather liked this cousin himself. Anyway, Bolingbroke and the fifth Lord Appellant, Nottingham later the Duke of Norfolk, were going to fight a duel. This duel the King did set up, as a spectacular pageant; and then, dramatically, at the last minute before it was fought, broke it up. He forbade it. Publicly, instead, he banished both the young men, Nottingham for life, Bolingbroke for a term of six—some say ten—years.

That took care of all five of the Lords Appellant who had controlled the King.

It may be that the King was a little insane by this time. Certainly there had been a considerable change in him. He had always had a violent temper; it was worse now, but perhaps that was only because the Queen's gentle influence was gone. It seemed more significant that, though formerly a rather silent young man, he was now an incessant, compulsive talker.

Everybody around him was very nervous, naturally. Nobody knew what might happen next. Nothing did, for a while. King Richard had governed very well—well enough, certainly—since taking over the government in 1389, and he continued to do well enough. But the change in his personality was too apparent to escape notice. He had lost the confidence of his people. Some historians think they grew contemptuous of him because he was a peaceful king, making treaties and not war, not following the gallant traditions of the Plantagenets.

(To some of the rest of us he seems quite sufficiently bloody.) Some sneer at him for being artistic (he remodeled Westminster Hall), fastidious (he used "little pieces made for . . . the lord King for carrying in his hand to wipe and cleanse his nose," perhaps actually inventing the handkerchief), and literary (he sponsored Chaucer, Gower, and Froissart). But it was really more held against him that he believed fully and firmly in the divine right of kings. He not only believed in absolutism, he practiced it. Taking over the government in 1389, he had summoned a hand-picked Parliament which took only three days to give him everything he asked. He was granted, for instance, a tenth of all national revenues and a subsidy on all wool, wool-fells, and leather. This was for life; he would not need to call Parliament again to ask for money. He would govern not with the aid of Parliament but with eighteen "advisors" chosen by himself, so in this too he was following the letter but not the spirit. Overcompensating for his years of being ignored and interrupted and countermanded, he had made himself a throwback, absolute king, with Magna Carta in a place of honor on the shelf.

And the nobility did not like it. The people did not like it. The nobility had not always discharged their obligations well, of course; the peasants had not always acted responsibly. But it seemed to all of them, on the whole, that anything was better than an absolute king again.

So King Richard's absolutism was the cause of England's turning against him.

The trigger was the death, in 1399, of John of Gaunt.

Richard acted as an absolute king would do—and went too far. He confiscated his uncle's estate. All that wealth and all those great possessions had been safe enough in the hands of a man who some historians—sneering again—say lacked the resolution to seize the throne. (There is another way of putting it; he lacked the treachery.) But great resources would not be safe in the hands of John of Gaunt's son, Bolingbroke.

Of course Bolingbroke was in exile, but only for a term of a few years. So King Richard extended his exile to life.

One does begin to believe that his mind was going, for on top of this he decided to lead a campaign in Ireland. It was quite unnecessary; it was much more important for him to stay close to London and see how Bolingbroke (who *was* one of the warlike Plantagenets) would take being stripped of his inheritance and being exiled for life—all because of a duel he had never even fought.

Bolingbroke showed quite promptly how he was going to take it. He returned from exile, landing at Ravenspur. He had only a few followers with him, but more joined him along the way. Finally he had an army of at least twenty thousand men. (Froissart said thirty thousand.) He moved rapidly north, making no mistakes at all. Richard came slowly south to meet him, making every mistake possible. He was neatly trapped in Flint Castle, one of Edward I's old fortresses, and taken as prisoner down to London, where he was shut up in the Tower.

On September 30, 1399, he was taken to Westminster Hall, open for the first time since its renovation. Undoubtedly King Richard had been looking forward to displaying his project in all its finished beauty, but not under circumstances like these. Richard was wearing his crown and royal robes, but he did not take his seat on the throne. He stood beside it and read his abdication. The Speaker of the House then read a much longer paper detailing why he had been asked to abdicate, Bolingbroke made an excellent short speech laying claim to the throne, the Archbishop of Canterbury led him to mount it, and former King Richard II was led by somebody else back to the Tower in London till the end of next year.

Then he was sent away, not seen again in London till the next year, when his embalmed body was shown to the people. The Plantagenets set great store by displaying a peaceful-looking corpse, as Richard's was. It covered the multitude of sins; not that they thought of them as sins, merely expediency.

Fortunately Richard had had his own tomb made before he died. Otherwise he might not have had such a fine one. He lies in effigy on it, beside his beloved first wife, Anne of Bohemia. Before the tomb suffered mutilation, later on, he and Anne were shown holding hands. Richard must have seen this often, looked at himself lying there dead, when he came to visit his wife's tomb. It must have been a very strange feeling for him. But then he was a very strange man.

Edward III

1312–1377

HE succeeded to the throne in 1327, upon the deposition and murder of his father Edward II.

It was his mother, Isabella of France, who had murdered his father. She did not do it personally; as a queen, she did not even put on her newfangled côte-hardie personally. Nor did her lover, Roger Mortimer, have to soil his own hands with King Edward's blood. They were the murderers nevertheless, and some historians have held it against young King Edward III (as he then became) that he kept on living with them for three years.

But he was only fourteen when his father died. Biding his time was about all he could do.

When he was seventeen he moved to avenge the murder. Mortimer, who had calmly assumed the regency with no authority at all, was arrested, tried before Parliament, and executed—the first hanging at Tyburn. Isabella was sent to a remote and very safe castle.

If this seems insufficient punishment, remember that she was still Queen Dowager and the young King's mother—he may have felt a delicacy (far in advance of his times) about belaboring her dirty linen in public. It is more likely, however, that he could not cut her down without cutting down his pretensions to the throne of France.

Back when Edward I had gone to war against that country, he had based his claim to parts of France on fairly remote inheritance. His great-grandmother Eleanor, wife of the Count of Anjou who became Henry II, had been Duchess of Aquitaine in her own right. But though four generations of her descendants had fought to keep their rights in France, none but Richard Lion-Heart spent much time there. They still spoke French, but they had lived in England since 1154, and France as home was long ago and far away.

Edward III, on the other hand, had been partly brought up in France. His mother had had him with her while she was living at the French court with her paramour Mortimer. And his mother was own sister to the last Capetian king of France, Charles IV, who had only daughters who could not succeed him (that was the Salic Law) and whose brothers had predeceased him.

So Edward III had no need to go back to whether or not what had belonged to his great-great-great-grandmother Eleanor still belonged to him. He claimed France, all France, in right of his own mother Isabella.

So Isabella in her distant castle was maintained in luxury and treated with respect, and her son the King even named her first little granddaughter after her. She repaid these favors by leading, for a change, a circumspect life. Eventually she became repentent in the religious sense of the word and, taking the vows of a lay order of nuns, spent her last years in a most exemplary and expiatory fashion. It is surprising that history has been so unsparing of her; surely nearly thirty years of respectability should triumph over her flyer with Mortimer. Of course she should not have been his mistress and she should not have conspired with him to murder her husband, but her son and her Church had both forgiven her and "She-Wolf of France" does seem a bit extreme.

The Salic Law also excluded descendants through the female line from the throne of France, but this could sometimes be got around; the main point, as Edward III himself put it, was that France was "too great for a woman to hold by reason of the imbecility of her sex." Edward could, and thought he should, be made an exception for because as a nephew he was the nearest male relation of the last king, Charles IV. Philip of Valois, the other claimant, was only Charles's first cousin.

All the medieval kings were close students of family trees. They remind one of ladies who are constantly working up new lines so they can get more bars on their DAR pins; but they were far less scrupulous in their conclusions. They were really more like the shady "researchers" who promise anybody with enough money a coat of arms and an awesome pedigree. They did not stick at twisting things around a little.

Unfortunately the Twelve Barons of France, who decided such matters, pitched for the cousin Philip of Valois instead of Edward. Philip duly ascended the French throne as Philip VI and Edward duly went to war to take it away from him.

There were other reasons for fighting the French. (There always were.) France had a treaty with Scotland, and Scotland was giving England trouble again. Then there was an economic impasse, a matter of wool which the English grew and sold to the Flemish weavers. Edward of England had married a Fleming, Philippa of Hainault, but, on the other hand, Philip of France was the Flemings' overlord. A crisis came when, in 1336, Louis of Flanders listened to his overlord and started arresting English wool-merchants. Edward of England, then, stopped exporting wool.

Edward's first great victory was a naval one, the Battle of Sluys, 1340. It ought to be as famous as Trafalgar. The French lost twenty-five thousand men, the English only four thousand. The huge French fleet was decimated. The English had, in what would become a proud national habit, swept the sea clean of enemy ships. Most interesting of all, the victory could largely be credited to a modern innovation, English archers with the new longbows. Longbows could shoot three arrows for every one that came from the cumbersome crossbows of the French, which had to be wound up between shots and were as heavy as lead.

Edward was less successful at Cambrai and Tournai, and great victory did not come to him again till 1346. Meantime Philip VI had invaded Gascony and Guienne, both English provinces, and was threatening Aquitaine. Philip's son, Jean of Normandy (the very name insulted, for they thought Normandy English too), had so far been able to handle Edward's captains, so he decided now to head his own expeditionary force. On it he took his own son, a blond fifteen-year-old also named Edward and called, from the color of his new armor, the Black Prince.

Having married at fifteen himself, before he even took over the rule of his own kingdom, King Edward had by this time many children. Most of them were breeding true to the magnificent, dominant Plantagenet genes. No matter whom the Plantagenet kings married— Philippa of Hainault was a stocky brunette, the kind of plain, sensible Flemish girl Henry VIII would reject in Anne of Cleves—the children were likely to be tall and blond and godlike. Edward III's boys were the height of a modern basketball team—five of them, too. Lionel was the tallest, six feet seven, but all of them fairly towered over the men around them, who in medieval times averaged several inches less than men do now. In any century they would have been impressive.

King Edward himself was very impressive indeed. At thirty-four he was not just a beautiful Plantagenet, he was a fine soldier, calm, confident, resourceful. Admirers of General Robert E. Lee will rise in wrath if I compare Edward to him, for Edward's virtues and ethics were strictly fourteenth-century, but I am not talking about his character, I am talking about him as a commander in the field. Edward sitting his horse waiting for the Battle of Crécy to begin looks very like Lee—outnumbered and unworried.

There are whole books written about Crécy. Edward had fought his way, literally—crossing the Somme under fire, to get out of a spot comparable to Dunkirk in World War II (except that no ships could stop there to take his army off)—to a spot of strategic brilliance. Philip's army had to make its way around the ten-mile-long forest of Crécy; and the way was narrow. Only two or three knights could ride abreast. One historian has found *les mots justes;* the road, he says, "was as narrow as the ramp to a slaughterhouse. . . ." As the French knights appeared around the bend, two or three at a time, the English archers cut them down—English archers using the longbow. The French, who had not learned from experience at Sluys, were still winding their heavy, cumbersome crossbows, and taking the English fire helplessly while they did it.

A thousand French knights fell at Crécy, and perhaps thirty thousand men. The English losses were negligible. Where the casualties at Sluys had been on a ratio of one to six, at Crécy it was more like one to thirty-five.

One of the decisive battles in world history, Crécy was the high point in Edward III's career. He was only thirty-four, and he would live to be sixty-five, but he would never touch this pinnacle again. Still, his fame and his legend were established; he did not need to.

Calais, however, redounded to his credit. He captured this stronghold the following year; it would be the one which England held till all the other French lands were gone. Edward had besieged it for months. King Philip, still licking his wounds after Crécy, did not even try to relieve his beleaguered city as it slowly starved. Finally they were forced to send to ask King Edward his terms.

These were very simple—unconditional surrender. But then he softened—or what was softening for him. We may imagine his looking, at this stage of the negotiations, much like the stylized bronze effigy on his Abbey tomb—mouth drawn down, face set in lines of royal sternness. He would permit six burghers of Calais to sacrifice themselves for their fellow townsmen. Let them present themselves before him, six rich, proud, prominent men. They would bring him the keys to the castle and the city of Calais. They would wear only their shirts—no shoes—and halters round their necks.

This was by no means a cruel and unusual punishment. By its long and stubborn resistance, Calais had put Edward to a great deal of trouble and expense, and nobody thought he was unusually hard-hearted because he was about to hang only six people. But Queen Philippa must have been unusually soft-hearted. Pregnant with her tenth child, she went down on her knees to ask for the lives of the burghers of Calais. You can see in Victoria Tower Gardens a copy of Rodin's monument to this so far unquestioned moment in English history. Unquestioned, too, is Philippa's place among English queens—she is one of the favorite and most famous.

King Edward was devoted to this excellent lady and would be buried beside her. But he had never been blind to the attractions of other ladies, and there were even rumors that the beautiful Countess of Salisbury had dropped her garter on purpose, and there was more to the King's founding the Order of the Garter than just the glorification of the age of chivalry. "Sing *Honi soit qui mal y pense.*"

Grandiose plans for making the Order a worthy successor to King

Arthur's Table Round, for enlarging Windsor Castle into a huge, imposing home for it, for spending money on it generally, were in line with Edward's way of life. He was an extravagant, luxurious king. Even on active campaigns he went in for silk pavilions; at home, it was enormous balls, enormous banquets, clothes, jewels, presents. Giving presents can be almost as expensive a habit as architecture—and Edward did not stop with Windsor Castle; he went on to authorize the enlargement and enrichment of Winchester Cathedral, Wells Cathedral, and so on. The sums he had cost the country had been naturally great when he was fighting in France; his peacetime expenses, added to them, now did much to cut away his wartime popularity. Especially at the time of the Black Death, with his country's poor suffering, it did not help the English people to hear details of the King's conspicuous consumption.

But King Edward had his problems and they began to take their toll. He was noticeably less optimistic and gay. In old age he became senile, and perhaps this took the edge off some of his bitter worries. He must have been sad and bitter, for instance, about the Black Prince. This firstborn son had proved a soldier as great as Edward I. He had fought first at Crécy: "Let the boy win his spurs," King Edward had said, refusing to rescue his hard-pressed son; and this the Black Prince had done indeed. In 1356 he was the victor of Poitiers, where the French King Jean showed he had learned nothing from his father's defeat ten years before. The French were still depending on crossbows, still sending knights to the slaughter two by two through a narrow defile. At Poitiers (Poictiers, then) the Black Prince proved also that he had *his* father's knack of beating a big army with a little one and losing, again, mere hundreds of men to the French king's thousands. In this battle he captured King Jean himself, and brought him and his young son back to London—not in chains, as most Plantagenets would have done, but with Jean riding a better horse than the Prince's own, so as not to hurt his feelings unduly.

But before long the Black Prince fell gravely ill. It was hard for King Edward to have produced an heir like that, brave and so much else besides, and now to know that he was dying, that he would not survive his father to rule England. This meant the long minority of a little boy,

Richard the Black Prince's son, with its attendant dangers. It meant—if King Edward knew his family—an endless wrangle among his other sons for control.

Then the Queen died, and it was apparent how King Edward had depended on her. Needing, at this stage, to be dependent on someone, he fell too much under the influence of his last mistress, Alice Perrers. She nearly ruined both him and his reputation; her rule over him became so complete that people suspected her of witchcraft. The witchcraft, of course, was only expertise in geriatrics; she knew how to manage an increasingly senile man. Enriching herself rapidly and efficiently, she knew quite well how much she was hated, and when King Edward finally lay dying, she stripped the rings off his fingers and ran for her life.

Edward II

1284–1327

H E succeeded to the throne in 1307, upon the death of his father, Edward I.

Before that he had been the first Prince of Wales. Born to a traveling mother who went everywhere with her husband, even on a Crusade, and had her children casually here and there, he had seen the light of day at Caernarvon in Wales. This was one of the places his father was building fortifications to keep the Welsh under control, after he had conquered them. According to the story—it has been questioned, like almost all the good stories in English history—he promised the Welsh a prince who could not speak a word of English or a word of French, so of course they thought it would be one of them. Instead, Edward brought out to show them, in his arms, his three-day-old son.

This little boy was the son and father of eminent kings, but he himself never amounted to much. Twenty-three when he ascended the throne, he was already under the influence of one of his notorious favorites, a young Gascon named Piers Gaveston. Trying to break up the connection, his father had exiled this undesirable, but as soon as Edward II became king he sent for him and created him Earl of Cornwall.

The new arrival was not exactly welcomed into the English peerage, and he did not exactly try to ingratiate himself. He went out of his way to insult everybody. His name for the Earl of Gloucester, for instance, was "whoreson" (which he occasionally varied with "cuckold's bird") and for the Earl of Lincoln "broste belly," which is more obscure but obviously impolite. "The black hound of Arden," which is what he called the Earl of Warwick, does not seem as bad as some of the other epithets, but it was Warwick who first reached the breaking-point and, after another attempt to get Gaveston out of the kingdom failed, had him murdered.

"By God, what a fool he was," King Edward said, when he heard it; "I could have told him never to get into Warwick's hands." But apparently he made no effort to punish his friend's murderer. This was not the Plantagenet way, and may have been one reason the question of Edward's being the true king, or an impostor, was sometimes raised. On occasion someone else calling himself the true king would appear and rouse momentary interest. But King Edward did look like a Plantagenet; the virtue of his mother Queen Eleanor of Castile had been famous; and everyone knew, of course, that excellent fathers often have worthless sons.

The virtue of the King's wife Queen Isabella is not famous at all. He had married this beautiful French princess soon after his accession, but he had been preoccupied with his favorite Gaveston and she never had much influence with him. In the year of Gaveston's murder, 1312, the Queen produced an heir and the legitimacy of this Edward was never questioned. But later, as the King found other favorites of his own sex, she learned to find outside interests herself. Queen Isabella has come down in English history as the "She-Wolf of France," but perhaps English environment as much as French heredity shaped her character. She was only sixteen (or fourteen, or seventeen—which chronicler do you read?) when she came to England to marry its king.

King Edward's later and even more famous favorites were a father and son both of whom were named, confusingly, Hugh le Despenser. They were fairly efficient businessmen and, though providing well for themselves, they also provided England with a better economic administration than, King Edward acting alone, it would have had. He was no executive.

Edward was not a good soldier, either. Attempting to conquer Scotland, he was vigorously defeated at the Battle of Bannockburn

(1314), and Bannockburn was followed by a series of less famous but significant defeats.

Like his father, Edward II had trouble along the Welsh border as well as the Scottish. There was a buffer strip, wild and wooded, not unlike the green belt that is now supposed to protect London, that was supposed to keep the Welsh more or less self-contained; it had been put under the control of several "Marcher barons" who had special strength and authority to handle the Welsh who slipped down from the mountains, did their dirty deeds, and slipped expertly back. This way the Welsh annoyed the Marcher barons but were not likely to annoy the English on the English side of the Marcher strip.

Generally, the idea—which went back to William the Conqueror—worked pretty well, but there was one disadvantage. If the Marcher barons were strong enough to handle the Welsh, they were strong enough to be something of a threat to their own king. One of them, Roger Mortimer, King Edward found particularly arrogant. Finally Roger and his uncle, another Roger Mortimer called Mortimer of Chirk Castle, were shut up in the Tower of London and kept there for years. Then Mortimer of Chirk died. Roger Mortimer, however, was too young and healthy to escape in this way, and the Tower was altogether too strong a fortress to break out of.

But, remarkably, young Mortimer escaped anyway. It seemed obvious it was an inside job, and as time passed it became more and more obvious who his accomplice might have been. The escaped prisoner soon showed up at the court of France, and soon after that Queen Isabella went to the court of France to visit her brother the French king. The Tower was a royal palace as well as a prison, and during the time Roger Mortimer had been shut up there Queen Isabella had been living in it. Though there is no evidence that these two were lovers in the Tower of London, it is accepted history that they were lovers at the court of France.

Edward II, at first, either did not know this or did not care. Ostensibly Queen Isabella had gone to France to remonstrate with her brother, who in 1324 had in a very unfriendly manner seized most of Gascony. It is hard to see how King Edward could have been induced to let the Prince of Wales follow her, but he did, on the theory that young

Edward's doing homage for the Duchy of Aquitaine would endear him
to or impress the French king. Gascony would be relinquished at once,
and Aquitaine and Ponthieu would not be invaded.

So the Prince of Wales joined his mother and her paramour at the
court of France, and there they all three stayed, and stayed, and stayed.

Still Edward II did not seem concerned.

But he did become concerned when Isabella and Mortimer, with the
Prince of Wales tagging along, finally left France and traveled not back
to England but on to the Low Countries. The Pope had threatened to
excommunicate the French king if he continued to harbor his sinful
sister. Why he did not threaten to excommunicate the Count of
Hainault, who harbored her next, we do not know. At any rate Queen
Isabella made Hainault her headquarters while she recruited an army to
invade England.

The nucleus of Isabella's army was foreign—soldiers of fortune,
knights looking for a romantic cause—but she expected to be joined in
England by many discontented Englishmen. Edward II's enslavement to
his favorites, his extravagance, his fecklessness, his basic inability as a
king had alienated almost everyone. Isabella had been in correspon-
dence, of course, with some of the more powerful English barons and
she knew she would have a good reception.

It exceeded all her hopes. She made what amounted to a triumphal
progress across England. She did not have to fight at all. King Edward
threw no armies into her path. He himself retreated from London
westward.

Isabella's army was increasing every day. Recruits by the thousands
fell into line, each baron bringing with him the men who lived on his
estates and owed him allegiance. The Tower of London, of sentimental
memory, was surrendered to her when she got there. At Bristol she
captured and hanged the older Hugh le Despenser. The younger one
was with King Edward. But not many people were still with King
Edward as he continued to retreat before the oncoming army. He
seemed to be heading for Wales. Finally, near Caerphilly Castle, he
surrendered to his implacable wife.

He was imprisoned in Llantrisant Castle temporarily. Later he was
taken to Kenilworth Castle and then to Berkeley. Apparently the idea

was to depose the King rather than murder him, but nobody knew this certainly, Edward least of all. He was left to think about it and many things.

The decision about the younger Hugh le Despenser was more quickly made, but he was not executed as quickly as his father had been. He was brought into London in the Queen's train, given a prejudged trial, and hanged, drawn, quartered, and disemboweled. The Queen gave herself the satisfaction of watching this sentence on her old enemy carried out.

Up to now everything had gone perfectly to suit her. The King, waited upon by a menacing delegation, "of his own good will" renounced the throne in favor of his son Prince Edward. But now something went very wrong. Parliament did not make Queen Isabella her son's regent, which she had certainly expected to be. It appointed, instead, a Council of Regency, with the new King's cousin, Henry of Lancaster, at its head. Isabella was not even a member.

It was unbearable and Isabella did not propose to bear it. She proceeded to usurp the regency as efficiently as she had just usurped, on behalf of her son, the throne.

Really, you can see her point. To have gone so far, to have planned and executed this whole revolution, and then to stand politely aside while somebody else governed England, was too much to expect of any victorious commander, much less Isabella of France.

It was also too much to expect of Roger Mortimer. Undoubtedly he had counted on being the power behind the power behind the throne. Parliament to the contrary notwithstanding, this is what he became.

It is known that it was Mortimer who appointed a new trio of keepers for the deposed Edward II. He had been transferred from Kenilworth to Berkeley Castle, and the quality of his accommodations had been drastically changed. At Berkeley they were, to say the least, unhealthy. But Edward II—now only Edward of Caernarvon—did not die of natural causes. His shrieks of agony were so loud that they were heard not only through Berkeley Castle but as far as the village.

The traditional story is that, to avoid making marks on the outside of his body, his murderers had burnt out his bowels with a red-hot iron inserted through a hollow horn.

Edward I

1239–1307

H E succeeded to the throne in 1272, upon the death of his father Henry III.

Edward got the news while he was out of England, actually on a Crusade to the Holy Land. But the monarchy happened to be stable at the moment. There had been times before, and there would be again, when it was purely necessary for the heir to be waiting, dagger drawn, on the very steps of the throne. Young King Edward was lucky—possibly because he had no paternal uncles. His only one, Richard of Cornwall, died just about the time his father did.

Mission accomplished in the Holy Land—Edward had personally captured the town of Nazareth—he and his queen turned back to England. As may be seen by her crusading with him, this unusual king (as he would prove to be) possessed an unusual queen. Eleanor of Castile, whose title, Infanta of Castile, has been immortalized in the pub and subway station Elephant and Castle, was a pious and beautiful lady who traveled with him all during her married life. He would go on many campaigns, and she would have her many children, fifteen or seventeen—the historians differ, and you can see how even Edward and Eleanor might lose count—wherever he happened to be.

The King's military problem was one of frontiers. In every reign there had been raids and depredations along the northern borders of

England. In Edward's time, as in his father King Henry's, the troublesome Welsh chieftain was Llewellyn ab Gruffyd. Edward defeated him in battle, cut off his head, and sent it to be stuck on a high pole in London.

Llewellyn's brother David was also eliminated. He was captured, tried, hanged, drawn, and quartered, his trophy-head going to London also.

At this time being drawn and quartered was a new thing in the administration of justice. It caught on immediately and became routine. But King Edward was one of those who held to the old ways, too. It was an old Saxon custom to flay anybody who sacrilegiously robbed a church and nail his skin to its door; Pepys described the great doors of Rochester Cathedral "as they say, covered with the skins of Danes"; and the son of a dean of Westminster remembered how "a portion of hard, dry skin was found underneath the bossed head of a huge iron nail that was fixed upon the door of the Abbey Chapter House. . . . Mr. Quekett, then Curator of the College of Surgeons, recognized this skin to be human. . . ." This may bear out the story that in 1303, while Edward I was fighting in Scotland, the King's Treasure kept here was looted and scattered—an inside job, made possible by some wicked monks—and this was Edward's furious response.

King Edward's wars in Scotland were long and hard and not over even when he died. He began brilliantly. He captured the Stone of Scone, to go under his coronation chair in Westminster Abbey. He captured Berwick, Dunbar, Addington, Roxburgh, Edinburgh, Sterling, Perth, Montrose, all these in only a few months; but Scotland did not stay conquered. William Wallace rose, and Scotland rose with him.

France, meantime, demanded King Edward's attention. He had in fact been on his way to fight the French when the Scottish situation intervened. But while the King was striking a blow for the Plantagenet interests in France, Wallace was systematically undoing all his work in Scotland. In weeks instead of months the same strongholds Edward had taken—Roxburgh, Sterling, Berwick, and the rest—fell to the native champion, and he won a spectacular victory at Stirling Bridge.

Back King Edward came from France. He was by now in his sixtieth year—old for a medieval man to be alive and active, much less belligerent—and he had a couple of freshly broken ribs. His horse had stepped on him during the night. But he was still in the saddle in every sense. He sat in it directing the Battle of Falkirk, and whipped William Wallace soundly.

It is no wonder the English take pride in Edward I as a soldier-king. He was a great one indeed, a tremendous strategist and a daring aggressor, brave as a lion. Ten thousand Scots were killed at Falkirk and the army was in precipitous flight. The only flaw was that Wallace escaped and it was six years—during which the mopping-up of Scotland continued—before he was finally betrayed, tried, hanged, drawn, and quartered, according to what was custom by this time, and his head stuck up on a pole.

Then Robert the Bruce rose in Wallace's place and was crowned at Scone. (But not on St. Columba's Stone, in the tradition of his predecessors—King Edward had that safely under his own new coronation chair in the Abbey.) Edward, now sixty-eight and not at all well, again went personally to war. The sharp edge was not, however, off either his mind or his enthusiasm. It was on this campaign that he had the Countess of Buchan hung up outside Berwick Castle in an iron cage. (He made other examples, too, but Lady Buchan is the best documented.) Her cage was built symbolically in the shape of a crown, for it was she who had actually set the crown on Robert the Bruce's head, thereby offending Edward of England. He had her shut in this cage "like a wild beast" and there she stayed for four mortal years. On nice days, she hung in it outside Berwick Castle; on bad days, inside. This was possibly because exposure in the worst Scottish weather might shorten the prisoner's life—more probably because in bad weather the visibility was too poor to point the moral. In any case, Lady Buchan encaged might be seen at any time by visitors to Berwick Castle. None doubted that King Edward, old and ill though he might now be, was unchanged from the King Edward who had had the skins of the robbers nailed up in the Abbey.

Edward had started out in a horse-litter, planning to direct others rather than take a painful active part in this campaign. But he soon found out that his commanders in the field were not fighting to suit him. After Aymar de Valence let the Scots defeat him twice in quick succession, the old King, in a rage, abandoned his prudent litter and took to the saddle again.

But this time he could not rise above his body's infirmities. Three days later, actually within sight of the Scottish border, even he realized he was about to die. He left instructions for his son, who would soon be Edward II—boil the flesh from his body, he said grandiloquently, wrap up his bones, and carry them at the head of the army into Scotland. He would reach his objective that way if in no other.

In English history everything that Edward II did was wrong and everything Edward I did was right, so there has been much criticism of the new King for not doing this. But there would have been much criticism, to put it mildly, if he had. When your father has been on your bones as much as the old King had been on young Edward's, about his favorite Piers and his extravagance and his gambling and all, you do not boil the flesh off his. So King Edward I was buried with dignity and respect in Westminster Abbey, in royal robes and crown. We know this because the English, who are not able to leave royal bodies alone, opened his tomb four centuries later, noting the trappings of royalty and the fact that Edward had been one of the tall Plantagenets, six feet two inches.

There is no effigy on Edward's tomb, though he liked effigies and had had a most beautiful one made for his queen, Eleanor of Castile, a bronze which is one of the great tourist sights of Westminster Abbey, as Eleanor is one of England's imperishably famous queens.

She had died many years before him. She had traveled so much with her husband that it was appropriate for her to have died away from home. Edward made her last journey, from Nottinghamshire back to London, lastingly memorable. Wherever the cortège stopped, he had erected "Eleanor Crosses" in her honor. Originally there were twelve of them, big, handsome, elaborate things. Northampton is left, and Geddington, and Waltham; the one at Charing Cross is only a reproduction to support the name.

People who know no other queen in English history have heard about Eleanor of Castile and how she saved the King's life, in the Holy Land, when he was hit by a poisoned arrow (or attacked with a poisoned dagger) and she sucked the wound. The fact that this story has been disproved by historians, and we are told to disregard it, is itself disregarded totally. Eleanor's legend is intact.

Hardly anyone knows, or is willing to admit, that this beloved Queen Eleanor had a successor, a deliciously pretty French princess named Margaret, whom King Edward married in his old age and who, also, traveled with him, bore him children, and made him very happy.

Like his having another wife, it is often overlooked that Edward had another specialty besides soldiering. Actually it is his peacetime achievements which make him one of the greatest English kings. His military successes were brilliant, but they did not last; Scotland, for all his efforts, achieved independence after his death; Wales produced in place of Llewellyn ab Gruffyd various troublesome Marcher barons, one named Mortimer; France, with whose king he had made a peace treaty (his charming Queen Margaret was part of it), was soon fighting England again, giving as good as it got in what King Edward, fortunately, did not know would be a Hundred Years' War.

But before fighting occupied him Edward had been constructively occupied with English law. He was not a student himself—it has been tauntingly said that he had only three books of his own—but he knew where to get hold of experts and how far to trust them. He had brought with him, on his first return to England as king, a Bolognese law professor named Francesco Accursi—English-speaking lawyers should remember him—and he appointed as his chancellor a bookish, hard-working young cleric named Robert Burnell. This Burnell may have been by coincidence a mystic as well as a student, but the abbeys and monasteries were full of able and intelligent men attracted to them because that was where the books were; this accounts for some of the highly secular types we are always encountering in the historical Church, this and ambition. But Edward was the true head of the combination. Never discount Edward, and never doubt that the fifty-one-point document he presented to his first Parliament represented his thinking. Duly enacted over a period of years, the contents of this document formed a new English code of laws, as great a legal landmark as the Justinian.

And Edward's Parliament evolved into the House of Commons we know today. In 1282 he convened at Shrewsbury a body that included two representatives from each of twenty towns and boroughs, as well as men of title and position. Eleven years later, at a Parliament at Westminster, there were men elected to represent the commons, as well as representative earls, barons, and knights, and a third category, churchmen—the famous Model Parliament.

Edward's care for legal and economic matters lasted through his long reign. As a young king, only just crowned, he had reformed the civil service; as an old one he set a ceiling on food prices. He was a builder; castles like Caernarvon and Conway are part of his monument. He was, in his strange medieval way, the most devout of kings. He loved his family and smote his enemies, and he left England better—much better—than he had found it.

Henry III

1207–1272

HE succeeded to the throne in 1216, upon the death of his father King John.

He was not as bad as his father but he was not as competent, either. Succeeding at the age of nine—a year after Magna Carta—and having fortunately no uncles, he grew up in no danger of being murdered. But the competent outsiders who ruled for him, William the Marshal, Gualo the Legate, and Hubert de Burgh, quarreled among themselves exactly like uncles, each trying to rule the country himself through the little king.

This little king grew up not only without uncles but without his mother. Isabella of Angoulême, the widow of King John, rather quickly married again. Her second husband was Hugh de Lusignan, Count de la Marche, to whom she had been engaged when John first caught sight of her and she first caught sight of the crown of England. This was fine, but Isabella should not have remarried without the consent of the English Council. She thereby lost her dower lands and her pension, and this kept her in a state of furious anger even after an adjustment was made.

By her second husband Isabella had numerous children, the half-brothers and half-sisters of her son King Henry III. (To call them stepbrothers, as some historians do, is quite incorrect. Stepbrothers are no blood kin; half-brothers have half the same blood.) The Lusignan family grew up in France, but when they were old enough they emigrated in a body to England, where their half-brother the King did everything possible for them.

He was also doing everything possible for his wife's poor relations. The young King had married Eleanor of Provence in 1236, jilting another lady to do so. It had all been very romantic. Henry had read a poem of Eleanor's and felt that her talents, in addition to her beauty, entitled her to the preference; and this love-match was, at first, very popular with his subjects.

Queen Eleanor was crowned in London with great pageantry, and naturally her father's relatives came from Provence and her mother's from Savoy to see it. What was less natural, or so it seemed to the English, was that hordes of these foreign relatives stayed permanently in England. They moved in. The King provided them with castles, pensions, offices, titles, sinecures, lands—everything they needed or wanted. Eleanor's grandfather, for instance, Thomas of Savoy, got a cut on sacks of English wool. Her uncle Peter of Savoy got the title Earl of Richmond and a strip of London along the Thames; where the Savoy Hotel now stands was his great Savoy Palace. Another uncle, William of Savoy (called William of Valance), was named head of the King's new Council. And it was the very last straw when her clerical uncle, Boniface of Bellay, was handed the see of Canterbury. This made this newly arrived Frenchman head of the English Church and, next to the King, the most important man in the realm.

The instant unpopularity of her relatives reflected on the Queen. Otherwise she was all the English could have wanted—elegant, beautiful, much in love with her husband, devoted to her children, as they came along, far beyond her century's idea of the call of duty. If she was also extravagant and arrogant, this was a traditional and occupational thing about queens. But because of her rapacious foreign relatives, who with the help of her husband's rapacious foreign relatives were skimming most of the cream off England, she was fervently hated.

A king with so many relatives and relatives-in-law to provide for would have done well to economize in other ways, but Henry was wide-open-handed in all. He too was extremely fond of his children, considering nothing too good or too much for them; he enjoyed having them weighed and giving their weight in silver to charity—like the Aga Khan—and when one of them died, he spent £700 on a solid silver effigy for her tomb. He was interested in clothes, furs, jewels, bibelots, interior decoration, imported wines and exotic foods, and especially architecture. He started a menagerie in the Tower of London and acquired three leopards, a white bear, buffalo, and actually an elephant. He gave spectacular banquets and balls. Everything he did was made into an occasion, and his special weakness was giving presents to everybody around him, not just to his family and foreign ambassadors.

Not for Henry, at least not merely, the cold wholesale charities to hospitals and almshouses, to "twenty poor old men" or "fifty widows of the parish." He did these conventional things, and he also threw his palaces open to the poor, inviting them to come in and be fed; but Henry took an interest in people personally, and his beneficiaries are often mentioned by name. There are many records of his gifts of specific things—cloaks with rabbit-fur linings, for instance—to people like his clerk's wife, the master janitor and clerk at Bristol Castle, miners named William and Walter, Adam and Richard, and even a "recluse." Perhaps it does not matter how a recluse looks, but this one must have been hiding out in a cold place, and the King was concerned about him. He wanted him to have a cloak with a lambskin lining.

It is hard for us to realize how very unusual this sort of thing was in the thirteenth century. If the measure of one's civilization is the measure of one's interested concern for other people and their problems, then Henry III was a very civilized man. A feckless, foolish man, perhaps, and not a very good king, but really a very nice one.

This personal touch extended to all King Henry's interests. There is a picture of him conferring, himself, with the masons who are carrying out some of his building plans. The King has an admonitory finger up and he is pointing out exactly what he wants done. He and the mason (who holds a compass and square) are standing toe to toe, their sleeves touching—this is no dictum handed down from the height of a throne. Clutching his flowing robes about him, King Henry, crown and all, is about to go climbing around inspecting the building.

The chances are that this building was Westminster Abbey. Henry

built and remodeled other churches and castles but this great Abbey—
the one we see today—was his life-work and his love. He did it in honor
of his royal predecessor and favorite saint, Edward the Confessor, for
whom he had named his eldest son. Ruth McKenney, whose account of
the design and building stands out among many, raises the question of
whether St. Edward would have liked Henry's tearing down the Abbey
which St. Edward himself had lovingly built, and substituting a new one
in his own taste.* It is unlikely, however, that this thought ever entered
Henry's mind. He was as sure of the excellence of his taste, and with
better reason, as he was of his grasp of everything else.

One of his weakest points, if he had only known it, was his grasp of
military matters. He had practically none. His reign is distinguished by
his badly planned, badly executed forays into France to defend the
Plantagenet lands, and by his inept efforts to control his barons at home.
Quite through his own fault, he finally had a full-blown civil war on his
hands. Fortunately his eldest son Prince Edward, learning through
experience and drawing on considerable natural talent he had inherited
from someone else, was becoming an excellent soldier; later he would
pull some of his father's chestnuts out of the fire.

Henry was lucky that his son loved him, for the relative young
Edward really admired turned out to be his father's worst enemy. This
was Simon de Montfort, Earl of Leicester, the husband of the King's
youngest sister. He was a strong, intelligent, energetic, and talented
man from whom Edward learned a great deal, but as the leadership he
gained among the barons became leadership against Edward's father the
King, he lost Edward. Meantime, there is no doubt that the boy's
admiration had seduced Simon de Montfort into thinking that, with
Edward in his pocket, he could depose King Henry and rule England
himself.

Even without Edward, he came dangerously close. By 1258, the King
had been expensively defeated in Wales as well as in France, and had
also been spending money like water trying to make his younger son
Edmund King of Sicily and his younger brother Richard Holy Roman
Emperor. (This was Henry for you, kindness with public money

* Ruth McKenney and Richard Bransten, *Here's England* (New York: Harper, 1955).

personified.) It was really rather plain that he could not manage the
affairs of England. When he asked Parliament for still more money, it
retaliated with the "Provisions of Oxford." The barons, headed by
Simon de Montfort, set up a council of fifteen men to "advise" the King
and if necessary veto him. They, not the King, would fill high offices.
And their first move was to order all royal castles returned to the
Crown. The Lusignans, the King's half-brothers, refused to give up
theirs and they were deported.

Eventually King Louis of France, asked to arbitrate between the King
of England and his subjects, declared (in the Mise of Amiens, 1264) that
Henry was entitled to rule without his fifteen-man council. But Louis
was not exactly a detached mediator; royalty cannot afford to condone
offense against royalty; and even when the Pope confirmed this ruling
Simon de Montfort would not accept it. He had already tasted power;
he had led an armed revolt, seen King Henry take shelter in the Tower
and Queen Eleanor, trying to leave it by the river, pelted with stones
and filth. Now he met the King's forces in an actual battle, the Battle of
Lewes, and defeated him and Prince Edward.

Prince Edward learned from it, however, as he learned much besides
warfare from Simon de Montfort. He loved his father; there was no
question of which side to choose; but one of the marks of his emerging
greatness was that he could learn from enemy competence. While he
was in custody, and his father was as real a prisoner, allowed to sign
everything but at the direction of a new council (this one of nine, and all
nine were really Simon de Montfort), he thoughtfully observed the
Parliament Simon convened. For the first time in English history there
was representation of a class of Englishmen who were neither nobles
nor clergy. Representation did not extend below the prosperous and
responsible middle class; this would have been too much of a sudden
revolution; but it was a great step forward, just as our American
Constitution was a great step forward even though it did not give equal
rights to Negroes and females. This, too, would have been too much to
be workable at the time.

Prince Edward thought over the matter of representation by someone
besides the dominant minority; he thought over the idea—which his
aristocratic father would have waved away—that a king should neither

claim nor possess absolute power but should be under the law himself; and it occurred to him, perhaps this early, that a strong king was actually strengthened by increasing the representation of his loyal people. Perhaps this early he began to think of the government and legal reforms he could put in hand when he was king.

Prince Edward had plenty of time to think, because he was kept in custody for a year, moved from one castle to another. (King Henry was in London with Simon de Montfort, because he was needed to sign everything and preserve the fiction that he, and not the Council of Nine, was ruling.) But Edward was not thinking merely along abstract political and legal lines. He was thinking about escape from captivity, and in May 1265 one of the schemes succeeded and he made his dash to freedom.

He attacked Kenilworth—the castle was one of the places he had been in custody—took some barons prisoner in their turn and then set out after Simon de Montfort.

They met at the Battle of Evesham and Prince Edward, quite brilliantly, won. His father, put into the front of the battle against him with nothing to distinguish him from the rebel barons, was fortunately recognized and unhurt. Simon de Montfort, of course, was hoping he would be killed by the army led by his son, and preferably by the son himself.

Instead, it was Simon de Montfort who was killed.

He had been a remarkable character with some very good points. But "the brave upholder of the rights of man," as one historian calls him? No, Simon was for Simon all the way. He was upholding himself. He used the methods and devices he thought would work for him. For nearly a year he ruled England, and did it very well; he would have liked to rule it in name as well as in fact.

Not even the sobering experiences he had lived through could make King Henry into a good ruler, but now restored to power he depended more and more, gratefully, upon his able son. His last few years were peaceful. The English then as now, perhaps, admired longevity nearly as much as eccentricity, and in his old age King Henry's good qualities, his outgoing kindness, his devotion to his wife, his active interest in beautification and improvement, were rather impressive. Westminster

Abbey, rising now to dominate the London skyline, was certainly to his personal credit.

Most of all to his credit was the reaction of his eldest son to the news of his death. This reached Edward on his way back home from a Crusade. Heirs to thrones are, very naturally and understandably, inclined to ambivalence; but those around him noticed that Edward, absorbed in his grief, did not seem to care or even realize that he had become King of England. It was noticed too that, even though he received news at the same time of the death of his baby son, it was the death of his father that bowed him down.

Perhaps Edward was right about King Henry III and all the rest of us have been wrong.

John

1167–1216

HE succeeded to the throne in 1199, upon the death of his brother, Richard I.

Historically, John is a stock character, the blackhearted king. He was a clown as well, the villain who laughs as he ties the heroine to the railroad tracks. (In John's case, spurned by a lady, he sent her a poisoned egg.) There is no denying he was bad. He ruled badly and he had many serious, as well as several minor, character and personality faults. But anyone who believes in a connection between character and environment can hardly be surprised. It only seems remarkable that he turned out as well as he did.

For one thing he was John "Lackland," so called; his father had made no provision for him. Later, he tried to take what belonged to his brother Richard. If he was blasphemous, it was something he heard at home. If he was quarrelsome, remember that his father was a violent man and his beautiful mother a shrew. She pointedly preferred his brother Richard to him, too. Richard had everything—he was the heir, after Young Henry died, and a popular hero. He was also a famous sodomite. Then there was brother Geoffrey, the sly and treacherous one; and, taking the place of the sisters who married early, the prospective sister-in-law Alais of France, who lived for years in this raffish household pending her marriage to Richard, and passed the time sleeping with his father, King Henry II. What was little Prince John doing, while all this went on? He was learning.

The youngest child of eight, he was physically unlike the other boys, who were big, godlike, handsome blonds, called commonly the Plantagenet type. He was not like his beautiful mother's family either. John was short and stocky, quite an interesting face, broad between the eyes, not unintelligent but not particularly civilized—even a little feral, like a jaunty, impudent puppy. We are not surprised to read that he clowned during solemn ceremonies. He looks arrogant, not regal; impatient, not thoughtful; and cruel, not just.

He became finally, in a purely negative way, his father's favorite. Henry had lost his original favorite, his eldest son and namesake, the Young King; and of the boys remaining, only John had not conspired against him—or so he thought. Actually, John had, but King Henry was on his deathbed before he discovered it.

John's brother Richard showed a similarly negative preference for him when, king himself and on his own deathbed, he said that he wanted the throne to go to John instead of to the heir next in line, their nephew Arthur. It was not that he wanted to do something for John, but that he wanted more to do something to Arthur's mother, Constance of Brittany.

Arthur was the posthumous son of Geoffrey, the brother who came after Richard in the family and ahead of John. Richard had originally intended Arthur to be his heir and had urged Constance to send him over for him, Richard, to raise; but Constance showed her intelligence by refusing. By staying with her in Brittany Arthur at least lived to grow up. When Richard died, however, this prince who had never lived in England was not a popular idea with the English. Richard himself had been an absentee king and had got by with it because he was a dashing and glamorous one, but Arthur got the backlash of his absenteeism just as John would get the backlash of Richard's wars and extravagances—Richard could get by with both, the unattractive John could not. But in the matter of inheriting the throne the barons, faced with the choice between the young foreigner Arthur (who would be dominated by his foreign mother) and the faulty but indigenous John (whose equally strong-minded mother they were at least used to), chose John. He looked better to them on the day of his coronation than he ever would again.

John's queen was a half-first cousin once removed, Isabella or Avisa or Hadwisa of Gloucester; her tenure was so brief that which name is best hardly matters. John, in France, was dazzled by beautiful young Isabella of Angoulême and promptly got a divorce from his wife to marry her.

It is easy to see why Henry VIII was so outraged when he was refused a divorce from Catherine of Aragon, a few centuries later, to marry Anne Boleyn. All this time such royal divorces had been sought and granted, fairly often, too, by Rome. John's mother had got one from her first husband the King of France. The grounds in the case of John's divorce were consanguinity; as in the case of Henry VIII's divorce, his family relationship to his wife had never bothered his conscience till he saw another lady he wanted to marry.

John's second marriage gave his nephew Arthur of Brittany a chance to make a real try for the throne. Isabella of Angoulême had been engaged to a Frenchman, Hugh de Lusignan, the Count de la Marche, when John met her; he married her in her fiancé's absence and the latter was understandably upset. He was not important enough for the French king to fight the English king in his behalf, but when Hugh de Lusignan joined forces with Arthur of Brittany, who had been betrothed to the French king's small daughter Marie, that was different. The King of France was not averse to seeing his son-in-law King of England, especially when he was entitled to be.

So Prince Arthur, with a French army behind him, began by besieging his grandmother, now aged eighty, in the castle-fortress of Mirabeau. Waste no sympathy on this poor old lady. Eleanor of Aquitaine would never be a poor old lady. Her teeth were not all she had kept—miraculous though this was for a twelfth-century octogenarian. Her verve was intact. She defended Mirabeau, sent to her son John for relief and got him there in two days. This was faster than King John habitually moved an army more than eighty miles. In fact it was unusual for John to move at all for anybody.

Arthur of Brittany was captured. Hugh de Lusignan was captured also, but later he was set free. (Isabella?) Arthur appeared in public once more—briefly—to put down the story that King John had had him blinded with a hot iron. Then he disappeared back into captivity and he was never seen again. Nobody really knows what happened to him.

But of course people thought he had been murdered by order of King John and at least one lady was bold enough to say so aloud. She was not about, she said, to send her son as a hostage—John had a system of keeping the barons in line by making them leave a child apiece in his custody—"to a king who had murdered his own nephew." But she was probably the last person to voice this sentiment. King John had her shut up in a cell in Windsor Castle and starved her to death.

Only the King of France was still asking "Where is Arthur of Brittany?" Still ostensibly on behalf of his son-in-law-elect he continued to press the war. He was winning—partly by default, for John went back to England even while his brother Richard's beloved Château Gaillard was being besieged. It was lost, of course, and so was the city of Rouen.

This meant the loss of the whole province of Normandy, and this in turn, though then considered a tragedy—by everyone but King John, who did not care—may have been a blessing in disguise. The Normans in England, its ruling minority, no longer had a divided allegiance with one foot in France. John's loss of Normandy had made them Englishmen. Incidentally, too, when Normandy became French again England first needed and first got a real navy.

John, turning his attention to domestic problems, promptly got himself excommunicated by interfering with the choice of a new Archbishop of Canterbury. The monks pushed their own candidate, the Pope, Innocent III, pushed another, and King John pushed a third. Both the Pope and the King were out of line; the selection was the monks' prerogative; but everybody got very angry. The Pope put England under an interdict lasting more than six years. He absolved the English people from allegiance to King John and (quite as drunk with fancied power as the King was) "deposed" him and "gave" England to the King of France. Very glad to have it on anybody's say-so, the King of France (at the Council of Soissons, 1213) got the consent of the French nobility to invade England and take over.

But again John was saved by being considered the lesser of two evils. His people frankly hated him, by this time, but they did not want to be taken over by the French. The war was carried, again, to France instead. John, again, was a failure at it. Worse, he gave in tamely to the Pope and declared England a papal fief. The Pope, ungenerous in victory, sent a much-hated cardinal-legate to England, and his candidate for Archbishop of Canterbury—the vacancy that had caused all the trouble—arrived to take over not only the English Church but English politics.

Stephen Langton, the new Archbishop (Cantuar, he signed now instead of Langton) was a highly competent, highly secular man. He lost no time in digging out a charter signed by Henry I, King John's great-grandfather, which had conceded certain basic rights John had been trampling on. He organized the barons to require a similar charter from John. He was the father of the confrontation at Runnymede.

John came to it with surprising meekness. One of the things that made him contemptible in English eyes was his tendency to fold up without warning. But when he saw the concourse of barons waiting on the field of Runnymede—hardly a one was missing, whereas only his closest staff and kin had come with him—nobody could criticize him for folding up and buckling under. There was nothing else he could do.

During four days they drafted and redrafted a document which John sealed on June 15, 1215, in the seventeenth year of his reign.

This Magna Carta covered great matters and small. The rights extended "to all the freemen of our kingdom." No man's wood could be taken "for our castles" without his leave. No widow would be compelled to remarry. There would be standard measures "throughout our kingdom" for wine, ale, corn—"to wit, the London quart." No freeman might be exiled, outlawed, or imprisoned "but by the lawful judgment of his peers, or by the law of the land." Twenty-five barons, chosen by them all, were to "keep and hold . . . the peace and liberties which we have granted and confirmed by our present charter," and they (or a majority of them) could force the king himself into line.

In closing, Magna Carta voiced the pious hope that "all ill-will, disdain, and rancour, which has been between us and our clergy and laity since the said discord began, we do fully release and pardon to them all."

King John left the field of Runnymede in good order, having

maintained his dignity in public; but as soon as he got home he had the temper tantrum of his life. It was said that he even foamed at the mouth.

The Pope did not foam at the mouth when he heard about Magna Carta, but he too was furiously angry. He "annulled" the document in August, suspended for two years the Archbishop of Canterbury (his own candidate for whom he had fought, but who was not acting now as if he considered England a papal fief), and incited King John to civil war with the barons.

Historically Magna Carta is usually translated, "And so they lived happily ever after." But they did nothing of the kind. The situation was more warlike than before.

John's new army consisted of foreign mercenaries. He could not get any Englishmen to support him.

He was afraid to leave his portable resources behind him so he took them with him on campaign. John was rich in personal treasure, gold and jewels and beautiful things, and he also had the crown jewels, the actual regalia, in his possession. The crown of Edward the Confessor, the Empress Matilda's crown, the sword of Tristan, the orb, the sceptre, all went lumbering and bouncing through the countryside in the King's wagon train. There were hundreds of gold and silver cups, crosses, chalices, the jewelry of Eleanor of Aquitaine who had been the richest woman in the world. These ornaments and the unset jewels were easily carried—one reason why jewels have always been a popular investment —but the cups and chalices, since John had so many of everything, constituted a burden as well as a security problem.

King John was no more successful on this campaign than on any of his others. But there was one thing about it—he was, at last, in good odor with the Church. The Church had swung around on his side. John had always been afraid of what would happen to him when he died—not enough to change his ways, of course, but enough to load himself with neutralizing relics. Now he did not particularly need them. This time it was the barons opposing him who were wrong, at odds with the Church, in danger of hell-fire. The Fourth Lateran Council had confirmed the Pope's annulment of Magna Carta and his suspension of the ringleading Archbishop of Canterbury. It endorsed his excommunication of the barons who, opposing good King John, had not laid down their arms.

The barons were, literally, between the devil and the deep blue sea, for, landing on the Kentish coast, here came the army of the French king. In their desperation, the English barons had finally appealed to him. But France would, of course, swallow up the barons if their side won.

King John solved the dilemma for everyone. Constantly retreating, harried, desperate, tormented by gout, ill but overeating and overdrinking as usual, he suffered a last catastrophe. When he was trying to cross the river at the neck of the Wash, the inlet of the North Sea between Norfolk and Lincolnshire, the tide came in too fast. The wagon train with all his treasure disappeared under the water. Gold and silver are heavy; the crown and orb and sceptre and all the other precious things have never been found again.

It is doubtful that John was sentimental about losing the regalia or his mother's jewelry, but he knew that without resources he could not pay the mercenaries, the only men fighting on his side. With the loss of all he had, he knew that he was beaten.

He knew he was dying as well. At least he was dying in the good graces of the Church. At least the French would not get England—for the barons had no quarrel with his son, and nine-year-old Henry would have the throne. In almost the only notice he had ever taken of this little boy, he made a will appointing a good man as his guardian.

Richard I
called Lion-Heart

1157–1199

He succeeded to the throne in 1189, upon the death of his father Henry II.

Look if you can at his great sword-uplifted statue in front of the Houses of Parliament. This is the King Richard, Richard Coeur-de-Lion, who for most of us epitomizes the Age of Chivalry, the Crusades, the fine flowering of the Middle Ages—for Richard was a poet, too, and a musician, as well as one of the great soldiers. His talents, his gestures, and his looks were all magnificent. It would be pleasant to be able to say that he made England a splendid king.

Instead he was one of England's worst. In a reign of ten years he spent only six months at home. Having been brought up in Aquitaine, because he would inherit that duchy, Richard was almost a stranger when he landed in England as unexpected king. But he was enthusiastically welcomed. His elder brother Henry, if he had lived, could not have commanded the adulation this gorgeous swashbuckler did. Even when he announced his intention of leaving, as soon as he could raise the money, for the Holy Land, everybody thought he was great. Nobody thought it odd that a complete egotist, whose favorite oath was "by God's feet," should consider freeing Jerusalem the most important thing in the world, and the Third Crusade, not governing England, his first duty.

For this project Richard had to raise vast sums of money. His father Henry II had left great treasure but it was not enough. The new King sold everything in sight. Manors, forests, patents, appointments to Church and public offices—everything had its price. In court cases, the verdict went to the litigant who had paid the larger bribe to the King. William the Lion, the King of Scotland whom Richard's father had taken prisoner, was allowed to buy back his independence. People began to wonder what Richard would stop at, and Richard gave them the answer—at nothing. "By God's feet," he said, "find me a purchaser and I'll sell London itself."

But though he was quite frank about how he felt about England—purely a source of revenue, or, in the splendid phrase, "the milch cow of the Third Crusade"—his people still thought he was wonderful. He had an able and unscrupulous chancellor, William Longchamp, who was his whipping-boy; all the unpopularity which slid off King Richard landed on this unattractive agent of his.

He also had strong backing from his mother. One of Richard's first acts as king was to order Queen Eleanor released from her confinement at Winchester. His father had kept her there for sixteen years. But she had not forgotten how to give commands, and, named regent for her son, the Old Queen took particular pleasure in setting many prisoners free. No one knew better, she said, that "prisons were distasteful, . . . and that to be released therefrom was a most delightful refreshment to the spirits." She was not indiscriminate. Many of those she freed had been unjustly confined, not having had the benefit of trials (this anticipates #39 of Magna Carta), or had suffered from the onerous forest laws which Henry II had so harshly enforced. In releasing these of her husband's victims, Eleanor, with pious malice, remembering her own imprisonment at his hands, required them to pray for his soul.

The Old Queen also took pleasure in sending to Winchester, to live in custody as she herself had lived for sixteen years, Princess Alais of France, her husband's mistress until his death but no longer her son's fiancée. She and King Richard were agreed that Alais as Queen of England simply would not do.

There was another, chaster princess in prospect. Richard was crowned alone, but soon afterward he sent his mother to open negotiations for Berengaria of Navarre.

She was his own choice. He was a friend of her brother Prince Sancho—Navarre was not too far from Aquitaine where Richard grew up—and he had met Princess Berengaria at a tournament. It was love at first sight; that is what makes their story so pitiful.

For Richard was a homosexual. His interest in Berengaria was mild. He knew it was his duty to marry; his preference was definitely for this princess; but he could not bring himself to pay much attention to her afterward. Incredibly, she never saw England. Richard himself, of course, was hardly in England at all during his ten-year reign. But she hardly saw Richard either. He was always preoccupied with campaigns. Once or twice he had seasons of violent repentance (coinciding with seasons of violent illness when even this brave man panicked) and made dramatic resolutions to reform his ways and live respectably with his wife. Good little Berengaria would hurry to wherever he was, happy to be noticed. But when the devil was well, the devil a saint was he.

At least his deviation was an anonymous army one, and would have been inconspicuous if his occasional repentances had not been so public. Richard had no favorites. There was no one like James I's Buckingham and Edward II's Piers Gaveston.

Women, of course, were not mentioned in connection with him either—only his wife, his mother, and sometimes his favorite sister Joanna.

Queen Eleanor, who had acted as regent when he first succeeded to the throne, before he could get back to England from France, was his regent also while he went to the Holy Land on the Third Crusade, while he was imprisoned on his way back through Germany—over a year, and the ransom England had to pay for him was twice England's revenue—and while he was fighting in France. Many people's impression is that the fight for the Holy Sepulchre took most of Richard's time as king. Actually that lasted only a few months. It was his struggles with the barons of his own Aquitaine that preoccupied Richard. He was like the early Hanoverian kings who, also, never bothered to learn English and always considered their original province more important, and home. And Richard's great motivation throughout his reign was not a Christian love for the Holy Sepulchre but a very un-Christian and personal hatred for the King of France, Philip Augustus.

Ostensibly the trouble was over the Princess Alais, Philip's sister, who had indeed had very questionable treatment at the English court. Sent there at the age of five, she had hardly learned promiscuity elsewhere, and anyway she was not promiscuous. She never noticed any man but King Henry II of England. The whole blame must lie on him. He took advantage of his role of guardian and protector to seduce the little French princess (fifteen by then), and he kept her from marrying his son Richard, or anyone else, for the incredible seventeen years of their relationship—which ended only when he died, when Alais was thirty-two. There is no excuse for him, even by twelfth-century standards.

But there is no excuse either for Alais's father King Louis or her brother King Philip. Successively, they knew quite well what was going on, and neither made any serious effort to stop it. The only person for whom allowances can be made was Richard, because, living in his detached homosexual world, he was simply not interested in Alais one way or another.

Richard was first and last a soldier. Fighting was his whole life. When he was young and only a prince, he had merely conspired with his brothers and fought to overthrow his father, but this was unworthy of his talents. When in 1187 Saladin seized Jerusalem Richard was delighted; here indeed was a worthy cause and a worthy foe, for Saladin was a tremendous soldier. Richard took the Cross—volunteered to go on a Crusade—without delay. At the Siege of Acre, which was his victory alone after his ally went home, and at Arsouf, he made his formidable reputation. For centuries thereafter Moslem women would hush their children with the name Malek-Ric which his enemies gave him: "Malek-Ric will get you!" or "England is coming!"

He was something to fear—terrible, all by himself, as an army with banners. The cruelty of this militant Christian and his followers made Islam appear peaceful. He was tall, strong, and beautiful, with a tremendous reach of long arms, and though his hair was "halfway between yellow and red," his favorite colors were crimson and pink—worn together. He really glittered in the sun. And his eyes were like blue flames. He appeared considerably more than human.

He had neither fear nor mercy. Not for Richard the Lion-Heart the straining at a gnat and swallowing a camel; he fought all the way, and when he saw Moslem women and children in front of him he saw the enemy and slaughtered them accordingly. Hanging ("including babies at the breast") became his trademark; after Acre, he ripped open the bodies of captured women and children hunting their gold and jewels. The legend of his ruthlessness and his invincibility grew—but he did not take Jerusalem.

Even then it was not his enemy Saladin who defeated him but his allies. Philip of France had been the first to go back home. Then Leopold of Austria, told by Richard to get to work rebuilding the walls of Ascalon—he himself, with his great strength, was carrying stones for it and using a pick—rebelled as generals under a supreme commander are still prone to do. Leopold took his army and went home too. Then it was the Duke of Burgundy who turned back, and Richard realized that he could never win. All this time, while he was losing his allied forces, Saladin was bringing up new ones.

It broke his heart—the Coeur-de-Lion—that he could not take Jerusalem.

But the heart was not the operative thing in Richard. That was will. Even a year in prison did not alter him. (It was Leopold of Austria, now his bitter enemy as Philip of France was, who captured him on his way home from the Crusade, and his minstrel Blondel, or so we still like to believe, sang under many castle windows until he replied.) With his tremendous ransom paid, he did not settle down thankfully in England as most English kings would have done. He did return there briefly, had himself crowned again in case people had forgotten him (they had not), and forgave at his mother's urging his treacherous younger brother John who, making a try for the crown himself, had conspired with Philip of France to keep Richard in prison.

Not many brothers would have forgiven this. What could Queen Eleanor have said, to soften the ruthless Richard? After all, John can't

help being a Plantagenet? You know, Richard, this sort of thing does
run in the family? *Every family has its ups and downs*

And what reason did Richard give for not having Queen Berengaria
come from abroad to be crowned with him? None, of course. Richard,
born, as he had remarked in prison, "in a rank which recognizes no
superior but God," did not answer even to Him very often.

Richard soon went abroad himself, but not to join Berengaria. He
went to France to fortify Normandy and to fight Philip. Almost as
much pure pleasure to him as the Third Crusade was the fortress he
built on the Seine south of Rouen—the Château Gaillard, 300 feet above
the water level, 600 feet long, 200 feet wide. One is prepared to believe
he had dreamed and planned this while he was in prison. Along with the
introduction of the crossbow, he is credited with many developments of
early stone machicolations.

"Comme elle est belle, ma fillette d'un an!" he exclaimed of his
fortification Château Gaillard—he who had no real children of his own.

The fighting in France was pleasant but minor. At Gisors late in
1198 he put King Philip "utterly to rout" and saw him, fleeing across
the River Epte, fall into it when the bridge broke under him and his
knights. Philip to Richard's delight "drank of the river" and had to be
pulled out. He escaped, but Richard personally unhorsed and captured
three knights on this occasion. Altogether a hundred and thirty knights
were captured, with two hundred warhorses and uncounted common
soldiers. This was not bad, even in comparison with the Third Crusade.

(Richard said, modestly, after this victory at Gisors that "God and
my right did this, not I"—and "Dieu et mon droit," which is the way
the French-speaking Richard put it, became the motto of the English
crown—just as Richard's new seal, with its three lions passant-gardant,
became their armorial bearings. Richard had had a new seal made so he
could have everybody's grant and charter and warrant resealed, and
charge accordingly. He was always in need of money to pay for his
fighting.)

He was fighting in France, besieging the Castle of Châlus, when he
got his fatal wound. Enjoying himself as usual, he had been watching an
ingenious Frenchman, almost out of ammunition, catching the English

stones in a frying-pan before hurling them back. It was a virtuoso performance and Richard loved it. He forgot about being cautious—if indeed he ever was. An arrow struck him in the shoulder. Trying to pull it out himself, he pulled off the shaft instead, leaving the head embedded. It would not come out; it would not heal. It took him twelve days to die. As he lay rotting with gangrene he not only drank heavily, as usual, but "desperately adventured his life by taking to himself a lover." He set his affairs in order and then sent for the man who had shot him.

"I forgive you my death," King Richard told the prisoner, in the words every English schoolboy memorizes. "Live on, . . . and by my bounty behold the light of day."

Did he feel pretty sure that, after his death, somebody else would take his revenge for him—that his sister, in fact, would tear the man's eyes out and flay him and have horses drag him apart? Richard being Richard, he probably did.

Henry II

1133–1189

HE succeeded to the throne in 1154, upon the death of his first cousin once removed, King Stephen.

There had been an arrangement between Henry's branch of the family and Stephen's. Henry's should have had the throne in the first place; his mother Matilda, Henry I's only surviving child, was not only in direct line of succession but had had fealty sworn to her by everybody else, including Stephen. Stephen had simply usurped her throne when her father died. Matilda had not reacted to this quietly; she gave the usurper no peace; and she the Queen (she said) and he the King (he said) fought it out until 1148. Then, Stephen's star in the ascendant, Matilda retired to Normandy acknowledging him king—but with the understanding that her heirs would succeed him.

It seems doubtful that Stephen would have kept this promise either, for he had two sons, Eustace and William. But in 1153 Eustace died and "generous provision" was made for William. Bought off, William amazingly stayed bought off, and when Stephen died, the following year, Matilda's precocious son came to the English throne as Henry II. It was the beginning of the Plantagenet or Angevin dynasty.

Angevin connotes from Anjou; Plantagenet was a nickname, derived from the sprig of broom (planta Genista) that Henry's father, Count Geoffrey of Anjou, going into battle, had stuck into his helmet.

King Henry arrived not quite a stranger in England, for he had made drumming-up-support trips in 1149 and 1153. Also, England had heard about him. Plenty. He was a burly, red-headed young man of great strength and force and the courage of his convictions. "Curtmantle," he was called, because he set a new style in men's clothes; Henry was too quick and vigorous in his movements to be hampered by the old-fashioned long tunic. Similarly, he had not let himself be hampered by the fact that the woman he wanted to marry was married already—and to a king. He himself, at that time, was only a count's son. He was only nineteen and she was thirty-one. But Queen Eleanor of France, in her own right the Duchess of Aquitaine, was motivated to get a divorce from King Louis and marry him.

This was a man, this young Henry, who knew what he wanted and went after it and got it, and he would make England a strong and able king.

Naturally, there was quite as much interest in the new Queen as there was in him. Eleanor was supposed to be the most beautiful and brilliant woman in Europe; she was also the richest; she was, like the new King, a miracle of energy and achievement. She had gone to the Holy Land on a Crusade. (Practically born in the saddle, she would, in her eighties, practically die in it.) She read books, and at her elegant court encouraged poets and musicians. And also—final hallmark of a successful queen—she was beginning now to bear sons. Though she had only daughters by the King of France, two little girls whom she abandoned without a qualm when she decided that the next King of England had more future, she had five Plantagenet sons, along with three Plantagenet daughters.

The first of the sons was a bit questionable; at least he seems questionable now; nobody dared to mention it then. During 1152, an *annus mirabilis* even for Eleanor, she divorced the French king in March, married the next English king in May, had her baby boy in August, and was crowned Queen of England in December. The baby boy was hers, yes, but whose else? Legally it would seem to have been King Louis's; little William was certainly conceived while she was married to him.

But by the time he was born she was married to Henry, so he passed as a Plantagenet; and anyway before long he died, and an indubitably legal son Henry took his place as heir. Then came more healthy children without any thought of dying, Matilda, Richard, Joanna, Geoffrey, Eleanor, and John. Henry, Richard, and John all were crowned English kings.

But Queen Eleanor, strong character that she was, virtual partner with her husband Henry in the great new empire of his England and Anjou and her Aquitaine, Maine, and Poitou, was not the ruling force behind the King. That was his new chancellor, Thomas à Becket.

Becket was Archdeacon of Canterbury when Henry noticed him, but not fully in holy orders and a very, very secular type. Certainly he had no bias for the Church's interests, for in the power struggle which began between this King and the clergy he fought well on the King's side. Henry was delighted with him. A wonderful idea came into his mind. The Archbishop of Canterbury was old and would soon die. When he did, why not his brilliant, hard-working, simpatico Thomas à Becket as archbishop as well as chancellor? With the chancellor also head of the English Church and on the side of the King, Henry's power troubles would melt away.

This wonderful idea was not new. Henry's grandfather had had a chaplain who was also chancellor, but there no consolidation of power had been involved; there was just the precedent of combining lay and civil offices. It was enough.

It had not occurred to Becket. Henry surprised him with it. He was more than taken aback. He did not want to be an archbishop. Apparently he had the quaint idea that the head of the Church should be a spiritual man. But he bowed to the King's will; and then something happened.

Thomas à Becket changed overnight, outwardly at least. He put aside his rich clothes and jewels and wore the rough robes of a monk, with hair-shirt underneath. He fasted, he prayed, he flagellated himself. Whether he had "got religion" like the American frontiersman at his camp-meeting, or like Saul of Tarsus on the Damascus road, or whether his outward and visible signs masked politics and ambition, nobody to this day really knows. His Church has given him the benefit of the doubt and canonized him. But there is more than a possibility that brilliant, hard-working, and self-seeking Thomas à Becket had not changed at all, that he had always resented being subordinate to the King, and that he had seen this way to meet and beat him on equal terms.

In any case, that is what he did. He resigned as chancellor—defeating Henry's whole point in making him archbishop. His effectiveness would have been in the dual role. Then he changed sides. He started standing for the Church, not the King. As archbishop he demanded from the King return of the church lands taken away at the Conquest. He defied the King to punish or even try anyone connected with the Church; down to the lowest clerk they were subject to Church law and courts, but they were above the law of the land. The King drew up the Constitutions of Clarendon; Becket refused to abide by it. The bishops of the English Church—envious, of course, and by no means convinced by Becket's sudden conversion—withdrew their support from him. The Pope wrote reproving him. The King had him summoned to trial for contempt.

This was the King's round all the way. Becket fled to Normandy, his family's place of origin. He stayed in exile seven years before he ventured to come back.

He came back fighting. In his absence the King, feeling the need to strengthen the succession, had had his eldest son Henry crowned King of England. This strange expedient was rather like consecrating a bishop-coadjutor, so there is absolutely no question of who will be the next bishop, when the bishop dies; and some clubs choose a president-elect, so called, at the same time they choose a president. This part was all right; it was a reasonable thing for King Henry to do, to insure being succeeded by a king who was already crowned and anointed.

The only flaw was that the Archbishop of York had crowned and anointed the Young King (with the Pope's special permission) in the absence of the Archbishop of Canterbury.

Roaring like a bull, the Archbishop of Canterbury excommunicated the Archbishop of York. (This does not sound very saintly. Except to a power-hungry man, what difference did it make?) He did stop short of excommunicating the Pope, but he also cursed in church (while ostensibly celebrating Christmas in Canterbury Cathedral) other prelates who, in the seven years he had been away, had made appointments without his permission.

Hearing about all this the King fell into a rage. "What cowards have I about me," he cried, "that no one will rid me of this lowborn priest?"

Afterward he claimed it was a rhetorical question, but courtiers then seized every chance and excuse to serve royalty. Times have changed; in our century no one even thought of murdering Captain Peter Townsend's divorced wife so the Queen's sister could marry him in her Church; but in the twelfth century, no sooner had King Henry's mouth snapped shut on "lowborn priest" than four knights leaped onto their horses and rode to Canterbury.

They murdered the Archbishop in the middle of divine service in his cathedral. Thomas à Becket died with great bravery and in dying won his long contest with the King.

Henry's penance was fixed by the Pope. In addition to sending crusaders to the Holy Land, having his son recrowned, and assuming the support of Becket's sisters, he had to walk barefoot, in a pilgrim's gown with a hair-shirt underneath, through the streets of Canterbury to Becket's tomb in the cathedral. There he confessed and asked for pardon. Then he bared his back and all the Chapter and monks at Canterbury lashed him seven times apiece—hundreds of welts and wounds. Henry was a strong man; this would have killed a weak one. When it was over, and again he had prayed and meditated, he was still able to walk back through the streets of Canterbury and then to mount his horse.

Back in London, he heard of the King of Scotland's defeat in battle, and he took this good news as a sign that his penance had been adequate, his sins were forgiven, and his troubles were over. But actually they were just beginning.

His family began to desert him. His son Henry, the Young King, was the first to go. He had always been arrogant—once he told his father to his face that he (King Henry) was only a count's son, while he (Young Henry) was a king's. Being crowned and anointed had definitely gone to his head. He now aspired to put his father aside and rule England as its sole king. (Young Henry's story—what he wrote to the Pope—was that he was usurping the throne because of Becket's murder.) Nothing came of this attempt; King Henry put a stop to it; but the Young King got away from him. Having a new Great Seal made, he turned up at the Court of France.

Queen Eleanor, very much involved in the plot to unseat her husband, was not so lucky. She was captured, the King sent her to Winchester Castle and kept her there in custody until he died—sixteen years. Nothing happened to their other problem sons. All of them except John had been in the conspiracy, Richard perhaps the ringleader. That was the real reason for his mother's treachery; she could never say no to this favorite child; but, as various historians have pointed out, she did have provocation.

She did indeed, but no more than other queens and much less than some. It was expected that healthy young men would have mistresses as well as wives, and though Eleanor was glamorous and beautiful and quite a lot, really, like Katharine Hepburn in *The Lion in Winter*, she was twelve years older than her husband and had borne ten children. She must have shown this a little bit. In any case, King Henry's affair with Rosamond Clifford, the "Fair Rosamond" of the legendary house in the maze, began before he married. Queen Eleanor, winding up a ball of silk, is supposed to have penetrated this maze and offered Rosamond the choice between a dagger and a cup of poison; instead, the latter entered a convent in excellent health and died years thereafter of natural causes. Henry's sons William Longuespée and Geoffrey the Chancellor were Rosamond's, I think; and, yes, it may have been trying for Eleanor that her husband kept the favorite one at court along with his legitimate children, one of whom had the same name—Geoffrey for Henry's father. But, again, this was and remained common practice. As far along as the nineteenth century Queen Adelaide was stumbling over *ten* Fitzclarences at court, the illegitimate children King William IV had sired while Duke of Clarence. And as for Henry's affair with Alais of France, that was terrible, but it was still new when Eleanor was shut up in Winchester Castle. How could she know it was going to last seventeen years, until her husband died?

When he did die, and Queen Eleanor was named regent by her son the new king, Richard I, one can hardly blame her for shutting Alais up in Winchester Castle, in her turn, just as soon as she herself got out of it.

But one must still say that as men and medieval kings go Henry might have been far worse. These two long affairs, Alais of France and Fair Rosamond, seem to account for most of his infidelity. He was not promiscuous; he was an emotional man who tended to fall in love.

He was a man who greatly loved his children, too, when they gave him a chance, and who felt it bitterly when they betrayed him and actually fought against him. At Gisors he took on and defeated three of them at once, Young Henry, Richard, and Geoffrey—along with his old enemy the French king. One of these family enemies was removed by death; the Young King died in his father's lifetime and then Richard was the heir. Allowances might be made for the Young King—it had perhaps been a mistake to have an already proud and obnoxious boy crowned—but the King could find no excuse for either Richard or Geoffrey. And when on his deathbed he heard that his youngest son, John, was also in a fresh plot against him he could not stand it.

"Not John!" he said. "Not John, my heart, my loved son!" He said to his illegitimate son Geoffrey the Chancellor, his mainstay during the sixteen years his sons by Eleanor had been conspiring and fighting against him, "Thou art my true son. The others, they are the bastards!" Perhaps this is the original use of bastard in the non-original sense.

Only this Geoffrey—typically—was with King Henry when he died. But when his body was lying in state in the Abbey of Fontevrault, his son Richard, now the king, came in to look at him. And—everyone knew what this meant—the nose and mouth of the corpse began to bleed.

Stephen

c.1097–1154

HE succeeded to the throne in 1135, shortly after the death of his uncle, Henry I. He did so by usurping it from his uncle's daughter Matilda.

King Henry had had premonitions that something of the kind might happen, and more than once had required his nearest and dearest to swear oaths of fealty to his daughter. Stephen was among those who swore to uphold and defend her.

But when King Henry died Stephen was conveniently nearby and Matilda was far away. Though she was still called Empress Matilda, because her first husband had been Holy Roman Emperor and she could not bear to give the title up, she was now married to Count Geoffrey of Anjou and was living with him in France. No sooner had she got the news of her father's death (December 1, 1135) than she got the second piece of news—Stephen had had himself crowned (December 22, 1135).

Stephen? But Stephen was not next in line for the throne, even if she and her two-year-old Henry were crowded out. Stephen was a younger son himself.

Stephen, however, was the one who wanted the throne enough to forget his oaths of fealty.

King Stephen, who was William the Conqueror's grandson by way of his daughter Adela, has been generously treated by historians. One calls him "a chivalrous gentleman" and another "mild, gallant, chivalrous and unfortunate." But if he was mild, gallant, and chivalrous he would not have snatched what belonged to his lady cousin.

One is reminded, as one so often is in reading history, of the Harrington quotation:

> *Treason doth never prosper; what's the reason?*
> *Why, if it prosper, none dare call it treason.*

Also, Stephen was no more unfortunate than he was mild, gallant, and chivalrous. He was fantastically lucky. What was it but luck that the legal heir was a woman and that she was out of the country when her father died? What was it but luck that an older brother did not try for the throne himself? What was it but luck that Empress Matilda's overbearing manners made everybody mad?

Stephen was also lucky in a positive way. His Queen, Matilda—with no thought of how confusing it would be for unborn historians he had married another Matilda—was a better strategist than he was. He was defeated at the Battle of Lincoln, early in 1141, and Empress Matilda sent him in chains to Bristol Castle; but Queen Matilda, rallying the forces which had let King Stephen rather badly down, reversed his fortune later that year. This time it was the Empress Matilda who was defeated—routed—and Robert of Gloucester who was taken prisoner.

This Robert was the oldest of King Henry I's twenty (*sic*) illegitimate children and therefore Empress Matilda's half-brother. He was also her firmest supporter and friend. So she exchanged prisoners with Queen Matilda—King Stephen for Robert of Gloucester—even though, with Stephen in irons, she had been closer to the throne than she ever had been or would be again.

In April 1141, after the Battle of Lincoln, she had been named "lady of the English"—they could not quite bring themselves to call her queen, even then—and in June entered London for, as she expected, her coronation. But it did not take place. London took an instant dislike to her "arrogance and tactless demands for money," and its citizens literally chased her out.

Stephen was unavailable at the time, shut up in Bristol Castle, so it was not a matter of choice between them. But if it had been, was Stephen really better? Apparently his manners were better, at least; but the *Dictionary of National Biography*, which is often acerb, precedes with the judgment that Stephen was "Brave, generous, high-spirited, warm-hearted, open-handed, courteous and affable to all classes" an account of his permitting his violent Flemish mercenaries to run wild; holding a forest court which involved his having "broken his vows to God and his pledge to the people"; despoiling "those he mistrusted for the benefit of his favourites" (taking their castles, etc.); hanging the uncle of the commandant of Shrewsbury Castle "with (it is said) over ninety comrades"; smoking out some people and starving out others; arresting bishops—one could go on and on, as Stephen did. For four years, too, he carried on a running feud with the Church and was placed under an interdict, the Pope refusing to let his son Eustace be crowned to insure the succession. This was when Stephen shut up all the bishops, to frighten them into submission—but the Archbishop of Canterbury, the only one authorized to crown a king, escaped overseas and Stephen did not, in this case, get what he wanted.

Does all this sound much better than the "arrogance and tactless demands for money" that got the Empress Matilda literally chased out of London? It really sounds much worse. The conclusions seem obvious—first, that King Stephen was one of those people who can, literally in his case, get by with murder, and second, that England in 1141 was not ready for Woman's Lib.

Eventually Empress Matilda realized this. After the exchange of King Stephen for Robert of Gloucester Stephen resumed the throne and Empress Matilda made no further effort to unseat him. She stayed five more years in England, Stephen making no attempt to molest her, either. Then she went back to Normandy and lived twenty more years. She lived to see her son Henry follow Stephen on the throne, but when she gave it up for herself she gave it up.

Stephen's own son Eustace, the one he had not succeeded in having crowned king, died before he did and evidently he had no ambitions for his son William. The death of his wife, Queen Matilda, also disheartened him. He was quite willing to come to terms with Empress Matilda's son, who visited England in 1149 and 1153. Perhaps it helped his conscience—if he had one—to know that the line which should have had the throne would come to it afterward, at least.

Stephen was not a bad king in the sense of being vicious (this sounds like the *Dictionary of National Biography et al.*, rising above little facts like the commandant's poor old uncle and the ninety others hanged with him) but he could not maintain law and order in England and it got to be a dangerous place. Geoffrey de Mandeville, Earl of Essex, was one who particularly ran wild between the orderly reign of Henry I and the orderly reign of Henry II, during the disorderly reign of Stephen.

Matilda

1103–1167

Sᴴᴇ succeeded to the throne in 1135, upon the death of her father, Henry I.

She was never crowned officially, though, any more than Lady Jane Grey was, and some historians do not even include her in the list of English sovereigns. *Burke's Peerage* does, which would gratify her.

She and her cousin Stephen competed, from her father's death onward, for the throne which he took without explanation or apology. "Never apologize and never explain, and you will be respected and admired by everyone"—it was not quite true of Stephen, but nearly everyone agreed that the idea of a woman on the throne of England was absurd and a male relative in usurping it had done the only reasonable thing.

Matilda, true granddaughter of William the Conqueror, "had the nature of a man in the frame of a woman," and she was a good fighter. But even defeating and capturing Stephen—at Lincoln in 1141—did not solve her problem. Partly it was her sex, partly her overbearing disposition (not softened when, in her first marriage, she became Holy Roman Empress) and partly, certainly, her hated second marriage.

Geoffrey of Anjou was only a count, but this was not what the English held against him. He was an Angevin and the Angevins were wild, violent people.

Since almost everybody else on the twelfth-century scene was wild and violent too, the Angevins, to have stood out, must have been spectacular.

The family's own story was that they were descended from the Devil. One of the remote Counts Fulke of Anjou had a beautiful wife of unknown background; this was odd enough, for the great families usually married carefully, but the oddest thing about her was that she never stayed in church for communion. By what seemed for a long time only a funny coincidence, she always had to leave for some reason or another before the consecration of the bread and wine. But Count Fulke's belief in coincidence finally ran out, and one day he instructed four knights to stand on the edges of the Countess's cloak, and thus physically prevent her slipping out of church as usual.

They tried, but the Countess frustrated them. With a shriek, she tore herself out of the captive garment and took off like a big bird. Holding two of her children by the hand, she soared still shrieking out the window. Obviously she was never seen again, and obviously this was just as well. By her inability to remain in the presence of the body and blood of Christ, the Countess had identified herself: she was the daughter of Satan.

The Angevins—Plantagenets—believed this family story. King Richard I would remark that they had come from the Devil and would go back to him and, planning his coronation, he specifically excluded Jews and witches from the service. Undoubtedly he was thinking of certain female relatives on his father's side.

England did not want the descendants of this devilish family on the English throne. Matilda had had no children by the Emperor, but by Geoffrey of Anjou she had four. The oldest, Henry, named for her father, was born in 1133, and this was the occasion of her father's making his barons repeat their oaths of fealty to Matilda.

Oaths did not mean too much to twelfth-century barons. Historians as eminent as Winston Churchill say just the opposite, but there were always a lot of broken oaths lying conspicuously around. These people believed that anything, absolutely anything, would be forgiven them if they made a deathbed repentance. They knew that death could come suddenly and violently, finding them unshriven, and they feared this.

But in Matilda's case and many others they were willing to take the chance.

Her French husband does not seem to have liked Matilda much better than her English subjects did. Count Geoffrey of Anjou was ten years younger than she was and their marriage had been purely political, a matter of territory. They quarreled violently. He sent for her to come back later, but in 1129 he actually drove her out of Anjou—just as the Londoners would later drive her out of their city. Something about the Empress Matilda certainly brought out the worst in many people.

Possibly her German manners irritated Geoffrey—for her first husband the Emperor, when she married him at age eleven, had "dismissed all her English attendants, and had her carefully trained in the German language and manners." Perhaps Geoffrey was irritated— being only a count—because she still called herself the Empress Matilda? But this kind of thing is still customary, and nobody else seems to mind. Americans registering at English hotels are still startled to note that Lady Whatever is staying in Room 27 with Captain Something Else; but it is quite all right; they are married, and etiquette and usage merely permit her to keep the higher rank of a previous husband.

Empress Matilda may have wanted a stable title to hold onto because her name was so fluctuant. A biography of her calls her "Matilda, Maud, Mold, Aethelic, Aaliz"—and Adela is still another version. In any case, all she ever had in her life, poor thing, was that fine title—never a kingdom. The Holy Roman Empire was a loose collection of politically allied countries, but their names are what appeared on the map, not the name of the Empire. It was rather like the English guinea, bigger and better than the pound sterling but not tangibly in existence as a bill or a coin.

The Emperor had been roughly thirty years older than Matilda, and about the time he got her educated to suit him, with her new German ways and manners, he died. Then she lost her mother, lost her brother—the legitimate one—had to marry again against her will, was done out of her father's throne and, when she laid claim to it, actually run out of her capital by the Londoners. She had had an exciting life, for a time; once, while she was contending with Stephen, she had escaped from a castle by having herself bound on a bier and carried out, like a corpse. Another time she escaped from another castle in the snow; she and three faithful knights in white robes that did not show against it, and with steps that made no sound upon it, walked to safety through Stephen's very camp.

But she had a long time, too long, to look back over this interesting part of her past. Even before her husband Geoffrey died, in 1151, they had made over the Duchy of Normandy to young Henry, and three years later, when Stephen died and Henry left for England to take up that responsibility, she let him go alone.

He took counsel with her before he sailed—the only person who advised him. She advised him later against invading Ireland, and she advised him again—unsuccessfully, unfortunately—against making Thomas à Becket Archbishop of Canterbury. But she herself merely lived on and on in Normandy, still the Empress, very charitable and religious in her old age, dying finally at sixty-four.

Henry I

1068–1135

He succeeded to the throne in 1100, upon the death of his brother, William Rufus.

Nobody has ever suggested that Henry shot his brother Rufus personally, and only a few have hinted that he put Walter Tiryl up to it. But he was indeed in the New Forest also, in the same hunting party, and the shot that killed Rufus made Henry king.

But not automatically, because he was not next in line. His elder brother Robert was away on a Crusade, however, and did not get back till the following year. By that time King Henry I was firmly established. Robert retired to Normandy—he was already Duke of Normandy—and Henry paid him a pension. But eventually he—Henry—decided this was a foolish thing to do and he could save money, and even pick up Normandy, by simply defeating his brother in battle.

Poor Robert, who seems to have been designed by nature to be a victim, was accordingly defeated at Tinchebrai in 1106. A handsome tomb in Gloucester Cathedral was the best thing that ever happened to him.

Henry I, firmly on the throne, made a firm, exacting king. He was a strict enforcer of the law, and some of his methods and punishments were severe. "The Lion of Justice," he was called. But England needed a firm hand and these methods and punishments promoted peace. "In his days no man dared to wrong another," a contemporary said. He also promoted peace outside his realm, preferring to get his way—as he usually did—by arbitration rather than battle. And he kept the barons firmly in their place. There were no uprisings in Henry I's time; authority was vested in the person of the King.

He made a likable as well as an excellent king. Bookish beyond custom (he earned another name, Henry Beauclerc) he also particularly loved deerslaying and he had a menagerie at Woodstock—long before Henry III's in the Tower, which is often said to be the first. He was hard-playing as well as hard-working.

He married rather late—at thirty-two—Edith of Scotland, who was a great-niece of Edward the Confessor. This was a popular marriage because it put the old English royal blood into his children. Edith for some reason unknown then changed her name to Matilda.

By Queen Matilda Henry had only two children, and the son, William, was drowned in 1120. Queen Matilda had already died by this time and the King, thinking it risky to fix his hopes of the succession on their daughter Matilda, was constrained to marry again. But Adelicia of Louvain gave him no children at all.

It is no negative virtue for a king to keep a barren consort, and it is much to Henry I's credit that he did not suddenly discover that he and Adelicia were too closely related or otherwise living in sin. Instead he sent for his now grown-up and married daughter Matilda and, as best he could, tried to insure that she would succeed him on the throne. He made all the barons swear fealty to her. But though the barons were very firmly Henry's men he had an excellent idea of how quickly they might change, once he was dead. He made the barons swear again, after Matilda gave him his first grandson, that they would be loyal to her and her heir and protect their rights. They did so unblinkingly and unblushingly.

It was said that King Henry never smiled again after his son was drowned. It gave him, however, an added incentive to make England strong; if he had any hopes of handing it down to a daughter instead of a son, it must be put in superlative condition. This Henry set himself to do. When he died in 1135, aged sixty-seven, he had given it thirty years of peace, had corrected the mistake of separating England's rule from

Normandy's, and had won less and less grudging respect for Norman rule in England. He himself was native-born—the first of the Conqueror's sons to be so—and he was married into the old line of English kings. It must not be forgotten, too, that the blood of these Normans was Norse blood rather than undiluted French, and that much of the so-called English blood was Norse too—so there was not really much difference between him and his subjects.

They mourned him sincerely. So soon after the Conquest, he had been a really great king to accomplish this.

William II
called Rufus

1056–1100

HE succeeded to the throne in 1087, upon the death of his father, William the Conqueror.

He built Westminster Hall. This is giving the good news first. William Rufus is so universally held to have been such a bad king, and such an unattractive fellow personally, that we should hold onto the thought that he did make some contribution to England. This Hall (1097, with probably the finest hammerbeam roof in all Europe) was saved by the firemen in preference to the House of Commons, when both of them caught fire during the Blitz. They were quite right. The House, which was only Victorian Gothic, has had very successful replacements made since. Westminster Hall was irreplaceable.

And William Rufus built it, but absolutely nothing else redounds to his credit. Surely there were some other things to be said for him, but history has stubbornly refused to say any of them.

Rufus—so called, by the way, because his face was so extremely red; his hair was blond—was William the Conqueror's second surviving son. To the first, Robert Curthose (he was short-legged, they say), he had given the Duchy of Normandy. This furnishes an idea of the relative value of Normandy and England, in the Conqueror's view. England regretted this opinion. They had no very great desire for Robert

Curthose, but they wished England had gone to him and Normandy to Rufus.

Rufus ruled England for twelve years. He did not marry. He was said to be a homosexual. He was not an idle king, and on the face of it the things he did were like those that would occupy many better-thought-of English kings. He put down baronial revolts (in 1088 and 1095) and also invaded Wales twice and built castles to strengthen the frontier. He had trouble with the King of Scotland, Malcolm II, who had done him homage in 1091 but in 1093 rose against him. Rufus killed him then, in a battle at Alnwick. All this sounds very normal, nothing unusually bad. But it was like the Empress Matilda later on. It was not what William Rufus did but what he was like—and apparently he was personally very bad. All the most unfavorable adjectives are brought out for him—nasty, brutish, blasphemous, cruel, violent, rude. It is not possible to disagree with them.

If he had been found dead there would have been an early English murder mystery, because a great many people would have liked to kill him.

Instead he was shot in broad daylight by a man named Walter Tiryl. It passed for an accident. An arrow went through Rufus's head as he was hunting with Walter, his own brother Henry, and others in the New Forest, in August 1100.

Tiryl took to his heels and was never seen or heard of again. This was natural, whether he had killed the King accidentally or on purpose. But the King's brother, too, left him just where he fell. Indecent haste was, Henry evidently thought, necessary. He rushed to Winchester where the royal treasury was, obtained it with some difficulty (for he was meeting the first of the people who thought that it, and the crown, belonged now to his eldest brother Robert Curthose), and had himself crowned, quickly, before Robert could get back from his Crusade.

Then, bethinking himself of his dead brother Rufus, so lately King, so suddenly nothing at all, he had William II of England, called Rufus, decently interred.

William I
called
The Conqueror

1027–1087

He succeeded to the throne in 1066, having defeated and killed King Harold Godwinson.

So he became William the Conqueror instead of merely William of Normandy, and King of England by right of the Norman Invasion and the Norman Conquest at Hastings.

William's invasion, however, was based on his belief that he was entitled to the throne. King Edward the Confessor, since whose death King Harold had occupied it, was William's cousin and had promised the throne to him. Harold's story, on the other hand, was that King Edward had changed his mind about that and on his deathbed said he wanted him, Harold, his brother-in-law, to have the throne. There was no reconciling these two pretensions peacefully.

William was not in any case a peaceful man. He had not been born into a peaceful situation. Not the Duke of Normandy's lawful heir but a bastard—his mother was a tanner's daughter—he had no right, many Normans thought, to get their duchy and they made him fight for it. Fortunately the King of France (Henri I, then) came in on his side, and he defeated his Norman barons at the Battle of Val-as-Dunes, in 1047.

But then King Henri turned against him as he grew too powerful for comfort. Under William the Bastard—still so called but strictly behind his back—Normandy became "the most vigorous military state in Europe." Nobody knew this better than King Henri, who in 1051 needed William to help him defeat Geoffrey of Anjou. Also, 1051 was the year William went by invitation to visit King Edward of England, who had had a Norman mother and was William's cousin. The looks of this King Henri of France did not like. Edward, celibate though married, needed an heir. It would be a melancholy day for the King of France if the Duke of Normandy, the most vigorous military state in Europe, became King of England too.

Doubtless Henri relaxed when Harold Godwinson, Edward the Confessor's brother-in-law, claimed the throne on his death and was elected king by the English Witan. But his relief was short, because William did not intend to take this lying down. He prepared a great fleet and sailed for England, landing at Pevensey and proceeding to Hastings.

William was lucky in several ways. The King of Norway had designs on the English throne too, and Harold had just fought off his invasion (killing him) when William of Normandy landed. So William fought a tired, decimated English army instead of a fresh one; he fought a leader who was brave, but also rash and hasty; he fought footsoldiers with cavalry. Harold had a few horses, for baggage only, but William's fleet had brought war-horses; you can see their heads sticking up in the Bayeux Tapestry. Three of William's horses were shot from under him during the battle, but, lucky in this too, he was unwounded himself.

But though luck and circumstances favored William, the military opinion is that he also outgeneralled Harold. His reluctance to leave the seacoast, proceeding from Pevensey only to another port, Hastings, could have conveyed some of his uncertainty to Harold; William was afraid to get too far from his ships, in case he should have to take to them. Harold could have profitably, his tactical critics say, waited for the invader farther inland—and rested his army while he waited. Each side had about the same number of men, six or seven thousand; it was the element of English fatigue that made them unequal. Also the tactic that William used most effectively was a very old one—feigned retreat. It is thought that the Normans' first retreat was a real and necessary one, but that William was encouraged to fake others because he had seen how eagerly the English took advantage of it. Again, the English were tired; they needed to try for a knockout because they might not outlast the Normans in rounds; but chiefly it was a matter of their—and Harold's—undisciplined enthusiasm. Defending their own country, men fight with a panache that has the defects of its virtues. They often lose, as Harold's army did, to cold, detached calculation. They often chase after an enemy with shouts of joy, only to have him turn on them and cut them to pieces.

Also William thought—if rather late in the day—to have his archers aim high, so that the arrows went over the wall of English shields. That was when Harold fell. The Bayeaux Tapestry shows him, shield full of arrows, trying to rid himself of the arrow lodged in his eye. Then it shows the mounted Norman finishing him with a sword.

Harold's body was stripped bare, like many other bodies, for the sake of its armor and rich clothes. His mother sent word that she would redeem his corpse by the payment of its weight in gold, but it could not be identified. His beautiful mistress, Edith Swan-neck she was called, wanted to try herself to find him, and she was successful. Harold was buried first, quickly, on the seacoast he had defended, but later his body was moved to consecrated ground.

William the Conqueror—as he now was—proceeded to London, and on Christmas Day, 1066, was crowned King of England in Westminster Abbey.

There was no dancing in the streets of London. It must have been much like the streets of Paris when the conquering German army marched in. The newsreels then showed us the faces of a subjugated people—some stoical, some in tears, some angry, all very scared. The French in 1940 knew, like the English in 1066, a good deal about their conquerors. They had heard the same stories of ruthlessness and violence along the way. They knew they could expect no mercy from the big, hard-faced man riding at the head of the column.

They could oppose him only in pockets of resistance, but like the French in 1940 the English in 1066 continued to fight the invader. That was why William the Conqueror built all those castles. The Tower of

London was the first. But you can see them, thirty or more, in all the important English towns, York and Windsor, Richmond and Ludlow, Chester, the last one to yield to him. All through his reign, over twenty-five years, King William was putting down sporadic outbursts of rebellion. He had to go back and forth to Normandy, too, for business and trouble that kept arising there, and when he did he took with him some of the important Saxon leaders; he was rightly afraid they would start something in England if he left them behind.

But, it is pointed out, he was also using these intelligent and influential men as part of his administration. Normans and Englishmen, victors and vanquished, were beginning, inevitably, to mingle. Their blood mingled in children born in and out of marriage. They began, however dimly, to understand each others' institutions and see each others' point of view.

King William made every effort to grasp the details of the problem of England. The most concrete example of this is the Domesday Book. You may see it in the Public Record Office in London. Unless you are a very dedicated and scholarly specialist you cannot read it with any degree of comprehension, much less pleasure; but you can see and be impressed by how minutely the kingdom is described, how thorough William's survey had been. As the chronicler said, "There was not one hide of land in England that he did not know who owned it and what it was worth, and then set it down in his record." * The Domesday Book (1086) makes our modern census procedure and result look amateurish. Primarily, of course, its aim was to look at taxable resources, but with this it gave England's thorough, able, and thoughtful King a broad knowledge he put to excellent use.

It is unlikely that Englishmen ever warmed to William the Conqueror, but certainly he earned their respect. To quote the chronicler further,

He was a very stern and violent man, so that no one dared do anything contrary to his will. He had earls in his fetters, who acted against his will. He expelled bishops from their sees, and abbots from their abbacies, and put thanes in prison, and finally he did not spare his own brother, who was called Odo; he

* Quoted in Winston S. Churchill, *A History of the English-Speaking Peoples* (New York: Bantam Books, 1963), vol. 1, p. 125.

was a very powerful bishop in Normandy and was the foremost man next to the King, and had an earldom in England. He put him in prison. Amongst other things the good security he made in this country is not to be forgotten—so that any honest man could travel over his kingdom without injury with his bosom full of gold: and no one dared strike another, however much wrong he had done him. And if any man had intercourse with a woman against her will, he was forthwith castrated.

William's stand on sexual morality was not just theoretical. He was sexually moral himself—no mistresses whatsoever. By his queen, Matilda of Flanders (his able regent when an alter ego was needed in Normandy), he had four sons and five daughters, and some of them he loved in the face of odds. His eldest son, Robert Curthose (they could have been socks; it is another case of historian blindly following historian to say that his legs as well as his stockings were short), was openly rebellious. He not only plotted against William, he actually fought him, putting himself on the side of his father's worst enemies. Yet William left him the Duchy of Normandy—in his view, a more desirable property than England.

He left England to his third son, William called Rufus. (The second son, Richard, had been killed out hunting.) Everybody else loathed Rufus. On the face of it it does not appear that he did anything worse than other eleventh-century people thought normal, but he must have been remarkably obnoxious personally, for this dog has a very bad name. However, his father loved him.

To his youngest son, Henry, the only one born in England, King William left nothing but money. Like King John later on, Henry might have been nicknamed Lackland. But Rufus's accident, or murder, brought him to the English throne and he became one of the greatest of English kings, his father's very worthy successor.

For William had, indeed, made England a splendid king. Against their will, the backward, oafish islanders learned continental civilization; with the feudal system, they acquired institutions we think of now as English innovations. In consequence of the Norman invasion and William's rule, they became for the first time a united nation.

Unification came in two stages. In the first, under the Normans, the Saxons and Danes and Angles and Celts and so on stopped indulging themselves in opposing each other; they were a conquered people all together; the cleavage was between the comparatively civilized, French-speaking Normans in administrative positions and castles, and the comparatively crude, English-speaking natives in no positions or castles at all. Then in the second stage water began to seek its own level and the cream rose to the top. Some of the English began to get knightly educations, to be clever about acquiring land and money and influential fathers-in-law. Some of the Normans became lax, slipped back, were no longer the very best people. Sometimes fustian went to armor in only one generation, or armor to fustian. It was a social revolution, much influenced in its nature and duration by the character and personality of the new English King.

There is no wealth of quotations from William the Conqueror. Such quotations, and many of them, give us very clear pictures indeed of rulers like Charles II and Queen Victoria—bringing them back to life as nothing else does. But we do have the account of William's landing on English soil. It is easy to fall on your face when you step off a beached boat, and this is what William did. What could have been worse? The mighty, warlike Duke of Normandy comes over to conquer England and falls flat. It was more than an embarrassment; to a superstitious people it was a bad omen. But William the Conqueror was, as always, master of the situation. He scrambled up. "See, I have taken England with both my hands," he said.

Harold Godwinson

c.1022–1066

HE succeeded to the throne in 1066, upon the death of Edward the Confessor, his brother-in-law.

He and his friends claimed that Edward on his deathbed had designated Harold. This was a reversal of his previously expressed wish, that William of Normandy, his cousin, should follow him on the throne. But it could have happened.

Actually Edward had no effective power to name either William or Harold as his successor. It was necessary, except in the case of a natural heir which Edward had not, for the Witan (the not very representative body) to elect a new king.

But this they promptly did. They elected Harold. There may have been a little intimidation. William of Normandy, the other kingly possibility, was far away; Harold was right there at the deathbed, and behind him was all the formidable power of his father, Earl Godwin, who had overshadowed Edward the Confessor himself. On Godwin's death, Harold had become "the first man in England after the King, and during the remainder of the reign was virtually ruler of at least the southern part of the kingdom." *

Now he felt himself ready to rule the entire kingdom.

* *Dictionary of National Biography*, VIII, p. 1302.

Edward the Confessor had died January 5, 1066. Harold had himself crowned the very next day. And this tremendously strengthened his position, for the English people, who believed that the rite that consecrated the communion bread and wine turned it actually and physically into the body and blood of Jesus Christ, believed similarly that the rite that consecrated and anointed and crowned a king turned him into someone very different and special, somewhere between men and the angels.

Whatever Edward the Confessor had preferred no longer mattered. After Harold had been elected and crowned he was, no doubt about it, truly king.

And, no doubt about it, he would have made England a strong and able king. Adjectives are heaped upon him. Tall, strong, handsome—on his mother's side, he was one of the beautiful Danes—wise, temperate, industrious. Firm, equitable. Loyal. Kind. Religious. Frank. Courteous. Brave, if also rash and hasty.

He was already a proven soldier. Having shared his father's banishment, he was also with the fleet when Godwin returned to be reinstated. The next year he led an English army against Aelfgar, the son of the powerful Earl Leofric, who with Welsh and Irish help had raided and burned Hereford. As William of Normandy's prospective subject—this was when it was assumed that William would succeed King Edward, before Harold had thought about succeeding him himself—he had helped William defeat an old enemy, Conan of Brittany.

Harold had married, after defeating her father, Ealgyth (or Edith), the daughter of Aelfgar, Earl of Mercia. She was also the widow of Gruffyd, an old Welsh enemy Harold had likewise defeated and killed. Beyond her willingness to let bygones be bygones, nothing is known about her; it was her husband's mistress, who unfortunately bore the same name, who was called Edith Swan-neck.

Queen Edith was to have only a few months upon the English throne. Harold soon heard that not only William of Normandy was preparing a fleet to invade England, but Harold Hardrada of Norway.

(Yes, in addition to the two Ediths we now have two kings named Harold.)

Harold of Norway struck before William of Normandy did. His fleet sailed up the Humber and he pitched camp near York at Stamford Bridge. Harold of England was in London when he got this news and he made it to York—with infantry—in five days.

In the great Battle of Stamford Bridge Harold of Norway was killed. Tostig, a traitorous brother of the English king who had joined his enemy, was killed also. But the victorious Harold let the defeated Harold's son Olaf go home free. At Stamford Bridge he had won such a great victory that he could afford to be generous.

The Scandinavians, who had invaded and ravaged and often ruled England for centuries before, would never be a real threat again. But their French relatives the Normans were a very real and immediate threat. Before the battle-stained Harold had even time to get his breath he got the news: William of Normandy had landed at Pevensey.

Back came King Harold from Stamford Bridge and York. He does not need alibis or excuses made for him, for he fought the Normans well and bravely; but he could not have been at peak. His victorious army had, certainly, suffered casualties of killed and wounded, and Harold urged them back almost as fast as he had marched them north. They got reinforcements, they got some replacements of the equipment they had lost, but time was against them.

The Norsemen and the Normans had not intentionally combined to defeat Harold of England, but both must get the credit. If Harold had not had to win first at Stamford Bridge, he might have won at Hastings.

He almost won as it was. His foot-soldiers were drawn up in a "shield-wall" which stood all day long against the onslaught of the Norman cavalry. If Harold himself had not been wounded—by one of the arrows William then ordered his men to shoot high in the air, so they would arch up behind the shield-wall—the battle might have been his. But the arrow got him in the eye and, struggling to pull it out, he could not fend off the mounted swordsman looming over him.

His two brothers—he had loyal brothers as well as the traitorous one of Stamford Bridge—had been killed already. The English fought on, fighting especially well as soldiers always do on their own soil, but with Harold dead and William very much alive they could not win.

The English have never forgotten Harold. One of the differences between them and the Americans is their awareness of history, and to many of them Harold is still very real. One such person inserts a notice every year in the *London Times'* column IN MEMORIAM. Between the remembrances of soldiers killed in Baghdad in 1917 and at Dunkirk in 1940, it reads:

> *HAROLD OF ENGLAND—*
> *killed in action defending*
> *his country from the in-*
> *vader. 14th October, 1066.*

Edward
the Confessor

c.1005–1066

HE succeeded to the throne in 1042, upon the death of his half-brother, Hardicanute.

This is the king whose tomb is the central shrine in Westminster Abbey—and very properly so, because he was the Abbey's founder. The structure he reared was not, however, the familiar one we see. Edward was the last of the old line of Saxon kings, but he was Norman on his mother's side, brought up in Normandy, in his thirties before he came back to England. So, naturally—years before the Norman Conquest, which we think of as the beginning of Norman architecture in England—King Edward built his Westminster Abbey in the Norman idiom, solid stone and round arches. It should have stood forever, as he intended. But King Henry III, meaning well, tore it down and rebuilt it only two centuries later. He thought St. Edward deserved a finer shrine.

For Edward the Confessor was by that time a saint. His Church canonized him within a hundred years of his death (Joan of Arc waited five hundred), and even now his tomb in the Anglican Abbey is a Roman Catholic oasis-shrine, with a special guidebook for pilgrims.

But it was not a very saintly young man called over from Normandy, at last, to reestablish his father's line on the throne. Danish kings, foreigners, had sat on it for twenty-six years. Danish invaders were the perennial problem of the Saxon kings, as Scottish and Welsh borderers would be their successors', and in Edward's father's time they had overrun the kingdom. (Schoolboys find it piquant that his obviously unprepared father was called Ethelred the Unready.) But Danish King Canute was dead now, King Harold Harefoot was dead, King Hardicanute was dead, and the Saxons were back in the person of King Edward.

One of his first acts on becoming king was to seize all his mother's property. Emma of Normandy was, politely speaking, a very strong and resourceful character. Playing both ends against the middle, she had married first a Saxon king of England (Ethelred, the father of her son King Edward who had just arrived) and then a Danish King of England (Canute, father of her son King Hardicanute who had recently died). This was pretty raw even in the eleventh century, and Edward may have resented it. There seems to be no doubt that he thought Queen Emma had favored his younger half-brother over him. She also may have been intriguing with King Magnus of Norway.

But do saints seize their mothers' property, whatever the provocation? And do they habitually swear "By the mother of God" and "By God and His mother"? Or dismiss their queens simply because they have quarreled with their fathers? If it comes to that, are saints likely to have quarreled with fathers-in-law? No, King Edward was not yet a saint.

Edward's father-in-law was the tremendously rich and powerful Earl Godwin, the strongest man in the kingdom, undoubtedly the moving force in bringing him home from Normandy when Hardicanute died. There were, after all, more Norse possibilities, as well as an older Saxon line. But there seems to have been some of the same thinking that prevailed after the Wars of the Roses, when Lancaster married York and the White Rose and the Red Rose bloomed (they said) on the same stem. Here was an available descendant of the old Saxon line of kings; marry him to a descendant of the Danish kings who had successfully invaded England and everybody on both sides will be satisfied and peaceful. It was even easy to produce a queen for Edward; Godwin's own daughter Edith happened to be descended, on her mother's side, from King Harold Bluetooth (King Canute's grandfather) as well as from Olaf, King of Sweden.

Edith was also said to be beautiful—no resemblance to Bluetooth at all. But soon the stories began to spread: Edward was celibate, he was not living with his beautiful Queen. And, certainly, no babies were born to disprove the tale.

Some people thought there might be something the matter with him physically—others, that he was merely too much like a monk. It was like the gossip that circulated around England when Queen Elizabeth I coyly declined to marry.

Edward's remarkable appearance, too, helped give credence to all kinds of wild surmise. It has been said repeatedly that he was a real albino, not just a blond Norman. If so, he stood out like a white crow.

While King Edward neglected his Queen but kept busy hunting deer and collecting religious relics, and of course building Westminster Abbey, his father-in-law was running the country, Mussolini to his Victor Emmanuel. There were many advantages to this arrangement, for the King was simply not interested and Godwin was an able man. If there had been trains in eleventh-century England Godwin would have made them run on time.

It must have infuriated him that, for one reason or another, King Edward had no children by the Godwin daughter who shared his throne. The simplest way for the Godwin quasi-kingly power to be continued indefinitely was in the person of the King's son, Godwin's grandson. But six years of the marriage passed without issue.

Then in 1051 the break came. King Edward suddenly put Queen Edith aside and exiled her father Godwin. He was capable of sudden and decisive action—witness his seizure of his mother's property—but this particular action seemed not like him. The theory is that there was a clever and ambitious Norman faction at court; having been brought up and educated in Normandy Edward would naturally be susceptible to it. But there are other possibilities. The simplest and perhaps the best is a quarrel with Godwin's authority. In the line of English kings there have been several who let themselves be manipulated up to a point, and then suddenly acted like kings. There is also the possibility that King Edward was taking an even firmer stand for celibacy. He was very sure, apparently, that he was not going to have an heir of his own body. For in this same year, 1051, he sent for a young man called William of Normandy to come to England on a visit, and he promised to leave him the throne.

This young Duke of Normandy was Edward's first cousin once removed. His grandfather, Richard II of Normandy, and Edward's mother Emma of Normandy had been brother and sister. He was, unfortunately, a bastard; except for that it was no wild idea that he should become King of England. Foreign royalty is often invited to fill a throne; this is the way the French Bourbons got the Spanish throne, the Austrian Hapsburgs the Mexican, the German Hohenzollerns the Rumanian, the Danish Schleswig-Holstein-Sonderburg-Glücksburgs the Greek. Even now there is a leftover belief in the divine right of kings. Also, a family reigning elsewhere is or should be expert because experienced in the art of reigning, and this may make them preferable to non-royal native talent however talented.

Nor was William a complete foreigner. He had no English blood, but the English, by this time, after two hundred years of successful Scandinavian raids and conquests, had a strong infusion of Norse blood—and Norman blood was Norse blood too, for the Normans were simply Norsemen who had settled and married in France. For that matter, the English and the French were alike, also, in sharing some Roman blood. Long before the Normans invaded England the Romans had conquered both their countries, and there never has been an occupying army that did not leave many babies behind. Perhaps the reason we have always understood the Romans so well, why Horace has been a universal solvent for so many generations of educated men, is that we are all some kin.

But King Edward could not effectively promise his throne to William of Normandy or anybody else. The Witan would have to make a choice. This was the way Edward had come to the throne himself, so nobody knew the procedure better than he did. After his half-brother King Hardicanute died, the Witan had voted for Edward as his replacement and then, while he was still living in Normandy, sent him an invitation to come to England and be crowned.

However, Edward did ask William of Normandy to succeed him; there seems no doubt about that. There would be dissension about whether or not he later changed his mind, but nobody questioned that he had made an initial commitment.

Meantime the Godwin family seethed in exile. But not for long. It took them only a year to come back. They came with a fleet, and a great show of force—which Edward, though he gathered an army together, decided not to test. Godwin came back. Godwin's able son Harold came back. Godwin's daughter Queen Edith came out of the nunnery Edward had told her to get to. One assumes that she and her husband were reconciled—as they certainly were later—at this time. If so, there was still the hope, however faint, that the marriage would be consummated and an heir born of it.

A child was never born, and King Edward did not change. He only grew more and more religious, more and more removed from the things of this world. His long white hair and beard were all his people needed, perhaps, to regard him with superstitious awe. But they began to come to him to have their sores and ulcers "touched." Many reported that they had been cured by having the King put his hands on them. Strangely, they did not seem to think of this talent for healing as a saintly attribute but as a kingly one; it became connected with the rank rather than with the ruler; and so as late as Queen Anne English subjects were flocking to be "touched" for "the King's Evil," as scrofula or any kind of skin disease came to be called. King Charles II, for instance, did not believe in this and absolutely hated doing it, but he had to. King Edward the Confessor loved it.

In everything he did now he was putting himself in line for this title, which most people find a baffling one. It seems to say so little. Of course King Edward was a confessor; he was a church member, and confessed when he went to church, before he took communion. Everybody did. To make a pretentious title out of this fact seems like singling out a child from a confirmation class and calling him Edward the Catechumen. There is a special definition for confessor, true (one who stands up for his faith in the face of persecution), but that does not fit King Edward—everybody around him was of his own faith and therefore no threat to his—and he was not, of course, a confessor in the priestly sense of hearing other people's confessions. Confessor is also a non-human noun, "the tomb of a martyred Christian; . . . an altar-tomb confessionary." King Edward was by no stretch of the imagination a martyred Christian, but miracles would take place at his altar-tomb just as if he had in fact been one, and the knees of the faithful would wear little hollows in the stone.

King Edward also dreamed dreams and saw visions. He dreamed once, for instance, that the Seven Sleepers of Ephesus had all turned on their left sides. Nobody, least of all the King, knew what this meant or portended, but it was all the more impressive for that. On his deathbed, he foretold a dark and troubled future for England.

As the King grew more and more mystical, the Godwin party—no doubt from necessity—grew more and more active. Somebody had to attend to the affairs of England. Earl Godwin died, but he left sons, and one of them, Harold, was as able and energetic as he. Descended through his mother from the Danish and Swedish royal houses, Harold like his sister Queen Edith bore no resemblance to King Harold Bluetooth; he was a tall, handsome man of the born-to-rule type that inspires devotion and confidence. He was making a very good job of ruling England, and as time passed it became apparent to many that this forceful man was not likely to step quietly aside, when the King did die, in favor of the King's faraway cousin who had no drop of English blood.

In 1066 King Edward had not seen William of Normandy for fifteen years. It had been in 1051, during the rift with the Godwins, that he had invited that young man to England and promised him the throne. It is entirely possible that he no longer cared whether or not William got it. He may well have come closer to his brother-in-law, as William receded in his memory. On his deathbed, entirely surrounded by Godwins— Queen Edith "warming his feet in her bosom," Harold Godwinson looming there the very ideal and image of a king—he very probably, as the Godwins said he did, repudiated his promise to William of Normandy.

Westminster Abbey had just been finished—just in time. The last hereditary Saxon king was the first of the Kings of England to be buried in it.

Suggested Reading

ELIZABETH II

Marion Crawford, *The Little Princesses* (Bantam, 1952)
Bernard Levin, *Run It Down the Flagpole: Britain in the Sixties* (Atheneum, 1971)
H. Tatlock Miller and Loudon Sainthill, *Undoubted Queen* (Doubleday, 1958)
Anthony Sampson, *The New Anatomy of Britain* (Stein and Day, 1972)

GEORGE VI

Angus Calder, *The People's War* (Pantheon, 1969)
Constantine Fitzgibbon, *The Winter of the Bombs* (Norton, 1957)
E. S. Turner, *The Phoney War* (St. Martin's, 1961)
John W. Wheeler-Bennett, *King George VI* (St. Martin's, 1958)

EDWARD VIII

A King's Story: The Memoirs of the Duke of Windsor (Putnam, 1951)

Lord Beaverbrook, *The Abdication of King Edward VIII* (Atheneum, 1966)

The Heart Has Its Reasons: The Memoirs of the Duchess of Windsor (McKay, 1956)

GEORGE V

Robert Graves and Alan Hodge, *The Long Week-End* (Norton, 1963)

Geoffrey Marcus, *Before the Lamps Went Out* (Little, Brown, 1965)

Sir Harold Nicolson, *King George V* (Constable, 1952)

Sir Frederick Ponsonby, *Recollections of Three Reigns* (Dutton, 1951)

EDWARD VII

Philippe Jullian, *Edward and the Edwardians* (Sidgwick & Jackson, 1967)

Philip Magnus, *King Edward VII* (Dutton, 1964)

J. B. Priestley, *The Edwardians* (Harper, 1970)

Sir Osbert Sitwell, *Left Hand, Right Hand!* (Little, Brown, 1944)

V. Sackville-West, *The Edwardians* (Doubleday, 1930)

VICTORIA

Robert Blake, *Disraeli* (St. Martin's, 1967)

Edward Boykin, ed., *Victoria, Albert, and Mrs. Stevenson* (Rinehart, 1957)

Lord David Cecil, *Melbourne* (Bobbs, 1954)

Elizabeth Longford, *Queen Victoria* (Pyramid, 1966)

Cecil Woodham-Smith, *Queen Victoria* (Knopf, 1972)

WILLIAM IV

Janet Dunbar, *A Prospect of Richmond* (Houghton, 1966)
Philip Ziegler, *King William IV* (Harper, 1973)

GEORGE IV

Terence Davis, *The Architecture of John Nash* (Studio, 1960)
Roger Fulford, *George IV* (Putnam, 1963)
John Gore, ed., *The Creevey Papers* (Macmillan, 1963)
Anita Leslie, *Mrs. Fitzherbert* (Scribners, 1960)
Donald Pilcher, *The Regency Style* (Batsford, 1947)

GEORGE III

John Brooke, *King George III* (McGraw, 1972)
Herbert Butterfield, *George III and the Historians* (Macmillan, 1959)
Alan Lloyd, *The King Who Lost America* (Doubleday, 1971)
John Summerson, *Georgian London* (Scribners, 1946)

GEORGE II

Alfred Bishop Mason, ed., *Horace Walpole's England* (Houghton, 1930)
John Fleming, *Robert Adam and His Circle* (Harvard, 1962)
J. H. Plumb, *Sir Robert Walpole* (Houghton, 1956)
Peter Quennell, *Caroline of England* (Viking, 1940)

GEORGE I

Roger Fulford, *Hanover to Windsor* (Wiley, 1960)
Henry M. Imbert-Terry, *Constitutional King: George the First* (Kenni-
kat, 1971)
R. J. Mincey, *No. 10 Downing Street* (Little, Brown, 1963)
Alvin Redman, *The House of Hanover* (Coward, 1960)

ANNE

Winston S. Churchill, *Marlborough*, abridged by Henry Steele Commager (Scribners, 1968)

Viktor Furst, *The Architecture of Sir Christopher Wren* (Lund Humphries, 1956)

David Green, *Queen Anne* (Scribners, 1972)

Louis Kronenberger, *Marlborough's Duchess* (Knopf, 1958)

Nikolaus Pevsner, *Christopher Wren* (Universe Books, 1960)

WILLIAM AND MARY

Elizabeth Hamilton, *William's Mary* (Taplinger, 1972)

R. J. Minney, *Hampton Court* (Coward, 1972)

Stuart E. Prall, *The Bloodless Revolution: England 1688* (Doubleday, 1972)

Nesca E. Robb, *William of Orange*, 2 vols. (St. Martin's, 1962, 1966)

Lawrence Stone, *The Causes of the English Revolution* (Harper, 1972)

JAMES II

The Memoirs of James II: His Campaigns as Duke of York (Indiana, 1962)

Graham Norton, *Discovering London*, vol. 5 (Macdonald, 1969)

V. de Sola Pinto, *Sir Charles Sedley* (Boni, 1927)

Joseph R. Tanner, *Samuel Pepys and the Royal Navy* (Haskell, 1971)

CHARLES II

Maurice Ashley, *Charles II* (Praeger, 1971)

Hester W. Chapman, *The Tragedy of Charles II* (Little, Brown, 1964)

Oliver Hill and John Cornforth, *English Country Houses: Caroline 1625–1685* (Country Life, 1966)

James Leasor, *The Plague and the Fire* (McGraw-Hill, 1961)
Gertrude Z. Thomas, *Richer Than Spices* (Knopf, 1965)

CHARLES I

Christopher Hibbert, *Charles I* (Harper, 1968)
Christopher Hill, *The World Turned Upside Down* (Viking, 1972)
C. V. Wedgwood, *The King's Peace 1637–1641* (Macmillan, 1955)
C. V. Wedgwood, *The King's War 1641–1647* (Macmillan, 1959)
Hugh Ross Williamson, *The Day They Killed the King* (Macmillan, 1957)

JAMES I

G. P. V. Akrigg, *Jacobean Pageant* (Harvard, 1962)
Miriam Allen deFord, *The Overbury Affair* (Chilton, 1960)
Catherine Drinker Bowen, *Francis Bacon* (Little, Brown, 1963)
David H. Wilson, *King James Sixth and First* (Oxford, 1967)

ELIZABETH I

Antonia Fraser, *Mary Queen of Scots* (Weidenfeld and Nicolson, 1969)
Elizabeth Jenkins, *Elizabeth the Great* (Berkley, 1972)
Robert Lacey, *Sir Walter Ralegh* (Atheneum, 1973)
Garrett Mattingly, *The Armada* (Houghton, 1959)
Willard M. Wallace, *Sir Walter Raleigh* (Princeton, 1959)
Neville Williamson, *All the Queen's Men* (Macmillan, 1972)

MARY I

David Loth, *Philip II of Spain* (Brentano, 1932)
H. F. Prescott, *Spanish Tudor* (Macmillan, 1940)

Thomas S. Szasz, *Manufacture of Madness* (Harper, 1970)
Milton Waldman, *The Lady Mary* (Scribners, 1972)

EDWARD VI

The Book of Common Prayer
Hester W. Chapman, *The Last Tudor King* (Macmillan, 1959)
W. K. Jordan, *Edward VI*, 2 vols. (Harvard, 1970)

HENRY VIII

Marie Louise Bruce, *Anne Boleyn* (Coward, 1972)
Arthur G. Dickens and Dorothy Carr, *Reformation in England to the Accession of Elizabeth I* (St. Martin's, 1968)
Garrett Mattingly, *Catherine of Aragon* (Vintage, 1960)
Lacey B. Smith, *Henry VIII* (Houghton, 1973)
Neville Williams, *Henry VIII and His Court* (Macmillan, 1971)

HENRY VII

S. B. Chrimes, *Henry VII* (California, 1972)
Roger Lockyer, *Henry VII* (Harper, 1972)
H. V. Morton, *In Search of London* (Dodd, Mead, 1951)
Graham Norton, *Discovering London*, vol. 4 (Macdonald, 1969)
A. L. Rowse, *Bosworth Field* (Doubleday, 1966)

RICHARD III

Paul Murray Kendall, *Richard the Third* (Doubleday, 1965)
Taylor D. Littleton, *To Prove a Villain* (Macmillan, 1964)
Clements R. Markham, *Richard III* (Russell, 1968)
Josephine Tey, *The Daugher of Time* (Macmillan, 1952)

EDWARD V

John Langdon-Davies, *Richard III and the Princes in the Tower* (Grossman, 1965)
Ruth McKenney and Richard Bransten, *Here's England* (Harper, 1955)
R. J. Minney, *The Tower of London* (Prentice, 1970)

EDWARD IV

Mary Clive, *The Sun of York: A Biography of Edward IV* (Knopf, 1973)
Paul Murray Kendall, *Warwick the Kingmaker* (Norton, 1957)
Paul Murray Kendall, *The Yorkist Age* (Norton, 1962)
J. R. Lander, *The Wars of the Roses* (Putnam, 1965)

HENRY VI

A. D. Browne and C. T. Seltmen, *Queens' College Cambridge* (Cambridge, 1951)
Philippe Erlanger, *Margaret of Anjou* (Miami, 1970)
B. J. W. Hill, *Windsor and Eton* (Batsford, 1957)
Edgecumbe Staley, *King René d'Anjou and His Seven Queens* (Scribners, 1912)

HENRY V

Christopher Hibbert, *Agincourt* (Dufour, 1964)
Harold F. Hutchison, *King Henry V* (John Day, 1967)
Enid McLeod, *Charles of Orleans* (Viking, 1969)

HENRY IV

J. L. Kirby, *Henry IV of England* (Shoe String, 1971)

RICHARD II

Roger Hart, *English Life in Chaucer's Day* (Putnam, 1973)
Harold F. Hutchison, *The Hollow Crown: A Life of Richard II* (John Day, 1961)

EDWARD III

Sir Arthur Bryant, *The Mediaeval Foundation of England* (Doubleday, 1967)
W. F. Grimes, *The Excavation of Roman and Mediaeval London* (Praeger, 1968)
Ranald Nicholson, *Edward III and the Scots* (Oxford, 1965)

EDWARD II

Harold F. Hutchison, *Edward II* (Stein and Day, 1972)
Graham Norton, *Discovering London*, vol. 3 (Macdonald, 1969)

EDWARD I

Sir Arthur Bryant, *The Age of Chivalry* (Doubleday, 1963)
Louie Butler Elwood and J. W. Elwood, Jr., *The Rebellious Welsh* (Ward Pitchie Press, 1951)
Theodore F. Plucknett, *Edward I and Criminal Law* (Cambridge, 1960)
L. F. Salzman, *Edward I* (Praeger, 1968)
Nigel Tranter, *Robert the Bruce* (St. Martin's, 1972)

HENRY III

Edward Carpenter, *A House of Kings* (John Day, 1966)
Frederick M. Powicke, *King Henry Third and the Lord Edward* (Oxford, 1947)

JOHN

Alfred Duggan, *Devil's Brood* (Arrow Books, 1960)
James Goldman, *The Lion in Winter* (Dell, 1968)
Alan Lloyd, *The Maligned Monarch* (Doubleday, 1972)

RICHARD I

John T. Appleby, *England Without Richard 1189–1199* (Cornell, 1965)
Philip Henderson, *Richard Coeur de Lion* (Norton, 1959)

HENRY II

Jean Anouilh, *Becket* (Signet, 1964)
Richard Barber, *Henry Plantagenet* (Rowman & Littlefield, 1972)
Thomas R. Jones, *The Becket Controversy* (Wiley, 1970)
Amy Kelly, *Eleanor of Aquitaine and the Four Kings* (Harvard, 1950)
W. L. Warren, *Henry II* (California, 1973)

STEPHEN

John T. Appleby, *The Troubled Reign of King Stephen* (Barnes, 1970)
R. H. C. Davis, *King Stephen* (California, 1967)

MATILDA

Christopher Brooke, *From Alfred to Henry Third* (Norton, 1966)

HENRY I

Winston S. Churchill, *The Birth of Britain* (Bantam, 1963)

WILLIAM II

Duncan Grinell-Milne, *The Killing of William Rufus* (Kelley, 1968)
Hilary St. George Saunders, *Westminster Hall* (Michael Joseph, 1951)

WILLIAM I

Denis Butler, *1066: The Story of a Year* (Putnam, 1966)
David C. Douglas, *William the Conqueror* (California, 1964)
Christopher Hibbert, *The Tower of London* (Newsweek, 1971)
The Last Invasion, 1066–1966: An Official Publication for the 900th Anniversary of the Battle of Hastings
Graham Norton, *Discovering London*, vol. 2 (Macdonald, 1969)

HAROLD

Alan Lloyd, *The Making of the King 1066* (Holt, 1966)
Hope Muntz, *The Golden Warrior* (Scribners, 1949)

EDWARD THE CONFESSOR

Frank Barlow, *Edward the Confessor* (California, 1970)
David Piper, *Fodor's London: A Companion Guide* (McKay, 1971)

An Index of People and Places

Abdul Karim (*see* Munshi)

Acre, Siege of, 203–4

Accursi, Francisco, 184

Act of Settlement, 3, 56–7, 68, 73

Adams, John, 46

Addington (Scotland), 181

Adela of England, Countess of Blois, daughter of William I, 215

Adelaide of Saxe-Meiningen, Queen of William IV, 28, 35–7, 212

Adelicia of Louvain, second Queen of Henry I, 223

ADMIRALTY, Whitehall, London SW1, 35. Nelson lay here after Trafalgar, in the Old Admiralty—the porticoed 1725 building behind the cobbled courtyard behind the Adam screen. (Notice the sea-horses.) The 1903 New Admiralty stretches out behind it; see this from St. James's Park (*q.v.*), where it forms the left side of Horse Guards Parade. Added on is the Citadel, built bomb-proof if not beautiful in World War II. None of this is for tourists inside; the Navy is busy. (Or the Ministry of Defence, which everything is under now.) Admiralty House, accessible only through the Old Admiralty, is private also. It was built (1786) for the First Lord of the Admiralty, but there is no such person any more. The Queen now holds the older title of Lord High Admiral and she lives elsewhere, so perhaps this beautiful house, with its splendid portraits and its horrendous gold furniture held up by dolphins, may yet be opened. Some very famous First Lords lived here—Earl Howe, the Earl of Chatham, William IV as Duke of Clarence, Winston Churchill (in both wars), Austen Chamberlain, Arthur Balfour, Brenden Bracken, W. H. Smith (the bookstore man) who never went to sea and was the model for Admiral Sir Joseph Porter in *Pinafore*.

beginning and end of the new Palace of Whitehall which James I was starting Inigo Jones to build in 1619. With his slightly earlier Queen's House (q.v.) at Greenwich, it revolutionized English architecture. The classical period had arrived. Outside, the Banqueting House is so perfectly proportioned that it looks plain, in spite of garlands and pediments and two kinds of orders; inside, there is only one huge double-cube room (over a vaulted undercroft) with a gallery as at Queen's House and the Rubens ceiling. This was an afterthought ten years later, when Rubens happened to come to London. "Read" its nine panels from the far end—not that they make too much sense in any order. Along with the good and the beautiful things about classical revival an infestation of gambolling Greeks had arrived, and politicians would soon be painted and sculpted wearing Roman togas. James I, the Defender of the Faith, is being received not by heavenly angels but by heathen gods, his family looking on; and all of them were looking on in 1649 when Charles I, his son, walked through this room and stepped out of an annex window to a scaffold and his execution. This event changed the character of the building; it has never been simply a banqueting house since; and there has been some uncertainty about what to use it for. George I converted it into a royal chapel; that lapsed; the Royal United Services had it for many years as a museum. At the moment it is empty again and, like Westminster Hall, this is the way it looks best.

Bardolf, Thomas, Lord, 160

Barnet, Battle of, 129, 144

BATH, Somerset, 80. Probably the most beautiful town in England, and the most un-English. Long before the Romans, people were attracted to the hot springs; but the Romans built the baths. They are an impressive layout, with a two thousand-year-old conduit still in use. There is a Roman museum. But Bath's greatest period was the eighteenth century, when the present city arose, a planned, sophisticated city built all of gold-colored Bath stone, and so unified, like Paris. The dandy Beau Nash, its social arbiter, made Bath the resort of resorts. Look at the houses marked with famous names, from Jane Austen to General Wolfe, Clive to Herschel, Gainsborough to Edmund Burke. Look at whole streets: Queen Square, North and

South Parades, Lansdowne Crescent, Royal Crescent, the Circus, and colonnaded Bath Street. Look at the Assembly Rooms, Pump Room, Guildhall, Octagon; at Pulteney Bridge with shops like a Georgian Ponte Vecchio. Bath Abbey, in clean matching stone, seems no older than all of these, but it was founded 1499 on the ruins of a Norman church. On the west front, angels ascend and descend a heaven-ladder. Inside, notice the Norman arch and pillar-base, the tombs of Malthus (political economy), of Pitman (shorthand), and of a royal American governor, Thomas Pownell. Obviously there is a nice memorial to Beau Nash, too.

BERKELEY CASTLE, Gloucestershire, 178–9. Built by the Berkeley family about 1155; they have kept it 800 years and preserved it beautifully. The room where Edward II was murdered is just the same, though some alterations in the castle were made in 1340. Circular keep, moat, dungeon, state apartments, great hall, tapestries —this castle has everything, even a bowling alley in the Elizabethan garden. Berkeleys are buried in the Norman-Gothic Church of St. Mary the Virgin, in nearby Berkeley; Edward, in Gloucester Cathedral (*q.v.*).

BERWICK CASTLE, Northumberland, 181–2. Fragments of the castle (two towers) and traces of the wall he also built recall Edward I, but the thrifty national habit of taking stones from an old building for a new building has made a ruin out of many a slightly damaged house. More interesting than the castle is its town of Berwick-upon-Tweed, founded 870, a bone of contention between Scotland and England because it stood on the border. Changing hands thirteen times before 1482, it has been English since. The town's Ramparts, famous among engineers as the earliest English example of "modern" military construction (over a century before Vauban), were begun in the first year of Elizabeth I's reign, 1558.

Bishops' Wars, 87

Black Death, 173

Black Prince (*see* Edward)

BLACKHEATH, Shooter's Hill, London SE3, 156. A wide open space near Greenwich, chiefly famous for eighteenth-century highwaymen. But it was also a famous campground. The Danes camped here in 1011, Wat Tyler's men in 1381, Jack Cade's in 1450. Here James I first showed the English the Scottish game of golf. Offside, notice some good Georgian domestic architecture, a crescent called The Paragon, and Morden College, a home for old merchants of the City of London. Sir John Morden, whose statue with his wife's is over the door, lost all he had in the world when his three merchant ships sailed over the horizon; after they turned up again he remembered how bad it was for a rich man to be suddenly poor. Morden College provides in a Wren building with Gibbons carving private suites for Sir John's friends and brothers, not just rooms; wine with their meals; a good library and a beautiful garden; and, the generous endowment having greatly appreciated, modern luxuries as well—in the chapel pews, for instance, individual "deaf-aids."

✓BLENHEIM PALACE, Woodstock, Oxfordshire, 67. Built by a grateful nation for the first Duke of Marlborough, the victor of Blenheim. Begun 1705. In spite of constant interference by the Duchess, it is Sir John Vanbrugh's baroque masterpiece, a heavy, impressive and depressing stone institution, not a house. (Sir John's position, of course, was that the Duke himself was an institution and that Blenheim was his monument, not his house. His taste in architecture, also, had been affected by his imprisonment in the Château of Vincennes.) The Great Hall is sixty-seven feet high. In the seven acres covered by the palace and courts, see the Thornhill ceiling, the battle flags, tapestries, the Long Library (180′ long), the chapel with the monument to "John Duke," as the family call him, the State Rooms, and the far from state bedroom where Sir Winston Churchill, always a young man in a hurry, was born to a beautiful American mother who had been dancing till the last minute, and was at least a mile from her own room. Sir Winston, incidentally, is not buried in the Blenheim chapel crypt but in the churchyard at Bladon, on the southeast side of the park—the park that was once Henry II's hunting preserve, now ceremonially landscaped with a triumphal gate, a victory column, a huge artificial lake, on which tourists can take cruises when they tire of the model railroad, and trees planted to show the way the troops were drawn up at the Battle of Blenheim.

Blitz, London, 10, 225
Blondel de Nesle, 204
Boadicea, 6
Boer War, 25, 33
Bohun, Mary de, Duchess of Lancaster, first wife of Henry IV, 159
Boleyn, Anne, second Queen of Henry VIII, 3, 95, 97, 103, 112–5, 195
Boleyn, George (*see* Rochford)
Bolingbroke, Castle of, 153
Bolingbroke, Henry of (*see* Henry IV)
Bombay, 82
Bonaparte, Napoleon, 47–8
Boniface of Bellay, Archbishop of Canterbury, 187
Bonnie Prince Charlie (*see* Charles Edward Stuart)
Book of Common Prayer, 9, 87, 108

√BRIGHTON PAVILION, Brighton, Sussex, 41. In this attractive seacoast resort George IV as a young prince installed Mrs. Fitzherbert and then began remodeling a house for himself. First Holland made it into a classical temple, with a rotunda and chaste small dome; then, during the Regency, Nash went whole hog with a huge onion-shaped dome and several smaller ones, pavilions with tent-shaped roofs, a forest of minarets, and an embarrassment of small detail. It is pre-Hollywood Indian, Arabian, and Turkish, and inside it is Chinese. No expense was spared, no surface left unornamented. The ceiling of the banqueting room is a huge palm-tree, its chandelier a frightening dragon, its painted walls not exactly background. None of this was Queen Victoria's taste. The Royal Pavilion was closed in 1845 and the town of Brighton bought it in 1850. Since World War II it has been brilliantly restored and, with many original furnishings and pictures returned by the present Queen, it must be seen to be believed.

BRISTOL, Gloucestershire, 178, 188, 215. The castle is gone; it will take a vivid imagination to see King Stephen's imprisonment here in 1141, fifteen years after Robert of Gloucester rebuilt it, and Prince Rupert of the Rhine's making it headquarters during the King's War. Oliver Cromwell unfortunately "slighted" it in 1655. But Bristol (half a million people by now) is also the seaport from which the Cabots sailed in 1497; it has a great cathedral, some of it dating from the twelfth century, and three important churches, All Saints, St. Mark, and St. Mary Redcliffe, the one Queen Elizabeth called "the fairest, the goodliest, and most famous parish church in England."

√BRITISH MUSEUM, Bloomsbury, London EC, 108. "The collections of the British Museum," says the official guidebook, in famous British understatement, "cannot be studied in a single visit." Tourists pressed for time usually want to see the Rosetta Stone, with its parallel columns of text that opened up the world of antiquity to the scholar; the blue and white glass Portland Vase; the Elgin Marbles (not Elgin as in America—hard "G") which Lord Elgin bought and paid for in Greece, though the Greeks still act as if he stole them; the recently reunited Venus; the Sutton Hoo ship-burial and the Mildenhall Treasure; Magna Carta; Nelson's log-book; the manuscript of Beowulf; the prayer book Lady Jane Grey carried to the scaffold; the Mausoleum from Halicarnassus, one of the Seven Wonders of the World; the punch-bowl from which Burns drank far too much— these are individually famous. People who are impressed by great quantities should look at mummies, maps, drawings, jewelry ("jewellery," the English call it), medals, coins, pottery and glass, stamps— and, of course, the books. Every book published in Britain must be sent free to the British Museum Library, which means they use more than a mile of new shelving every year. Sir Robert Smirke's fine colonnaded building, only a hundred and fifty years old, already winged and annexed, is constantly being outgrown; with London University it is about to engulf Bloomsbury. Its center, the Reading Room, is a sight not to be missed, even by non-readers with neither time nor inclination to get a ticket from their Embassy—dome 140 feet in diameter, 106 feet high, raised supervisory desk ringed round with catalogues and desks for readers, a fine hush, a special smell. In seat G7 Karl Marx wrote *Das Kapital*; some of the present occupants appear to be up to something similar; others are plainly by Daumier. Most British Museum readers are, of course, perfectly respectable and level-headed and even eminent scholars, but there is always, with books piled high around him, at least one descendant of Edward V or Mrs. Fitzherbert or the Sobieski Stuarts, feverishly working to fill in one last little gap because then he will be King of England.

Mary's the Great to the Church of the Holy Sepulchre, one of the few left that were built round, like the original in Jerusalem. This one dates back to c.1130 and stands in a rose-garden.

Cambridge, Adolphus, Duke of, 35

Cambridge Terrace (*see* REGENT'S PARK)

Campeggio, Lorenzo, Cardinal of Santa Anastasia, 112–3

Canada, 10–1

Canning, George, 35, 42

Canterbury, Boniface of Bellay, Archbishop of (*see* Boniface)

✓CANTERBURY CATHEDRAL, Canterbury, Kent, 126, 136, 210–1. Begun about 1070 near the site of a fourth-century Christian church; since 1072, when William the Conqueror put his mark to a document settling an un-Christian quarrel over supremacy between the archbishops of Canterbury and York, the seat of the primate of the Anglican Church. Since 1170, when the Archbishop Thomas à Becket was murdered, and Henry II was scourged in punishment here, it has been a shrine. Canterbury, so much more accessible than Jerusalem or Rome, combined miracles with pleasure. Picking the nicest time of year—Aprille with his shoures sote—taking it at the easy, natural gait which they called the Canterbury gallop and we call the canter, enlivened by story-tellers, jugglers, minstrels, and frequent stops for refreshment along the way, the pilgrims arrived finally to a real tourist welcome. Only a city by-law checked the Canterbury innkeeper's urge to "catch them by their reins, their clothing or their Staves and try to make them come into his Inn, . . . shouting at the said Pilgrims and strangers passing along, inviting him in. . . ." But inside the Cathedral, then as now, silence fell. The spot where Thomas à Becket stood, backed against a pillar to fight off his murderers, is marked with a small stone slab. He became St. Thomas; his shrine was built behind the high altar, soon enriched by such offerings as the gold crown of Scotland (Edward I) and the famous jewel called the Regale of France (Louis VII). At the Reformation, the Regale appeared on the thumb of Henry VIII, the shrine was ordered destroyed (though people kept coming, anyway), and Becket's tomb was obliterated. You cannot find it now. See, however, the magnificent tomb of the Black Prince, the tombs of Henry IV and his Queen, of Cardinal Pole, of many archbishops; the screen with statues of Edward the Confessor, Richard II, Henry IV, V, VI; the portrait windows of Edward IV and his Queen. Look particularly at Canterbury's wonderful painted glass, taken out before the air raids of 1942 and 1943; it took four years to fit it back in.

CHARING CROSS, Charing Cross, London WC2, 183. The very center of London. The name Charing comes from chèrereine, the beloved queen it recalls; the cross is a reproduction of the one erected by Edward I in 1291, and removed by Cromwell, 1647. The Albert Memorial is also modeled on these crosses; Anthony Eden's father said he would like to see "all the bad architects of Britain buried at the foot of the Albert Memorial." *Amen!*

underneath the towers, a fifteenth-century piece of artillery named Mons Meg (not the thing they shoot off at one o'clock every afternoon), a banqueting hall, a war memorial, and the room in which Mary Queen of Scots gave birth to her son James. It is Holyrood Palace, however, that seems most associated with this most famous queen. Here she came to live after her French widowhood, here she was berated by John Knox, saw the murder of Rizzio, and was married to Bothwell, who had probably raped her at Castle Dunbar, only three months after the mysterious murder of her first husband. It is interesting, incidentally, to notice that holier-than-thou inscription on John Knox's house in the High Street—"Lufe God abufe al. . . ." If you read that second *f* as a long-tailed *s* you have a thumbnail sketch of John Knox. He had a nice house, though, and so did Lady Stair and the Achesons and Huntlys and Queensberrys along the Royal Mile. Deacon Brodie lived here too, the sanctimonious hypocrite they hanged in 1788. But Canongate is only one of the teeming streets in Old Town, which has "the most beautiful slums in the world" as well as, in the space between Princes Street and The Meadows, things like the Scott Monument, the National Gallery, the Royal Scottish Academy, and New College. As for New Town, you have seen it before, in Paris, in Bath, a regularly drawn design predicated on the level ground which Old Town did not have, Charlotte Square at one end, St. Andrew Square at the other, George Street linking them, the longest street in town. Look at the north side of Charlotte Square, by Robert Adam himself (1791) and most beautifully restored by the fourth Marquess of Bute, whom Scotland must thank also for the time and money he spent on Caerphilly Castle. Here is the rational, civilized architecture you may prefer; here are some of the best restaurants in town, and good hotels; whether you have come to the Festival, or to see the soldiers drill on the Castle Esplanade, or to look up your ancestors in Register House or buy a cairngorm brooch or try a tartan, you will understand in New Town as well as Old how very national Scotland still is, and why it is just as non-U in Scotland to say "British" as it is in England. Scots who ha' wi' Wallace bled will bleed again if you call them anything else.

they were building the tomb with its elaborate stone canopy and beautiful recumbent figure—surely this alabaster head is a likeness— they also remodeled the east end of the church and the cloisters. The beautiful east window, its original glass intact, dates from this time, and the cloisters show the earliest fan-vaulting which survives in England. Notice the carvels (what modern libraries call carrels), the Norman lavatorium (frankly a trough), and especially the tomb of Robert Curthose, Duke of Normandy. This tomb too has a recumbent effigy, painted in gorgeous colors and with a gold coronet, and shows poor Robert Curthose, too late as usual, in the act of reaching for his sword.

✓ HAMPTON COURT, Middlesex, 59, 72, 80, 117. Most beautiful royal palace. Built by Cardinal Wolsey for himself in 1514; with 280 guestrooms and 500 servants, it was obviously more suitable for a king than for a churchman. So Henry VIII thought and showed, and Wolsey rather hastily gave him Hampton Court for a present. Henry added to the palace—an indoor tennis court, for instance, 1529 and still in use. He decorated it here and there with "devices" entwining his initial with Anne Boleyn's, and then changed the queen's initial whenever he changed queens. (See one example outside the chapel door.) Five of his six queens lived here, and one of them haunts it, Catherine Howard, who runs screaming along a corridor. Here Henry's son Edward was born, his daughter Mary honeymooned with Philip of Spain, his daughter Elizabeth had smallpox. Anne of Denmark died here, Charles I took refuge from a London mob, Cromwell was mortally stricken, Charles II brought poor little Catherine of Braganza, whose rivals' portraits fill a special gallery called the Hampton Court Beauties. (If they disappoint you, remember that double chins were then in style, as shaved foreheads had been in Plantagenet times.) James II did not live at Hampton Court as king, but when his daughter Mary and her husband took over they moved there at once. William III suffered from asthma and could barely get his breath in London. They called in Sir Christopher Wren and built a huge new palace onto the old—tearing some of it down. You still come over the moat (noticing the Queen's Beasts) and through the Tudor gatehouse, but when you have gone through Base Court and Clock Court and Fountain Court you are in an entirely different kind of building. William's greatest enemy was Louis XIV, so he was trying to overcome Versailles too. The state rooms are spectacular; most people think they have too much of everything, and prefer Henry VIII's Great Hall. No royalty has really lived at Hampton Court since George II, but many old friends of royalty occupy "Grace and Favour" apartments, so some parts of the palace are not open. But much of it is, and with its gardens, orangery, tiltyard, banqueting house, and Great Vine (planted in George III's time, now the size of a tree, still loaded with grapes you can buy) it will detain the visitor at least a day—more, if you get lost in the maze.

The builder of new Hardwick (who had been born in the old) started marrying at the age of twelve and buried four husbands, getting richer every time. Elizabeth Hardwick Barlow Cavendish St. Loe Shrewsbury, "Bess of Hardwick," was a high-nosed, hard-nosed old lady who enters history as the co-jailer of Mary Queen of Scots. Her fourth husband, the Earl of Shrewsbury, had been given that unenviable task by his own queen; and there was, of course, trouble. One complication was the fact that Bess Shrewsbury's granddaughter, Arabella Stuart, was very close to the English throne. Her father was Lord Darnley's brother. There was considerable hope that Queen Elizabeth, not liking James—she had never wanted James—would name Arabella her heir; but Arabella herself scotched that. She got the idea of marrying young William Seymour who as Lady Catherine Grey's grandson was also very close to the throne, and the Queen hated that family even more than she hated James. At this very idea, Arabella was put in prison. She escaped; she did marry her young man; but she was captured again and thrust into the Tower. She died there four years later, quite insane. Her grandmother's dearest dream was at an end. But she was not the type that dies of bitter disappointment. The pleasures of building could take the old Countess's mind off almost anything. She had built or altered everywhere she lived—at Chatsworth, Bolsover, Welbeck, Oldcotes, Worksop, Tutbury; but Hardwick Hall (1591–96) was her masterpiece. She signed it proudly, ES and a coronet standing out against the sky on all of the towers, not just one. Next most noticeable are the tremendous windows. The famous Robert Smythson is supposed to have been the architect, but is not supposed, by those who know Bess of Hardwick, to have been on the decision-making level.

where Elizabeth stayed on two occasions; she was staying there when she got the news of her accession.) But the house itself, not the contents, is the great attraction at Hatfield. In the early nineteenth century the second Marquess was moved to embellish and improve; he had the white ceilings so beautifully and expensively painted and gold-leafed that it would be out of the question to restore them to their original state; and the family who now walk in comfort from one wing to the other are not likely to make the armory an open portico again, with the wind whistling through as it did before the second Marquess filled in the floor-to-ceiling arches. But try to imagine Hatfield House without these well-meaning improvements. Notice the imaginative fireplaces, one with a double shell over it, one with a mosaic portrait inlaid, one with a plaster statue of James I, one a carved stone coat of arms. Notice particularly the Grand Staircase —Italian Renaissance in English oak—with an intricately carved pair of gates at the bottom, to keep the dogs downstairs. Notice the galleried library; this is one great-house library which has been used, for the building ancestor and his father, Lord Treasurers (Prime Ministers) to James I and Queen Elizabeth respectively, were not the last intellectuals in their family. The third Marquess, three times prime minister himself, was also a distinguished chemist, and his grandson, Lord David Cecil, is the author of the classic biography *Melbourne.*

HEVER CASTLE, Edenbridge, near Tonbridge, Kent, 115. If you saw the movie *Anne of a Thousand Days* you have already seen Hever Castle. Built in 1453 by Sir Geoffrey Boleyn, Lord Mayor of London, it was remodeled about 1584 and, having become a ruin by that time, extensively done over three hundred years later by a rich American. Lady Astor's father-in-law, who became the first Viscount Astor, came to England in 1890 and had a very fine time buying real estate. In addition to Lansdowne House he bought two other houses in London; he bought Cliveden; but Hever Castle seems to have been the most fun of all. He diverted the course of the Eden River—it took 1,500 men five years—to create a new forty-acre lake; he renovated the castle, with particular attention to the gate, drawbridge, and moat; and safely on the outside of this (he had the drawbridge pulled up every night) he built a Tudor-style village for the accommodation of his guests. Why Mr. Astor, a man who slept with two revolvers at his bedside, invited these dangerous people to visit him we do not know; nor why the ruins on his property of an earlier castle, built by

Westminster Hall offers nothing so lightminded. Its past includes banquets, celebrations, and, judging from tennis balls found lodged in the roof, games; but solemn legal processes and lyings-in-state (George V, George VI, Sir Winston) are more generally associated with it. Here Sir William Wallace and Sir Thomas More, the Earl of Strafford and King Charles I, were tried for their lives, and the Duchess of Kingston for bigamy. Here were seen Cromwell's greatest triumph and greatest ignominy; he was inaugurated Lord Protector in Westminster Hall, and then after the Restoration his body was dug up and decapitated and the head hung here for twenty years. But almost all the time, now, Westminster Hall is empty. The business of government goes on in the Gothic buildings (1840–49) of Charles Barry, who had won a competition. You will see his House of Lords, but his House of Commons was destroyed by enemy action in 1941. Sir Giles Gilbert Scott designed its worthy successor and it was built 1948–50. It is impossible to describe briefly. Every meticulous detail is loaded with symbolism, from the Woolsack stuffed with every kind of British wool to the conference table inlaid with two hundred woods, one from each territory. An iron lantern lit in the clock tower shows when the Houses are sitting at night; in the House of Commons there is a green bag behind the Speaker's chair for the reception of petitions; snuff boxes are still provided for members, and red tape in the members' cloak-room for hanging up their swords; there is a certain prayer used since 1660. The whole idea is to make everything seem unchanged, and it does. It is mildly shocking to be reminded how new the buildings are, how much older our own Capitol in Washington is.

This is, of course, the castle of Sir Walter Scott's *Kenilworth*. Read it when you get home. Built in the twelfth century by Geoffrey de Clinton, it belonged in the thirteenth century to Simon de Montfort and in the fourteenth to John of Gaunt, Duke of Lancaster. It was John who turned the big keep into something more than a fortress by adding a two-storied wing, called Lancaster Building later if not then, with a Great Hall 90 x 45. Kenilworth was still not quite fit for a king, though, and Henry VIII's Lodging was built, a Tudor wing at the other end of the keep.

Then in 1563 Queen Elizabeth gave the Castle to her favorite, Lord Robert Dudley, whom she soon after created Earl of Leicester. He made still another addition, joining the Lancaster and Tudor wings to make the Castle into a hollow square. In 1570 he fortified it, engaging the Italian military engineer Julio Spinelli; and he furnished it most beautifully and expensively. Leicester was one of the first people to use oriental rugs on his floors instead of rushes. In 1575 he gave for the Queen a house-party that is still talked about—eighteen days at £1,000 a day, fireworks, tumblers, bear-baiting, plays, dancing—and he need not have bothered, because then he married somebody else and she never forgave him. His castle never had another such master; though it had withstood attack in Simon de Montfort's time, it was partly destroyed in Cromwell's, and nobody lived in it after the Restoration. After three hundred years it is a romantic ruin.

Kennedy, Mrs. John F., 18

KENSINGTON PALACE, Kensington Gardens, London W8, 37, 54, 72. It was not always practical for William and Mary to shuttle between London and Hampton Court, so they put another palace in hand. Nottingham House, renamed Kensington, was much closer in but still beyond the urban pollution which aggravated William's asthma. Again, Sir Christopher Wren was the architect. Again, you cannot see the whole of the Palace, for there are people living here, among them Princess Margaret and her family; but the State Rooms are open, the Cupola Room where Queen Victoria was baptized (this is later, c.1720, and by Kent instead of Wren), and her nursery and adolescent bedroom. This is where the Princess Victoria was sleeping when the official gentlemen came to tell her she was Queen of England. But like George III, who would never live at Hampton Court because George II had boxed his ears there, Victoria as Queen had no idea of living in Kensington Palace, the scene of her mother's snubbings and domineering. These rooms are an informal museum, but there is also a regular museum housed in Kensington Palace, the London Museum which is to London what the Carnavalet is to Paris, devoted to the city itself and nothing more. The dioramas are the most attractive—one of the Fire, one of the winter when the Thames froze over and little shops were built on the ice, one of London

Bridge covered with half-timbered houses, one of nineteenth-century Piccadilly traffic. There is a gorgeous collection of costumes, with always a few people cooing over the long ivory-lace sheaths the little princesses wore to the coronation of George VI. There are artifacts from every period of the history of London; now that the buildings are getting taller, the digging is getting deeper, and all kinds of things are turning up—a Neolithic bowl, for instance, on the site of Heathrow Airport.

Kent, Edward, Duke of, father of Queen Victoria (1767–1820), 35–6

Kent, George, Duke of (1902–1942), 8

Kent, Joan, Countess of (*see* Joan)

Kent, Victoria of Saxe-Coburg-Saalfeld, Duchess of, Princess of Leiningen, mother of Queen Victoria, 28, 36–7

Kenya, 5

Keppel, Alice Edmonstone, the Hon. Mrs. George, 24, 26–7

Kéroualle, Louise de, Duchess of Portsmouth, 76, 80

KEW GARDENS, KEW PALACE, Kew, Surrey, 48. The most famous botanical gardens in the world, laid out in 1759 by George III's mother. It was just a garden then. Since then it has spread to 288 acres, acquired a palm house (Decimus Burton), a pagoda (Sir William Chambers), very extensive big glasshouses, a herbarium (7,000,000 plants), a library (50,000 volumes), and the tallest flagpole in the world. A great deal of valuable scientific research goes on behind the scenes. But tourists can see the flowers, which are spectacular, and little Kew Palace, which "Farmer George"—George III—loved. It is the most unspectacular palace anywhere. Built in 1631, it looks more like its other name, Dutch House.

Kielmansegge, Sophie Charlotte, Countess of Darlington, 57

King James Version, 91, 94

"Kingmaker" (*see* Warwick)

King's Bench, Court of, 76

King's College, Cambridge (*see* CAMBRIDGE)

King's War, 87

Kitchener, Field Marshal Sir Horatio Herbert Kitchener, later Earl, 20

Kneller, Sir Godfrey, 57–8

√ LINCOLN, Lincolnshire, 218. The town gate the Romans left is probably the most interesting thing in town. Look at the Newport Arch spanning the main road to the north; its inside face is Roman. There is another good town gate, Stonebow, thirteenth and sixteenth centuries; but the emphasis here is Roman. Under the Romans Lincoln had colony status; they called it *Lindum Colonia*. William the Conqueror built his castle here on a Roman site. See the tunnel-vault of the east entry (though the façade is fifteenth-century) and another Norman gate; see also three towers on the walls, Lacy or Lucy (c.1200), Observatory and Cobb (both c.1400). John of Gaunt was constable here before 1400 and may have built one or both of these. The castle belonged to the Duchy of Lancaster till 1831 and then was sold to the County of Lincoln. The high spot in its history is King Stephen's capture here, 1141. Far more impressive than the castle is Lincoln Cathedral, enormous, commanding, visible from any spot for miles around. It too was originally Norman and there are still Norman features in the west end, but there was an earthquake (or something) in 1185 and they had to begin almost all over. The Angel Choir, very elaborate, was added in 1256–80; thereafter no serious changes were made until the great Storm of 1548 blew down the spire which then crowned the middle tower. If it was as high as the tower itself, the Cathedral looks better without it. See in the Cathedral Treasury gold and silver altar vessels and also one of four prime copies of the Magna Carta. Outside the Cathedral, see the Usher Art Gallery if you are interested in Alfred Lord Tennyson. Look at the City and County Museum as well as its notable Roman contents; it is thirteenth century, formerly a church; and if you want an idea of what London Bridge used to look like, look at Lincoln's. It has sixteenth-century houses and shops built on one side. Finally look

at the two stone twelfth-century houses (on Steep Hill) that have
survived especially well because they were built especially well, and
built especially well because they were built by Jews. Until Edward I
expelled the Jews in 1290, Christians borrowed from them but hated
them, and anti-Jewish riots were frequent. Jews built solidly not only
because they kept large sums of money on hand, but because they
hoped to survive.

but the collection's prize is Lady Arabella Stuart, painted in the Tower in actual process of losing her mind.) Inside, there have been more alterations than out; the hammer-beam roof of the Hall was closed in c.1700, the architect Wyatville made extensive alterations 1800–10, and in 1860 the fourth Marquess of Bath had the ceilings painted and gilded in the Italian Renaissance taste, possibly not yours, certainly not mine. But, as at Hatfield House (q.v.), the decision to whitewash over is not lightly made. (Also spared, so far, are the present heir's extensive murals, a mixture of oil and sawdust.) A particularly interesting and beautiful room at the top of the house, "Bishop Ken's Library," is not shown to tourists—too far off the beaten track. Not many of them have heard of Bishop Ken anyway, but most have sung in church at least one of his hymns, "Praise God from Whom all blessings flow." Substantial blessings were channeled to Bishop Ken through the master of Longleat in 1689; in that year, still a stickler for principle (he was the one who had "refused poor Nelly a night's lodging"), he refused to acknowledge William III's right to the throne, and lost thereby his Bishopric of Bath and Wells. He was invited to move to Longleat, and spent the rest of his life there in peace and quiet. There were then neither tourists (millions of them) nor lions. The present Marquess of Bath is raising lions at Longleat now. With the advice of the famous Chipperfield circus family (Mary Chipperfield has written a book about it, *Lions on the Lawn*), he is not only providing a tourist attraction but helping a threatened species survive. Approach the lions cautiously; the Longleat staff have trouble with some people who want to take close-ups. But enjoy the gardens freely, see "Capability" Brown's characteristic park and the orangery and the pets' cemetery and especially the stable courtyard, which is very chaste and choice.

planned it—some say Lord Pembroke and Roger Morris, some Henrietta Howard herself—it had only the rarest and most expensive materials and the finest workmanship. Mahogany had not been used for structural work, like doors and floors, before this; but at both Marble Hill House and Houghton Hall (1723) it was used as freely as native wood. Actually the naval officer in charge of importing it almost involved England in a war with Spain, for he accidentally or otherwise had it cut on Spanish territory; and he cut plenty. Notice the staircase for its beauty, but note that the whole thing is solid mahogany. Notice the decoration in the salon—the big room overlooking the river, on what the English call the first floor—and on the pediment of the overmantel especially. Grinling Gibbons had died in 1721, but James Richards, the new Master Sculptor to the King, was a worthy successor. To this small-but-charming example of pure Palladian architecture came Henrietta Howard's friends, her antidote to George II—Pope, Gay, Swift. And, of course, Horace Walpole was her neighbor at Strawberry Hill. The Countess of Suffolk—to give her her well-earned title—retired from court in 1734 and lived at Marble Hill House until she died thirty-odd years later. Still later, Mrs. Fitzherbert was installed there by her royal quasi-husband; Lord Wellesley, the Duke of Wellington's older and less imitable brother, was a tenant after her. But in this case the people are less important than the house. Chiswick is just as pure Palladian, but it is icily regular, splendidly null compared with Marble Hill. See Marble Hill and you have seen in microcosm the best architecture of its period in England.

MARLBOROUGH HOUSE, Marlborough Road, Pall Mall, SW1,
25. Much changed from its original appearance—only two stories
high over an unimportant basement, with a galleried flat roof and five
rather lonely looking chimneys. It is a tall building now and the
proportions are ruined. Sir Christopher Wren drew the plans, having
been commissioned in 1709 by the Duchess of Marlborough—not by
the Duke, as is usually said. She was very pleased with him at first but
finally had to let "the poor old man" go and finish it herself; even so,
it was done in a phenomenal two years and (she thought) knocked
the spots off Blenheim Palace, the Duke's project. Since the Duchess's
time, Marlborough House has had a succession of royal tenants—
Prince Leopold, the widowed Queen Adelaide, Edward VII as Prince
of Wales (this was when the fast Marlborough House Set made a
name for itself), and finally Queen Mary from her husband's death
till after her granddaughter's accession. Though not one of the horsey
members of her family, and Marlborough House walls are frescoed
solid with horses and soldiers and blood and gore and the triumphant,
untouched Duke, Queen Mary was very much at home in Marlborough House and the Londoners still miss having her there. Since her
death Queen Elizabeth has given Marlborough House as a Commonwealth center for government conferences and it has been considerably done over, sparing the horses but augmenting the "one-bar
electric fire" heating with which Queen Mary, Queen Victoria's true
descendant, was perfectly happy. When it is not being used it is open
to the public. Open also, for part of the year, are services in the
Queen's Chapel, Marlborough Gate, one of the most beautiful things
in London. The queen for whom it was begun and named never
materialized—this was back in 1623, when Charles I, then a young
prince, had gone to Spain with the Duke of Buckingham, both of
them in disguise and Charles with the Infanta Maria in view. But he
married another Catholic princess later, so the little masterpiece of
Inigo Jones, which is also a very big milestone—the first classical
church built in England—had plenty of use and became a *cause célèbre*.
Historically this chapel has no connection with Marlborough House,
but physically it is right alongside, and if you are given a tour of the
Commonwealth Center you may be shown the chapel too.

This is a bit off the beaten track, and it is true the Castle is in ruins. But they are impressive ruins, as Middleham in its day was an impressive place. A Norman keep, one of the largest in England, walls ten or twelve feet thick, inner and outer wards, guard tower, drawbridge, moat, it was the stronghold of the great Earl of Warwick, the Kingmaker. This, not

Warwick Castle, was his family's usual home, and here little Richard of Gloucester, a close kinsman because his mother was a Neville, spent the formative years from nine to thirteen. Later Richard married the Kingmaker's daughter (Anne Neville), and they lived here at Middleham, where their son Edward was born. (Edward died here, too, Prince of Wales, before he grew up.) One way or another, Richard and Anne held on to Middleham. But Anne certainly did not inherit it; Warwick the Kingmaker was attainted, stripped of all he had, when he switched sides and died fighting for the Lancastrians. His castles reverted to the Yorkist crown, and Middleham was given to Richard.

MILFORD HAVEN, Pembrokeshire, 131. The forces of Henry II set out from here to conquer Ireland; the forces of Henry VII (then only Earl of Richmond) landed here to conquer England. Sir William and Lady Hamilton are buried here in St. Katherine's churchyard; Nelson wasted his time leaving Lady Hamilton to a grateful nation, for England had no intention of burying her beside him in St. Paul's, and very properly ignored the whole thing. But there is some little connection here, because Nelson had laid the cornerstone of St. Katherine's.

MONTROSE, Angus, 181. A pleasant harbor town with some eighteenth-century architecture left, but the Castle, where Balliol submitted personally to Edward I, is gone. In the Old Church, from which the curfew bell tolls at ten o'clock every night, undoubtedly waking up a lot of people, notice the chandelier shaped like a hearse.

---

* This is the Roger Mortimer who was involved with Queen Isabella. He became Earl of March only a short time before his death and is generally known as Mortimer, not March, in history.

forest less than fifteen years old. (William's son Rufus was also killed
in New Forest while hunting, but even in 1100 there would have
been better places.) New Forest now is reduced in size, but still
nearly a hundred thousand acres. There are good roads through this
and some interesting towns—Lyndhurst, Brokenhurst. Bucklers
Hard is not a town, just one eighteenth-century street, but its
shipyard has been restored and there is a maritime museum. At
Beaulieu, which like Bucklers Hard is on the Beaulieu River where it
flows into the Solent, Lord Montagu of Beaulieu has a famous motor
museum which unwilling tourist husbands really enjoy. There is also
a thirteenth-century church, once part of a Cistercian abbey.

NEWSTEAD ABBEY, near Nottingham, Nottinghamshire, 118.
Nottingham is also the owner, and the beautiful gardens, nine or ten
miles out by bus, are a popular municipal park. There is a
manor-house of mixed ancestry, mostly Tudor and Georgian, where
the Byrons in general and the famous poet in particular lived. The
abbey church is a ruin, but young Lord Byron approximated the altar
and put his famous monument to his dog Boatswain there. Since the
English are much inclined to spell dog backwards, this is less shocking
than Lord Byron hoped it would be. But he kept on trying. It seems
quite possible that he cared nothing at all for his half-sister Augusta
but, trying to find something shocking and different, suddenly
thought, Ah, incest. His great-uncle, from whom he inherited his title
and this estate, already had earned the name of "the wicked Lord,"
already had done everything possible in the way of wild spending and
extravagant remodeling of gardens, making lakes, etc.—in fact, he
had brought the family to the brink of ruin and it was this old man's
excesses, not the poet's better publicized ones, that made it necessary
to sell Newstead Abbey in 1818. Byron had never got to live there
much. He inherited when he was ten, but sometimes they needed to
rent it out, and then of course he was away at school and college, and
had the itch to travel, and really needed to be in London to sell books.
But any feeling about England he had was for Newstead Abbey, and
it is evident in some of his poems.

Oudenarde, Battle of, 49, 54

Overbury, Sir Thomas, 91

OXFORD, Oxfordshire, 87. Oxford is hopeless. If you believe you can
see it in any reasonable time, or having seen it will know one college
from another, look at Oxford from a height. (The best place is the
cupola of the Sheldonian Theatre, which you should see anyway—
1664–68, Wren, honorary degrees.) Look at that jigsaw puzzle of
quadrangles, buttresses, spires. Then come down and try, which is all
you can do. Carfax is the big downtown intersection. There is a
Norman cathedral and famous churches, St. Mary the Virgin, St.
Michael, St. Peter in the East. The Ashmolean Museum could detain
you all day. The Botanic Gardens are the oldest in the British Isles.
The University has thirty colleges; some of them, including the five
women's colleges, are comparatively new and others, though of old
foundation, have replacement buildings. The oldest complete complex
of college buildings, designed as a unit, is unhappily called New
College. It was founded in 1379. See the chapel, garden court,
cloisters, part of the old city wall, Treasure Room with gold, silver,
and a unicorn's horn. At Balliol College, founded 1282, look at the
cross set into the pavement outside; this is where Bishops Ridley and
Latimer were burned to death. Look at the door that used to be one of
the college gates—it was charred by the heat of that fire. All Souls,
founded 1483, has a fifteenth-century and an eighteenth-century
quadrangle. This college has only fellows, no undergraduates. See
Magdalen College, founded 1458; writers get maudlin over this one's
beauty. See the cloisters, Magdalen, Muniment, and Founders'
Towers, and deer in the hundred-acre park. At Christ Church,
founded 1525 and 1546, Tom Tower has a famous 18,000-pound
bell, Great Tom, and the quadrangle is called Tom Quad. In another
quadrangle, Peckwater, notice the statue to Dr. John Fell (1660–
1686), who was dean of this college; he looks no more unlikable than
anybody else. In Merton College, Queen Henrietta Maria lodged
during the Civil War, when Oxford was her husband's capital. It was
founded 1264, has the oldest quadrangle in Oxford (Mob Quad),
finished 1311, an even older chapel and the oldest library in all
England. This is open to the public. See there the astrolabe that

Chaucer, more versatile than you thought, wrote a treatise about. The versatile Sir Christopher Wren is of course prominent at Oxford, where he was Professor of Astronomy and also designed the Garden Quadrangle of Trinity (founded 1555) and the Hall and chapel of Brasenose (founded 1509). St. John's, founded 1555, has a quadrangle by Inigo Jones. Look at more colleges, of course, if you can— Queen's, founded 1340, is by Hawksmoor and Corpus Christi, founded 1517, has a 1581 sundial in the quad—but in any case end your Oxford sightseeing with another overview, this time from the gallery of the Radcliffe Camera. This classical rotunda, masterpiece of James Gibbs and built 1737–49, is a reading-room for the Bodleian Library, named after Sir Thomas Bodley who gave its books and an endowment after it was ruined in the Dissolution. But the first founder was Humphrey Duke of Gloucester, Henry V's younger brother. The section of the Bodleian called Duke Humphrey is not open to tourists. Scholars may use it freely if they bring letters from, say, the Library of Congress.

remains of Pevensey Castle, begun 1080, with a thirteenth-century gatehouse and inner bailey, and surrounded by a Roman wall still as much as twenty feet high in places. It was pretty well decayed when the Armada threatened, in 1588; it was refortified then and again in World War II, though not repaired that time. Nobody attacked it, anyway.

Philip II of France (*see* Philip Augustus)

Philip II of Spain, 96, 104–5

Philip IV of France, 184

Philip VI of France, 169–70, 172

Philip of Austria, 123

Philip, Prince, Duke of Edinburgh (*see* Edinburgh)

Philip Augustus, King of France, 195–6, 199, 203–5

Philippa of Hainault, Queen of Edward III, 170–2, 174

PICCADILLY, London W1, 13. An important street and a circus, which many people consider the real center of London—not Charing Cross. It may have been circular once, but it is now an irregularly shaped maelstrom with a small statue in the middle. Called Eros, this is actually the Angel of Christian Charity. It honors a famous philanthropist, Lord Shaftesbury. The angel is supposed to be shooting to bury a shaft in Shaftesbury Avenue, a theater street leading off the Circus, but unfortunately for the pun is aiming the wrong way. This little statue, probably the first one anywhere to be made of aluminum (English: aluminium), is a beloved London mascot and was accordingly hidden during the bombing; it is almost hidden again by the hundreds of shaggy boys and slovenly girls who stand by the hour on the steps of the monument, which is conveniently located over a big underground station with shops, restaurants, lavatories, cinemas, everything. They may eventually be asked to move if the new Piccadilly Circus development scheme is approved. Though the statue of Eros will be carefully put back, a grandiose design may take away the assorted surrounding buildings and, of course, their insistent signs. (Chesterton said the lights must be a wonderful sight if you can't read.) But many perverse people like Piccadilly Circus just as it is. Architecturally there is nothing to lose, but if the rebuilding of

QUEEN'S HOUSE, Greenwich, London SE10, 92. This is the house
visible from the river between the two framing sections of the Royal
Naval College. Their placement shows how important it was
considered then, under William and Mary. Already about a hundred
years old, it was that pace-setting piece of architecture that, with the
Banqueting House in Westminster, Inigo Jones had built to start a
whole new style in England. It was planned for Anne of Denmark,
but left unfinished when she died in 1619. Later it was finished for
Henrietta Maria, so it was still the Queen's House; and Mary of
Modena lived there too. This pure and beautiful building should be
seen for its own sake; but worth a river trip to Greenwich is also the
museum of the Royal Naval College, its Painted Hall, where a
hundred officers can dine under a Thornhill ceiling, and its chapel.
Peter the Great, making his famous tour of the world outside Russia,
was impressed with it; he told William III that if he were King of
England he would turn Greenwich Hospital into a palace and make
St. James's Palace a hospital.

Quekett, John Thomas (1815–1861), 181
Quennell, Peter, 55

Radcot Bridge, Battle of, 162–4
Raleigh, Elizabeth Throckmorton, Lady, 94
Raleigh, Sir Walter, 93, 97, 101
Ranelagh, 54
Ravenspur, 167
Reformation, 138
Reform Bill, 36
Regency Act, 47
REGENT'S PARK, north of Marylebone Road, London, NW1, 41.
This was not planned as a park at all, much less a public one. The
Prince Regent was going to build there not merely a palace for
himself, but twenty-six separate "villas," two crescents and two
circuses of rowhouses, with terraces of still more houses all around the
edge. Very little of this materialized, the Prince's own palace least of
all. But see the splendid terraces that John Nash did build,

George and Queen Mary lived here when they were Duke and
Duchess of York, and the Duke of Windsor was born here; King
George and Queen Elizabeth, also as Duke and Duchess of York,
lived here for three or four years after their marriage. It is hard to
judge White Lodge, because it was much altered and added to by
Princess Amelia, George III's daughter, when she was Ranger of
Richmond Park—but George II, who may or may not have been
responsible for Marble Hill House, undoubtedly built White Lodge.

ROCHESTER CATHEDRAL, Rochester, Kent, 181. Begun 1082 by
the monk Gundulf who was architect of the White Tower in London
and of Rochester Castle here; this is the tallest keep in England, 120
feet high. The Cathedral was originally founded by St. Augustine in
604, but depredations by the Danes gave Gundulf a clean slate to
work on. See Gundulf's statue, the tomb of Bishop Walter de Merton
who founded Merton College at Oxford, the stalls and monks'
benches (thirteenth century, probably the oldest in England), the
vaulting and graffiti in the crypt, and the beautiful doorway, 1160. In
the town of Rochester, see in the High Street the Guildhall (1687)
and Corn Exchange (1706). Both were given to Rochester by
Admiral Sir Cloudesley Shovell, the one with the pretentious tomb in
the Abbey. These buildings are pretentious too. See Restoration
House, about a hundred years old when Charles II stayed here on his
way home to London, 1660; Minor Canon Row, 1736; King's

imagination to people it with determined barons and a faulty king. You will want to see the marker that Queen Elizabeth dedicated in 1965: THIS ACRE OF ENGLISH GROUND WAS GIVEN TO THE UNITED STATES OF AMERICA BY THE PEOPLE OF BRITAIN IN MEMORY OF JOHN F. KENNEDY. . . . If you are a lawyer you will be interested in the Magna Carta Memorial erected by the American Bar Association. But if it is King John and the barons and Magna Carta you are really interested in you should go far from Runnymede, to the town of Bury St. Edmunds in Suffolk, which considers itself the birthplace of Magna Carta and can show the abbey church on the high altar of which, in 1214, the barons swore to force the King to accept Magna Carta. Part of the municipal motto is *Cunabula Legis*, Cradle of the Law.

A leprosarium dedicated to St. James the Less once stood here; when Henry VIII chose this site for a palace to please Anne Boleyn, the name was ready-made, and apparently all the germs were dead. The gate-house and the Chapel Royal (ceiling attributed to Holbein) are the only real survivals of Henry's building. Neither is open to tourists. Surprisingly, though, tourists may wander through the arches into the courts, right under the eyes of the guards. Nothing seems to be going on inside. The glory has, of course, long since departed from St. James's. It was never anybody's favorite palace; Richmond and Placentia were more to the Tudors' tastes, though Mary I did die here; it was just a convenient London *pied-à-terre*, small and simple as palaces go. The first Stuart's interest was in Whitehall Palace across the Park, which he was starting to rebuild with a new architect, Inigo

Jones. His son Charles, before being executed outside Whitehall
Palace, spent the last night of his life at St. James's; and the last of the
Stuarts, James III, the Old Pretender, was born there. Generally,
though, the focus was on Whitehall. But then Whitehall burned, only
the Banqueting House saved, and the Court moved overnight into
small, simple, inadequate St. James's. Naturally it was much remodeled and altered, by Wren, by Kent, by its occupants—one that we
know of felt perfectly free to tear out and replace her staircase. All
the Georges lived here, not to mention George I's mistresses. But
then Queen Victoria strongmindedly moved into Buckingham Palace
and that was when the glory departed. For some reason the Court is
still called the Court of St. James's, but ambassadors so accredited to it
never see the place, the State Rooms are hardly ever used, and the
Chapel Royal is no longer popular for royal weddings. Certain
royalties well down the line of succession still live there, and Edward
VIII both as Prince of Wales and King occupied York House, part of
the complex which may also be said to include Clarence House
(where the Queen Mother lives), Marlborough House, and the
Queen's Chapel built for Charles I's bride. Also there are houses in
the various little inside courts, comparable to houses inside a cathedral
close; the people living in them mean "as much or as little" to each
other "as any ordinary neighbors in an ordinary street." Some live
there by "Grace and Favour"; Loelia Duchess of Westminster, in her
autobiography of that title, tells of being born in Ambassadors' Court,
St. James's, in a house provided for her grandmother as the widow of
the Queen's Secretary, and of growing up in another house, "a bit of
the palace known as Queen Anne's Bower," which was one of the
fringe benefits of her father's position as Equerry. Members of the
Household still live in these houses inside St. James's; there is a room
for the young officers in charge of the guard, and the Lord
Chamberlain—his talons now, however, drawn—still maintains his
office.

connecting Ludgate Hill and Cannon Street), London EC4, 10, 21,
41, 156, 160. Christopher Wren built fifty City churches (you will
find one at every turn) and many other buildings too, but at first he
was an astronomer mainly, an architect only by avocation. The Dean
of Windsor's son was, naturally, interested in church architecture,
and his uncle, the Bishop of Ely, gave him his first commission. He
had submitted a plan for remodeling Old St. Paul's, in need of work
even before Cromwell's men tore it up inside and stabled their horses
in it. But then, suddenly, came the Great Fire, 1666, and a cathedral
had to be built from the beginning. Wanting to mark the spot, Wren
sent a workman to bring him a stone, and the man came back with a
tomb-fragment saying RESURGAM. The real cornerstone was laid
in 1675. Wren's design was classic, rather than Gothic; this was
controversial, and controversy there had certainly been. The wooden
model the architect had first made (see it, eighteen feet long, in the
library) is very different from the cathedral that actually arose. You
are there; *circumspice*. That is what his son wrote for Wren's
tombstone in this building: *Lector, si monumentum requiris, circumspice*, if you want to see his monument, look around you. At St.
Paul's, the building is the thing. The tombs do not detract from it, as
they do in Westminster Abbey. Look up at the dome, two domes
really, one inside, the other outside a brick cone, a masterpiece of
engineering. Climb the stairs, if you want to project your voice across
the Whispering Gallery. (You can climb still higher for a beautiful
view, but the views from Westminster Cathedral and Post Office
Tower are good too. Those buildings are, respectively, inferior and
perfectly terrible, but they have elevators.) Look at the Grinling
Gibbons carving, notably in the choir. Look at the Tijou ironwork,
the organ that Handel played, and of course the eminent tombs.
Westminster Abbey has the poets, but the painters are in St. Paul's.
So is the Duke of Wellington, a tremendous monument, Admiral
Earl Howe, who came unsuccessfully to our shores, Field Marshal
Earl Kitchener, John Donne, wearing a shroud and standing on a
funeral urn (he posed for this himself, and his expression shows he
enjoyed it), Nelson in the crypt precisely under the dome. Also in the
crypt is the tremendous catafalque (eighteen tons) that carried

Wellington's coffin. The last great man's funeral here was Sir Winston Churchill's; if you saw it on television you saw St. Paul's at its best. The bomb damage is not apparent anywhere. The new American Memorial Chapel is imposing. But the new building development around St. Paul's is more depressing than the rubble it replaced. St. Paul's rises in the midst of that like genius rising above mediocrity.

St. Stephen, 91

Saladin, 203–4

Salic Law, 169

√SALISBURY, Wiltshire, 77. The spire is the tallest in England, 404 feet. Except for this spire, which was added in the next century, Salisbury Cathedral was built exactly according to plan—it rose very fast, 1220–60, because nobody was arguing or changing his mind. This was good. Some cathedrals point out rather plainly what happens when you change horses in midstream or let a committee design a horse. Notice this integration inside and out. Notice the tomb of William Longuespée, Earl of Salisbury. He was the first to be buried in the new cathedral. He stood witness as his half-brother King John sealed at Runnymede; he lies here in effigy wearing full armor and something very strange on his right hand. Notice also the monument to Bishop Wyville, c.1375, which shows him standing inside a castle. Outdoors, notice the wall that makes the cathedral premises a close. It is Edward III, and many of its houses, like the Bishop's house and the old deanery, are basically the same period. The Chapter-house is thirteenth-century too, and the cloisters. But notice #68 in the close; it was built in 1720. You will not notice any Norman work anywhere, which is unusual; Salisbury was not built on the ruins of a Norman predecessor. It had one; you can still see its outline in the grass; but they left this Norman site and started over again elsewhere. The place they left was Old Sarum, the place they built this new cathedral was New Sarum—Sarum being the ancient name for Salisbury. There is a limerick, much beloved by the people who know this, which begins, "There was a young curate of Salisbury, Whose manners were quite halisbury-scalisbury. . . ."

Salisbury, Catherine de Grandison, Countess of, 172

closed into a little cramped, sunless space, accessible through a half-timbered Elizabethan house. (This, incidentally, was invisible too, until in World War I a bomb knocked off the modern front.) Notice in St. Bartholomew's the tomb and colored effigy of the founder, the Augustinian Rahere; the font where Hogarth was baptized; Prior Bolton's window; the Chamberlayne and Mildmay tombs; the Lady Chapel, where Benjamin Franklin worked as a printer. By that time the church had fallen into disuse and decay, and though this part has since been restored a great chunk of the church has entirely disappeared. You can see how foreshortened it looks. Actually it is still too big for the kind of congregations they have now in London. Having the same name as the church, and the same founder, Rahere in 1123, St. Bartholomew's Hospital, "Barts" to its students, is the oldest London hospital on its original site—though the building is new for London, 1702. You may go in. The hall is by Gibbs and the little church—St. Bartholomew the Less, inevitably—remodeled finally by Hardwick. But the greatest pride of this famous teaching hospital is Dr. William Harvey, chief physician 1609–43, who unfortunately preferred to be buried with his family instead of among his friends.

The stately but not very homelike home of the Dukes of Northumberland, Syon was built as a monastery. The Bridgettine Order of nuns moved to this site in 1431, so this may be the date of at least part of the house. Famous occupants and/or owners include Elizabeth Barton, "the Holy Maid of Kent," a nun here before her execution at Tyburn; Queen Catherine Howard, who also went from here to her death; the Protector Somerset, who had begun to build or rebuild when he got in trouble and was executed too; the Duke of Northumberland, Lady Jane Grey's father-in-law, who at Syon House urged her to accept the crown she knew belonged to Mary Tudor. Persuaded—or rather coerced—she set out from Syon to the Tower and her coronation. It turned out to be her death instead, and her husband and his father the Duke were executed also. By this time Queen Mary Tudor was firmly on the throne and Catholicism was back in; the Syon nuns came back from the Low Countries, Mary died, and Queen Elizabeth sent them packing again. At this point you would think nobody would want Syon House as a gracious gift; too many Syon people got their heads cut off; but the Percy family accepted it and have lived there ever since. (The Northumberland title as well as the house had been taken away from Lady Jane's father-in-law, a Dudley, when he was convicted of treason, and the Percys were given that too.) They have done a great deal to the house. In 1632 they had Inigo Jones make some repairs and changes, and in 1762 an equally famous architect,

Robert Adam, did the state rooms so completely over that they were—and still are—sensational. The Great Hall, the State Dining Room, the Red Drawing Room, the Long Gallery, and especially the Anteroom all belie Adam's reputation for the sweetly pretty. Nor is the gateway he made for the house sweetly pretty, especially since Northumberland House in London was torn down and the big iron lion that identified it was brought out to Syon and put on top of the Adam gate. See also the gardens, naturally by "Capability" Brown, the impressive glasshouses, and the lake; you might at the same time look for traces of the sixty-nine bombs that fell on these grounds during the war. But the house was fortunate. To date, the worst thing that has happened to it was the explosion of Henry VIII's body, in 1547. It rested here on the way from Westminster to Windsor, and during the night the bloated, decayed mountain of flesh really did explode, all over the floor; the dogs found it first; and the prophetic curse of a displaced monk was recalled—"the dogs would lick his blood as they had Ahab's."

Tangier, 82

TEMPLE GARDEN, Victoria Embankment, London EC4, 140. This is one of the most unchanged parts of London. It was dreadfully bombed during the war and a great deal of it is gone, but what remains is excellently restored and the atmosphere of withdrawal and study is intact. To turn into Middle Temple Lane from Fleet Street (or into Inner Temple Lane with Prince Henry's Room over the arch) is to escape from all you may dislike about the twentieth century. The order of Knights Templar had this riverside site originally. They were dissolved in 1312, and by 1338 some law professors had leased it and moved in. They are still there. They early developed four great Inns of Court, Middle Temple, Inner Temple, Gray's Inn, and Lincoln's Inn. The two Temples lie side by side nearest the river; the visitor cannot tell one from the other, and they are both served by Temple Church. See this first; it is a relic of the pre-law, Knights-Templar days—round like the Church of the Holy Sepulchre in Jerusalem, but with additions hardly less distinguished.

It was really gutted in the war—only one Templar's tomb-effigy out of nine survived intact—but it has been very successfully restored. See also in this area Middle Temple Hall, where Shakespeare is supposed to have played in *Twelfth Night,* 1602. See the houses along King's Bench Walk, Inner Temple Lane, and the Courts—Goldsmith died in 1774 in Brick Court, and quiet descended on the studies of his more serious neighbor Blackstone, whom he had often disturbed. You cannot see Crown Office Row, the most famous range of houses; it was wiped out in the Blitz; in fact, all three of the places the Lambs lived in the Inner Temple are gone. To see the other two Inns of Court you must cross Fleet Street where, almost opposite the Middle Temple Lane exit from the Temple, you will see Chancery Lane with access on the left to Lincoln's Inn; cross High Holborn beyond that and, again nearly but not quite opposite, Fulwood Place will take you to Field Court and the edge of Gray's Inn. If you could ignore Fleet Street and High Holborn, you could easily see how the Inns of Court ran north away from the river, a continuous line; though physically separated now, they still act together in the matter of legal training and practice. Via the Inns of Court is the way—the only way—to the English bar. They house, train, and examine candidates for the law. Even if the student goes to school elsewhere, as in these days he is quite likely to do, he must be passed on by an Inn of Court; and after he is admitted to the bar, he may well have an office here in the Temple, and perhaps live there too, on an upper floor.

Tennyson, Alfred Lord, 32

Test Act (Oath), 75–6, 83

TEWKESBURY, Gloucestershire, 144. See first the House of the Golden Key and Ancient Grudge, if only for the name. See the field where the Yorkists defeated the Lancastrians—if, again, you have a good imagination. See the road-marker to the east of town, Tibble Stone, which is mentioned in the Domesday Book. But mainly see the abbey, where Edward Prince of Wales was buried under the tower. This is an enormous church—dimensions and plan are almost like Westminster Abbey's—and it has the largest Norman tower in existence. Notice the high altar, Purbeck marble; this too is unusually huge, but at the Dissolution in 1539 the monks, before leaving, managed to get it down and out and bury it. (The whole church might have been wrecked at this time, but the strong-minded townspeople claimed that part of it, at least, was the only parish church they had and succeeded in buying the whole thing for £453.) Behind the high altar you can look through a grating in the ambulatory floor and see, displayed in a glass case, the bones of George Duke of Clarence, the one who may or may not have been drowned in malmsey, and those of his wife Isabel, daughter of Warwick the Kingmaker who was also lord of this manor. Another gruesome tomb is that of Abbot Wakeman, who is depicted with five different kinds of creepy, crawly things—worm, mouse, snake, etc.—hard at work on him, assisting the natural processes of decay. Not gruesome at all, admirable and in Edward's case rather funny, are the Despenser tombs. Edward, one of the original Garter knights and in his day Lord of the Manor of Tewkesbury, is kneeling on top of his chantry chapel. Everybody is very surprised to look up and see him there, in full armor and with an elaborate canopy over his head. Edward le Despenser died in 1375. He was the great-great-grandfather of Isabel the Duchess of Clarence, who was granted the Manor of Tewkesbury after her father the Kingmaker was killed and attainted and she could not inherit it from him. Edward le Despenser was also the grandson and nephew of the two Hugh le Despensers who influenced Edward II and so met their deaths at the hands of Queen Isabella and Roger Mortimer—the younger Hugh, in fact, is buried with his wife Elizabeth Montacute in another beautiful Despenser tomb here; their recumbent effigies are alabaster. And if you think this sounds like a small world—it was, indeed—hear also that this Tewkesbury Abbey was founded in 1092 by Robert Fitzharmon, the great-grandfather of King John's first wife, Isabella of Gloucester (his half-first cousin once removed!) and the work was carried forward after his death by his son-in-law, Robert Fitzroy, Earl of Gloucester, the illegitimate son of Henry I, the Robert of Gloucester who worked so hard to put and keep his half-sister Matilda on the throne Stephen had taken.

since disappeared, but it is still the preferred designation. It has to
have some description because another church is called All Hallows
on the Wall.) This is one of the most interesting and attractive
churches in London—it *is* London, in readable layers. In the crypt,
under ashes from the 61 A.D. fire, was found a piece of Roman
pavement you can see, together with a tombstone—Demetrius's; he
was namesake of a king. The wall is Saxon down here, and in the
main church there is a seventh-century Saxon arch, the oldest in
London. Then there is some Norman work, eleventh or twelfth
century. The walls, severely damaged in the Blitz, are fourteenth and
fifteenth century, the tower 1659—said to be the only surviving piece
of church architecture from Cromwell's period, which was a time of
tearing down rather than building. From this tower, as Samuel Pepys
wrote in his diary, he watched the Great Fire (1666) burn to the very
edge of the porch of this church. So rebuilding was not required then;
but after 1941 everything was needed. William Penn was baptized in
this church and John Quincy Adams was married, and other famous
people, like Bishop Fisher and Archbishop Laud, paused here on their
way to the scaffold, or lay in the churchyard briefly, headless, on their
way back. The scaffold site is at the west end of Trinity Square
gardens, a little bricked rectangle which is a Roman Catholic shrine
because their St. Thomas More was beheaded here. Almost all of the
Tower prisoners were beheaded here on Tower Hill. Only if you
were a queen, like Anne Boleyn, or a man the Queen had loved, like
the Earl of Essex, were you granted the privacy of a death inside the
Tower.

TOWER OF LONDON, Tower Hill, London EC3, 80, 93, 95, 98,
101, 114, 116, 126–30, 133–9, 141, 143–4, 151–2, 156, 159, 167,
177–8, 188, 190, 223, 229–30. The White Tower, the central one,
not whitewashed any more, is Norman. William the Conqueror built
a wooden fortification here immediately after arrival; it was necessary; but then he sent for stone from Caen in Normandy and his
architect Gundulf, the same bishop who built Rochester Cathedral
(*q.v.*) began the permanent building. (Another bishop, Ranulf
Flambard, had to finish it for another king; he also had the honor of
being, in 1101, its first prisoner.) Except for the windows, which Sir

Christopher Wren enlarged when he was Surveyor of Works (but he skipped four on the south side), it looks about the same now as then. See the Chapel of St. John, the oldest church in London, absolutely pure and untouched Norman. Here Henry VI, murdered in the Tower, lay in state; so did Elizabeth of York, the Queen of the next Henry; and the Knights of the Order of the Bath kept their vigil. In the crypt of this peaceful, high-minded chapel are kept the instruments of torture used on prisoners, and the block, last used for Lord Lovat in 1747. Also in the White Tower is the magnificent armor museum, started under Charles II. (Armor and weapons used to be made in this fortification—the later Bowyer Tower gets its name from this—as well as coins.) The center of attraction here is Henry VIII's armor; there is a suit that he wore as a young prince, another made for him after he grew to be a monster. If you are pressed for time, the White Tower is of course the one to see, though the Little Princes are associated with the Bloody Tower and Henry VI with the Wakefield, and there is not a single one of the towers that does not repay your interested and prolonged scrutiny. There are twenty towers in all. Richard I, who had seen a lot of castles on his Crusade and his other fighting travels, is supposed to be responsible for the concentric plan that developed the simple White Tower into a complex; but it was the next generation, Henry III, John's son, that did most of the building. The palace Henry III built inside the walls has vanished, and you may not see inside Queen's House, where Anne Boleyn stayed before her coronation and again before her death, so the Tower really gives you no idea of what it was like to live there, either for royalty or for the large and busy community seeing to their needs or making arrows or coins. The moat was drained at the insistence of the Duke of Wellington in 1843; this spoils the medieval effect but people no longer get typhoid from it. Traitor's Gate, so nearly connected with fatality that Princess Elizabeth hysterically refused to go up the stairs, is a replacement—Barnum bought the original, it got lost somewhere, and may yet turn up in America. See the Crown Jewels in their super-safe new cave under Waterloo Barracks; they are replacements too, most of them, but dazzling. See Raleigh's Walk, and the ravens, and Tower Green, and

St. Peter ad Vincula (rebuilt 1305, restored 1512), where Anne Boleyn, Catherine Howard, Jane Grey, and the Duke of Monmouth lie headless under the floor. Sir Walter Raleigh's son, born in the Tower, was baptized in this church. Later if you have the time you can come back here for a Sunday morning service—the Yeoman Warder's spiel will have taken the edge off your necessarily guided tour of this part of the Tower—and if you really want to get the feel of what you are seeing, you can come back some night at nine for the Ceremony of the Keys.

Townsend, Captain Peter, 211

Trafalgar, Battle of, 47, 170

Tranby Croft Scandal, 25–6

Tristan, 198

Trooping the Colour, 11

Troyes, Treaty of, 156

Tudor, Edmund, Earl of Richmond, 122

Tudor Family, 97, 102, 122–3, 126, 128

Tudor, Henry (see Henry VII)

Tudor, Margaret (1) Queen of Scotland (2) Countess of Angus (3) Lady Methven, 89, 102, 117, 123

Tudor, Mary (1) Queen of France (2) Duchess of Suffolk, 123

Tudor, Mary (see Mary I)

Tudor, Owen, 122, 148

TUSSAUD'S, MADAME, Marylebone Road, London NW1, 137. This famous waxworks museum should be taken very seriously. It is only incidentally for children (Cinderella, Alice in Wonderland) or for murder addicts (Neill Cream, Doctor Crippen). All the rest is current events and history, both extremely well done and educational. Political and sports figures stand here, dressed in their own clothes, just as long as they are in the public eye; some of them remain after that, having become timelessly famous; others are relegated to the basement while the new Prime Minister and the new Wimbledon champion take their place. It is not safe to melt anybody down, because sometimes people work their way back up from obscurity, the way Mr. Churchill did. Permanent figures on display include all of the sovereigns of England from William the Conqueror down to the present Queen, with some of the more famous consorts. In every case a true likeness has been earnestly sought; Madame Tussaud was a perfectionist, and her family have inherited her standards as well as her talent. She got her start at the Court of Louis XVI, teaching the ladies of the royal family to make wax flowers; her next assignment was making death masks from the severed heads of Louis and Marie Antoinette. She did the dead Marat still lying in his bathtub. As soon as she could get away she came to England, where she modeled Lord Nelson from his death-mask, John Wesley from a portrait, George Washington from a life-bust. Madame did Lord Byron from life; she went to Paris to do Napoleon from life also, and returned to do George III, Queen Charlotte, and George IV. Her elder son did the Duke of Wellington from life; they were famous, no one refused the Tussauds. Their scope is remarkable, the list is, obviously, endless. See this museum, along with the National Portrait Gallery, first of all—not just first among museums, but even before you see the Tower and Westminster Abbey—and they will help you enjoy and understand everything else you see.

TWICKENHAM, Middlesex, 54. In addition to Marble Hill House (*q.v.*), see Horace Walpole's creation of Strawberry Hill. This started out as a "little plaything house," a simple cottage when Walpole (*q.v.*) acquired it. From 1749 to 1776 he worked on it, never quite sure whether he wanted a castle or a cathedral and ending with some of each, a domestic neo-Gothic of a complexity and detail which, like the Brighton Pavilion (*q.v.*), must be seen to be believed. You must write ahead though; a training college for priests now occupies the house.

Tyburn, 116, 168

Tyrell, Sir James, 136–7

United Nations, 11

United States, 10

Urban IV, Pope, 190

Utrecht, Treaty of, 52, 72

Not as big as some, more beautiful perhaps than all, this might be the best cathedral to see, outside of Canterbury, if you could see only one. It is wonderfully complete. The Chapel of Our Lady by the Cloister was destroyed in 1552, but another Lady Chapel is left, the cloisters, chapter house, Bishop's Palace, with gatehouse and moat (do not waste time waiting for the famous swans to pull the bell-rope when hungry), the Cathedral School, canons' houses, Vicars' Hall, Vicars' Row, where only one householder has had the courage to ruin the concept, the Archdeacon's House (now the Theological College), the Chancellor's House (now the Museum), Prebendal House where the principal of the college now lives. Access to the Cathedral Green from the Market Place outside is through Penniless Porch, which is not a porch and not built by a penniless chapter, and to the Bishop's Palace and the Cathedral Cloister through the Bishop's Eye, an even larger and handsomer gatehouse. The Cathedral itself, begun 1184, has a famous façade with three hundred statues on it. There used to be four hundred but it is still quite a crowd. There are two very famous clocks, one inside and one out; the canons are rather bitter about the proportion of people who come just to see the little knights joust on horseback every hour. Inside, the unique inverted arches confront you. In 1338, only twenty years after the central tower was added, the cathedral was in real danger of a collapse, and these strengthening arches were added as an emergency makeshift. But they turned out to be beautiful, and they keep you from confusing Wells with any of the other English cathedrals with vaulted ceilings and fourteenth-century stained glass and alabaster tombs. You are also unlikely to forget the curve of the stair to the chapter house, exquisitely worn, the roof bosses conveniently placed for your inspection on passage ceilings, and the atmosphere you expected to find all over England concentrated here over Wells as thick as a cloud of smog.

Wells, H. G., 4

Wessex, Earl of (*see* Godwin)

WESTMINSTER ABBEY, Broad Sanctuary, London SW1, 5, 13, 15, 41, 89, 123–4, 126–7, 133, 139, 143–4, 159, 161, 172, 181–3, 188–9, 191–2, 229, 237, 239, 242. Try to see the Abbey first and not the tombs, which would have been better restrained. What you are seeing is Henry III's monument, as St. Paul's is Wren's. See St. Edward's Shrine, which he built this church to house fittingly. Note the pointed openings underneath the tomb; here people in desperate need of healing were left overnight, one hopes with a mortal friend or relative nearby, his knees fitting into the depressed places in the stone. See how Henry III and his royal successors are grouped around the Confessor's shrine; here are some of the most famous tombs in the whole Abbey, all except Edward I's with effigies. See the chantry chapel that Henry VI built nearby for the repose of his father's soul, and note the new head and hands on the effigy of Henry V; originally of silver, they were of course promptly stolen, and were not replaced till 1971. (These are polyester resin, so nobody will be tempted to steal them.) Built for Henry VI in his turn, but more truly for himself and his own new Tudor dynasty, is the chapel added on by Henry VII, replacing the smaller Lady Chapel he pulled down. This is the great glory of Westminster Abbey, "the most beautiful chapel in Christendom." The banners of the knights of the Order of the Bath flank a miraculous ceiling; you cannot believe that fan-vaulting is stone; and here too are some of the most important Abbey tombs. Henry VII and his consort Elizabeth of York, in bronze by Torrigiani, lie in the place of honor behind the altar; but the sculptor's masterpiece is neither of these but Lady Margaret Beaufort, Henry's mother, whose tomb is in the south aisle. In the south aisle you will find also the mother of James I, Mary Queen of Scots, brought here from Peterborough Cathedral (*q.v.*), and in the north the elaborate tomb in which Queen Elizabeth was buried directly on top of Queen Mary her predecessor. This was an ugly thing to do, an insult to both of them; the Henry VII Chapel was not that crowded. At the end of this aisle lie two infant princesses, the daughters of James I—Sophia's cradle-tomb especially, with the three-day-old baby tucked under a coverlet, is a place of sentimental pilgrimage for many visitors. (These should also see at this point the burial place of the Little Princes of the Tower.) Then there is a famous tablet marked, with a simplicity rare in Westminster Abbey, "Jane Lister Dear childe Died Oct. 7th 1688." But the list of tombs is endless. If you cannot, *Blue Guide* in hand, go up one aisle and down the other and see absolutely everything, at least let your fingers do the walking and see where you must go to find your favorite historical or literary or other character, whether it is Major André or Doctor Johnson, Sir Isaac Newton or Charles James Fox. (More recent than the *Blue Guide,* though, is a slab in the floor, not a tomb, REMEMBER WINSTON CHURCHILL.) In the eighteenth century monuments to people buried elsewhere began to appear, in addition to the tombs. In both there has been a great deal of pecuniary emulation, the memorials have grown bigger and more grandiose, and the size and cost of the marble is not necessarily in ratio to the importance of the deceased. One man, Thomas Thynne, of the Longleat family, was buried under a monument showing the most dramatic scene in his life, his assassination; his coach was stopped in the road and he was then and there done to death. There is a fine likeness of the coachman, whose descendants used to brag about its being on a monument in Westminster Abbey. But try, try not to get so preoccupied with any and all of these monuments that you are not constantly looking at the Abbey. No part of the Confessor's Norman church is seen above ground; but the "Dark Cloister," the undercroft with its museum, and the Chapel of the Pyx are his. (See particularly in the museum the funeral effigies of Charles II, Lord Nelson, its hair arranged by Lady Hamilton, Mary II, Henry VII, Edward III with his mouth twisted down from a stroke—perhaps a fatal one, perhaps an earlier one which had left him at the mercy of Alice Perrers.) As for the main body of the church abovestairs, it is Henry III all the way, and, really, his historical image does need revising; but outside Westminster Abbey is much changed. The familiar twin towers are actually eighteenth century. The alterations and improvements— some the latter, some merely the former—were all optional, not undertaken because of a fire or an earthquake or Cromwell's men. Nor did Westminster Abbey suffer in the Reformation. It is a Royal Peculiar. This does not mean somebody like James I or Edward II, but a church whose dean is directly responsible to the sovereign. He does not go through a bishop and certainly not through the Pope; so why, vindictive elements have reasoned in the past, tear it up?—the royal tombs were there, Parliament was meeting in the Chapter House and they were stamping out silver coins in the Chapel of the Pyx. Tourists are always horrified, however, at the small vandalisms; the Coronation Chair, for instance, with the Stone of Scone underneath, has been carved all over with initials just like something in America.

Kings who
preceded the kings of this survey lived here—it was King Alfred's
capital, and at the east end of the High Street is his statue, erected
1901 on the thousandth anniversary of his death. But Saxon kings had
been there before Alfred, and the Romans before that; in fact, the
settlement of Winchester is something no historian remembers; it was
already there. See the "miz-maze" on top of St. Catherine's Hill,
which may be prehistoric; Town Cross, fifteenth century but much
restored; Pilgrim's Hall, fourteenth century; Church of St. Cross,
Norman with fifteenth- and sixteenth-century embellishment; Wol-
vesey Castle, where the Bishop of Winchester lives in the remaining
wing of a 1684 episcopal palace, which takes its name from a Norman
castle demolished in the Civil War; St. Swithin's Church (if you can
find it); St. Cross Hospital, where any wayfarer, including tourists,
may still receive a dole of bread and ale. The old men who are cared
for in this almshouse (the English call a spade a spade) wear medieval
uniforms of two kinds, black gown with silver Cross of St. John for
the foundation of 1136, mulberry with a tasselled hat to match for the
foundation of 1445; they brighten the streets of Winchester the way
the pensioners do in Chelsea. The big sights in town are Winchester
College, founded 1382 with the motto "Manners Makyth Man," a
tower built 1481 and a chapel with fan-vaulting which served as the
model for Eton's; Winchester Castle, with an early but not early
enough Round Table on the wall of the Great Hall, where Sir
Walter Raleigh was sentenced to death (1603) and Judge Jeffreys
held a "Bloody Assize" (1685)—this is also the castle from which the
aspiring queen Matilda was carried in a coffin; and the cathedral,
begun 1079. Mary I and Philip of Spain were married here.
Winchester Cathedral is the longest in Europe—556 feet. It has a
thirteenth-century Lady Chapel and was extensively reworked in the
fourteenth by William of Wykeham, its famous bishop who was also

the founder and architect of Winchester School (whose boys are called Wykehamists) and of New College, Oxford (*q.v.*). Winchester's most famous bishop, though, was pre-cathedral, the Saxon saint Swithin. Swithin (*fl.* 860) did not exactly do anything about the English weather—he got his sainthood in connection with the Danish invasion—but for forty days after St. Swithin's Day, July fifteenth, the English at least know what the weather is going to be. See in the cathedral statues of James I and Charles I, a brass tablet to Jane Austen, a window to Isaak Walton, and a fine tomb which may or may not be William Rufus's. (His being buried in this cathedral, 1100, was said by some to have caused the central tower to fall in 1107.) King Canute's bones are supposed to be here also, but this too is uncertain, and Winchester has enough certainties not to have to clutch at these.

WINDSOR CASTLE, Windsor, Berkshire, 10, 18, 28, 30, 33, 62, 128, 159, 173, 196, 230. The stone castle replaces William the Conqueror's quick wooden fortification, and Henry I, his son, seems to have been responsible for its beginning. We know he lived at Windsor at least part of the time, for he also built the first King's House, close to the big Round Tower we see today. (Incidentally, this tower is not round.) And we know that this royal residence must have disappeared within about a hundred years, for Henry III then built another King's House in an entirely different place. In the meantime Henry II had also been adding to the stone castle, and it may surely be assumed that his son Richard Lion Heart, the nearest thing to a real military engineer his century could produce, also had a hand with the fortifications. The three drum towers seem to date from the Henry II–Henry III period. By this time the Castle grounds were clearly divided into Upper and Lower Wards on either side of the Round Tower; and so they remain today. It was Henry III, a compulsive and creative builder, Edward III, who wanted to make Windsor into a setting for the Order of the Garter, and George IV, "whose restlessness leaves nothing quiet" (as the doggerel says in connection with this very thing of re-doing Windsor Castle), who rounded out the spectacle of the largest inhabited castle in the world. There is much to see, even if the Queen is in residence and you may not see the State Apartments. You will go in through Henry VIII's Gate. See St. George's Chapel, where the banners of the Knights of the Garter hang above their carved stalls; and if you are in time for Evensong, when tourists are not shown around but may take part in the service, most of the tourists will melt away and the few remaining may be seated in the Knights' stalls instead of in the body of the chapel. Many kings and queens are buried in St. George's. Poor Henry VI and his successor (a polite word) Edward IV are both here; Henry VIII, having never forgotten the perfect wife who gave him his only legal son, had directed that he be buried in the crypt beside Jane Seymour. The friends of Charles I, for the reception of whose body no provision had been made, found a place for him beside them. George III, Edward VII, George V with Queen Mary, their effigies startling because they seem still real to their people and not historical characters, George VI—but Queen Victoria and the Prince Consort, though she did the Chapel built by Henry III over into a Memorial Chapel for him, both lie at Frogmore in the Home Park, which can only be visited two or three days in the year. (At Frogmore, too, the Duke of Windsor was recently buried.) Again, do not let its historical aspect obscure for you the architecture of St. George's—this is one of the most beautiful churches in England. Leaving it by the stone stairway which gives so much dignity to the Garter processions, see next something very different—Queen Mary's Doll's House, not a childhood plaything but a miniature mansion designed by Sir Edwin Luytens. Everything in the house is an exact reproduction, reduced in scale, and the functional items function. Famous authors contributed books—all except George Bernard Shaw, who refused—and Rudyard Kipling rewrote "If"; then all the books were bound with an M and a crown on each, and bookplate inside. Famous painters did portraits for the walls. The carpets and curtains were specially woven, a linen tablecloth was borrowed from Buckingham Palace and reproduced in Belfast, two-inch size. King George's red dispatch boxes were also borrowed and reproduced in miniature. All the furniture shows the meticulous skill that you have noticed all over England, in life-size scale, in the invisible repair and replacement of bomb or woodworm damage—and this is the whole point of Queen Mary's Doll's House. Though Shaw was not, naturally, the last person to sneer at it, the House is like Madame Tussaud's, only incidentally for the children. It can tell you a good deal about England. Returning to Queen Mary's actual house, for she was the first chatelaine of Windsor Castle to explore the whole place, turn it inside out, and evaluate and rearrange what she found, so that it became very much hers, you may be fortunate enough to see the State Apartments—though the present Queen uses Windsor a great deal. It was her home during the war years, and Prince Philip enjoys the polo in Windsor Great Park. See the Garter Room, St. George's Hall, the Grand Corridor where Queen Victoria's court so suffered from draughts ("that cave of the winds," Disraeli called Windsor Castle), the Grand Reception Room, the Waterloo Room honoring the famous victory, the White, Red, and Green Drawing-Rooms—you will be gently but firmly guided, so you need not fear missing anything. Finally (and this is optional) you might climb to the top of the Round Tower, 230 feet high. You will not only see the whole plan of the Castle, which you can see no other way—Upper, Middle, and Lower Wards, Horseshoe Cloisters, towers, everything—but you will see why William I thought, in 1066, that this was an inevitable place to build a castle.

Windsor, Bessie Wallis Warfield, Duchess of (*see* Warfield)

Windsor, Duke of (*see* Edward VIII)

Windsor Family, 20

Winter's Tale, The, 39

Witan, 228, 233, 240

WOBURN, ABBEY, Bedfordshire, 118. Half of the Stately Home of the Russell family, Dukes of Bedford. The other half was pulled down by the father of the present Duke because dry-rot had been discovered, but this could have been treated and the loss of most of the bedrooms, a fine riding school and other features is regrettable. Everything possible, however, has been done to recoup this disaster and Woburn is the very first in popularity with tourists. Unencumbered by their children, whom they may confidently drop off at the playground or the Pets' Corner, they should see (in addition to the state rooms themselves) Queen Elizabeth's Armada portrait (left background, the Armada gallantly approaching, right background, the Armada breaking up on the rocks), the double portrait of Mary I and Philip II, the Holbein of Jane Seymour, the silver-gilt toilet set, the Chinese wallpaper imported in 1753, the unbelievable shell-lined grotto, the Flitcroft stables, the most complete Sèvres dinner service, of its quality, in the world, presented by Louis XV, the portraits of Queen Elizabeth's Earl of Essex and of Sarah Duchess of Marlborough, two of whose granddaughters married Dukes of Bedford. There is also a portrait of the family's most undesirable connection, whose daughter was another Duchess of Bedford, the notorious Frances Howard. She is England's most famous murderess, though for some reason she is not in Madame Tussaud's. You will have no trouble finding this portrait; look for the one with practically nothing on above the waist; she looks quite bold and depraved enough to have practiced witchcraft and helped to murder Sir Thomas Overbury. And indeed she was guilty, she pleaded so and with her second husband the Earl of Somerset (James I's favorite, Robert Carr) was sentenced to be hanged. She was released from the Tower, however, and died insane. But her daughter by Somerset, Anne Carr, who would become the Duchess of Bedford, had actually (Burke says) been born in the Tower. You can see why William Russell's family fought this marriage wildly; and you will be interested to see the portrait of Anne at Woburn, beautiful and good, in a white satin dress.

YORK, Yorkshire, 117, 230, 235. After London, perhaps the most mandatory English city. The Romans' Eboracum; Hadrian came here 121 A.D., two other emperors, Septimius Severus and Constantius I, died here; Constantine the Great, the latter's son by St. Helena, the one quite possibly born at Caernarvon (*q.v.*) was proclaimed emperor here at York. Under the Romans this was a walled city, and it still is. See the Multangular Tower, early fourth century, still standing in the museum gardens—for that matter, see the museum—and walk along the walls. They afford splendid views and a slight, very slight grasp of the impact of the Romans on the rest of the known world. The Normans raised two mounds with two castles on them; Baile Mound or Hill survives but Clifford's Mound, across the river from it, also has Clifford's Tower. This is not the original keep, however; that was wooden, and burned in the Jewish riots of 1190. See the churches: All Saints, St. Mary's, St. Michael-le-Belfry, Holy Trinity; the Treasurer's House, St. Anthony's Hall, King's Manor, Mansion House, Guildhall (1448 and heavily bombed, but restored), St. William's College, Merchant Adventurers and Merchant Taylors' Halls, both fourteenth century, Assembly Rooms, Debtors' Prison—this one does not sound very inviting, but it is 1705 by Sir John Vanbrugh, who remember had been a prisoner in the Château de Vincennes; it has a collection of costumes, a collection of weapons, and a collection of toys, so that it happily engages tourists of both sexes and all ages; and it is also the prison where Dick Turpin served time and Eugene Aram came, with gyves upon his wrist. But of course York Minster is the big sight in York—not just another Gothic cathedral but the biggest one in England, and the oldest foundation in England; it was to York and London that St. Augustine's mission to convert England (597 A.D.) was directed; the church was to be governed, according to the instructions, from these two former Roman capitals; and though the Archbishopric of London did not materialize the Archbishopric of York did. Under other cathedrals you can see Roman ruins that are purely coincidental, but at York they are the ruins of the earliest Roman Christian church. Inside, notice the great stained-glass windows, taken out for safekeeping during the war; the chapter house (1286–1307) without the usual central column, an awesome feat of engineering; tombs of the bishops; the tomb of William of Hatfield, Edward III's son; the rood screen (1473–1505) with life-sized statues of the kings from William I to Henry VI. Edward III married Philippa of Hainault here, after which there were no royal weddings until that of the present Duke and Duchess of Kent.